considering traveling in Vietnam and being open to Vietnamese perspectives."

— Jan Barry, co-founder of Vietnam Veterans Against the War, co-founder, 1st Casualty Press

"For more than thirty years, I taught college-level literature and writing classes on the war in Vietnam. My only regret is that students did not get to read, to experience, *Seeking Quan Am*, a beautifully written, intensely honest book by combat Vietnam veteran, Mark Smith, and Vietnam era civilian, Susan Dixon. Their book will take you back, break your heart, and make you laugh and cry. I recommend it highly, especially for veterans and civilians who continue to suffer from the physical, emotional, and spiritual wounds of war."

Fred A. Wilcox, author of *Waiting for an Army to Die: The Tragedy of Agent Orange* and *Scorched Earth: Legacies of Chemical Warfare in Vietnam*

"I was privileged to travel to Vietnam with both these authors and see the 'American War' through their eyes. Despite different perspectives, their laser vision penetrated the fog of war, the souls of the fallen and forgotten, and the personal pathos of a generation supporting and resisting war in Indo-China. Smith and Dixon give us a memorable double helix of stories about an offshore war that spawned a war at home."

Charles C. Geisler, Professor Emeritus, Cornell University

Praise for Seeking Quan Am

"I was in Vietnam twice. The first time was in 1967-1968 participating in combat operations with Mark. The second time, by reading Susan's and Mark's story, I was transported to Vietnam as part of their group. In spirit, I was there again. Their courage and search for understanding, brought, in no small way, peace to this old trooper's heart and mind."
— Captain Robert Alekna, US Army

"*Seeking Quan Am* opens passageways between different worlds. It connects the lives of war veterans and civilians, Americans and Vietnamese, past and present. It demonstrates a deep commitment to reconciliation and to learning from people we may once have perceived as inhuman, something our world desperately needs more of today. But this is not to say Dixon and Smith's memoir offers easy answers. Perhaps its strongest parts are those that expose the contradictions we often don't see, or choose not to see, both in war and everyday life. Highly recommended."
— Kevin Basl, Iraq War veteran and co-editor of *Warrior Writers: A Collection of Writing and Artwork by Veterans*

"Even though I only served with Mark Smith for about eight weeks, that eight weeks was a period in both of our lives that we both will never forget and will forever bind us together as friends. This is Mark's story of his two tours in Vietnam. For me it is a memorial to those that made the ultimate sacrifice and those that made it home."

— Marvin Hasenak, Vietnam Veteran, 1968-69

"As a commander, I looked for NCOs to take over a platoon if the leader was either wounded or killed in action. I knew I would get accurate information and update status from Mark so I could make a sound tactical decision. I had total faith and confidence in his ability to make a sound assessment of the tactical situation and recommend what action we can take to complete the mission. Mark was a consummate soldier and respected by all. He would have made an exceptional officer. Your work accurately describes the time that I was with C Company 2/7th."

— Colonel Robert Meager, US Army

"Unlike many works that reflect on the war experience, Susan Dixon and Mark Smith have created a unique dialogue between peace advocate and war veteran that expands our sensibilities about the complex personal issues involved. It is also the story of their journey to explore beyond memories and ideals to look at the truth of what war really is and what it means to be human in its midst."

— Kate Dahlstedt, MA; Founder, Soldier's Heart

"*Seeking Quan Am* does a great service to veterans by going beyond simply listening to their stories. It does a great service to war resisters and military family members by examining and reexamining thoughts about the war and its impact on soldiers, civilians, Americans and Vietnamese, and sharing this jumbled progression. It does a great service to Americans

SEEKING QUAN AM

A Dual Memoir of War and Vietnam

SUSAN R DIXON
MARK M SMITH

Copyright © 2019 by Susan R Dixon and Mark M. Smith

All rights reserved. No part of this book may be reproduced in any form or by any electronic or mechanical means, including information storage and retrieval systems, without written permission from the author, except for the use of brief quotations in a book review.

Cover Design by Anna Gallow, Flourish Design Studio, Ithaca, New York

Cover Photographs by Mark M. Smith: L.Z. Jill, near Song Be along the Song Saigon and Quan Am

Find supplementary material at www.seekingquanam.com

Published by ATI Books, Ithaca, New York.

Everything is held together with stories. That is all that is holding us together, stories and compassion.
   Barry Lopez

Contents

A Note About Names	xi
1. The Southern Part of Heaven	1
THE NORTH CAROLINA VULTURE	5
2. Slipping into Harmony with History	6
3. February 1967	10
4. Nui Mieu	14
5. Tan An Village	16
6. Duster Hill above LZ Uplift	21
7. Tiger Mountains	24
8. An Khe Bridge	27
9. An Khe	29
10. An Khe, LZ English	30
11. Van Thien Village	32
12. LZ Dog	43
13. An Hoa and An Quang	46
14. to LZ Horvath	53
15. Night March	56
16. North Tiger Mountains	60
17. Hoai An Valley	63
18. Tiger Mountains	65
19. LZ Horvath	69
20. September 1967	71
21. LZ Horvath Basin	72
22. LZ Pony	75
23. Outpost Harry	77
24. XYZ Ring [An Khe]	78
25. Tiger Mountains	81
26. LZ Ollie	83
27. Phu Cat Air Force Base	85
28. LZ El Paso to Camp Evans	87

29. The Tet Offensive	89
30. Quang Tri to Danang	101
31. An Khe	104
THE RETURN	107
32. Why I Went Back	108
THE WAR IN THE JUNGLE	115
33. The Dream	116
34. The Month Everybody Got Shot	118
35. War Zone C	127
36. May 1969	130
37. 1st Platoon	133
38. Along the Saigon River	138
39. Line One	143
40. Death's Golden Eyes	155
41. The Grim Landscape	163
WAR AND MEMORY	193
42. What's War Got to Do With It?	194
43. The Monster in the Labyrinth	205
44. Finding My Way Back To a Place I Had Never Been	219
45. Survivors	235
46. Looking for Answers	271
47. Ghosts	279
48. The Old Veterans	300
MEDITATION	303
49. Seeking Quan Am	304
Acknowledgments	313
About the Authors	317

A Note About Names

Because Seeking Quan Am *is an account of experience rather than a documentary, we have chosen to retain place names as we knew them. We use "Vietnam" rather than "Viet Nam," for example. "Danang," rather than "Da Nang," "Saigon" and "Hanoi," rather than "Sai Gon," and "Ha Noi." For the most part we do not use diacritical markings because at the time we knew little about them.*

We encountered more difficulty with the pejorative term commonly used by soldiers for their Vietnamese counterparts and so heavily present in the majority of veteran memoirs. Mark used the term almost casually and without evident malice when he wrote in the 1970s and although it was painful, we decided to retain it. We did so not so much in the interest of historical accuracy per se, *but to prevent his accounts from being inaccurate, of reflecting back on that time an evolution of thinking that had not yet occurred.*

As for the names of the men Mark served with, the reader expecting introductions of characters and clear movement into and out of the story may find themselves disoriented. This, again, reflects the reality Mark experienced: men arrived and left with little fanfare. Such was the reality of life in the field that they may have been known by first name, or last name, or nickname, or some simply by their job within the unit. When their time was up they might or might not have had the opportunity to say goodby. Worse, if they were injured or killed, they were taken out quickly and were just gone, with little opportunity for those left behind to observe their loss. (One poignant exception occurs in Mark's second tour.)

While neither of us is Buddhist, the humility we felt in encountering Vietnam as we wish we had decades ago allowed us to be open to Vietnamese values and spirituality. From small private images to majestic statues such as one that stands above the harbor at Danang, we encountered the bodhisattva of compassion, the best known of the enlightened beings who give of themselves to help humanity. In Vietnam this being is understood to be female and is called Quan Am.

SEEKING QUAN AM

1

The Southern Part of Heaven

IT IS JUNE 8, 1966, GRADUATION DAY FOR THE SENIOR CLASS OF Chapel Hill High School. The ceremony is not taking place in the auditorium of the old building on Franklin Street, the one set back across a lawn with a low stone wall along the sidewalk that the cool kids sat on before school, smoking or just hanging out. That building would be torn down a few weeks later in what feels like a metaphor, the old structure making way for the new, like something they might have done themselves, or were about to do.

Instead, the graduating class is in the main auditorium on the university campus, which lends the proceedings an unfamiliar *gravitas*, the larger stage signaling the one the graduates are being told will now be theirs. They are leaving the boundaries of childhood and entering the world where anything is possible no matter what path they choose. The speaker is the university chancellor and the father of one of the graduates. "Find your passion," he says. "Do what you love and use that to make the world a better place." It is all in the spirit of John F. Kennedy's boundless enthusiasm: find a problem and solve it, say you will get to the moon and do it. "Climb every mountain," the choir sings. Dream the impossible dream. They all remember where they were, though, in which room of the old school building, when the voice on the intercom announced Kennedy's assassination.

As a class they have had the usual high school experiences: sports, dances, clubs, and community activities, along with the usual mix of academics and the usual division of social labor. There are the outgoing kids, the introverts, the "most" everything, and the ones who hung back while they figured out what road to take. There are the worker bees, the team members, the club members, the future this and future that, the chorus, the band, the debate team, and the main office assistants. The boys wear suits for their pictures in the year book. The girls wear identical round neck sweaters with a short string of pearls. It is the mid-60s, but it is the South and in some ways it feels like still breaking up with the 50s.

Within all this, two seniors stand out by being who they are and helping to make up what the yearbook describes as "the one face of the student body." There is nothing particularly exceptional about either one, except in the usual way. If their high school experience groomed them for what is to come next it is only in that they have both participated in and resisted high school life, using strategies that are going to come in handy.

Mark Smith is holding court somewhere in the fourth row. He has stomped around the high school halls in combat boots and worn four of his own teeth on a necklace, so no graduation ceremony is going to tame his spirits. He has been an indifferent student in spite of a natural intelligence and a quick mind. He fell into the role of photographer for the school newspaper by accident and from then on the camera was his entrée into every space in the school and any event taking place there. He took candid shots in the hallways, in classrooms, on the bus to away games. He caught the girls being silly and the boys being serious. He didn't have to sit with everyone else during assemblies–in other words he didn't have to sit *still*–because he was in the balcony taking pictures. The camera became so much a part of his identity that a friend called it his "one-eyed girlfriend." Now though, the graduation gown depriving him of his usual prop, he is amusing himself and everyone around him by passing around a book of cartoons called *No Spitting on the Sheriff*.

Meanwhile, up on the stage, but off to the side, Susan Dixon sits at the grand piano, where she is accompanying the chorus. The supporting role suits her, as it gives her an excellent vantage point for observing the action. She studied her way through high school, loving French so much she took summer classes at the university so she could place into a higher level where she read French fashion magazines and memorized the lyrics to *Les Parapluies de Cherbourg*. Other than serving on the honor council, she kept a low profile, wishing she wanted to go to dances, games, and pep rallies because in some ways they looked like fun. The simple, soaring melody of "Climb Every Mountain," which builds to an uplifting crescendo about finding one's dream, gives her hope that she can transcend anything. Even a war.

Outside the auditorium, diplomas awarded and the ceremony ended, the seniors disperse into the tumultuous world they are now empowered to tackle. Reactions against the civil rights movement have grown violent, the KKK has marched in Durham, and in just three weeks the United States will begin bombing Hanoi. "Climb Every Mountain" will have to compete with everything from Barry Sadler's "Ballad of the Green Berets" to Barry Maguire's "Eve of Destruction." It is confusing knowing how to be a woman, no better knowing how to be a man, and events are not going to make either any easier.

Susan's application to a small college in New England has

recently been rejected, which means she will not get out of town as she hoped. Instead she will attend the University of North Carolina in the fall and live at home. Mark, on the other hand, disdainful of any further limitations of the classroom, has enlisted in the Army and will volunteer to serve in Vietnam. There are no goodbys or promises to write between the two, as there are among some of their mutual friends. In spite of the small size of their class and the links between them that will prove significant, Susan and Mark barely know one another. It will be many years before that will change, years in which the dark side of the graduation ceremony's optimism have laid bare the ways in which stories fall apart and must—and at what cost—be pieced back together again.

THE NORTH CAROLINA VULTURE

MARK M. SMITH

2

Slipping into Harmony with History

1965 - 1966

NOTE: MARK WROTE ALL OF THE FOLLOWING TEXT IN THE 1960s and early 1970s. Susan edited it for length and narrative consistency.

In the late fall of 1965, as American and North Vietnamese troops fought a bitter campaign in the Central Highlands of Vietnam, I had already set my course for the Army. As wars go, Vietnam was nudging middle age but my acquaintance with it had begun long before. From 1962, when as an eighth-grader I saw John F. Kennedy speak at the University of North Carolina's Kenan Stadium and noticed some South Vietnamese officers who had been brought up from Fort Bragg for the occasion, until 1975, when communist tanks rolled into Saigon and put an end to the thing, the Vietnam War was almost as much an institution as school, marriage, or anything else that was taken for granted in American life. For thirteen years it simply was—day after day, month after month, year in and year out, if not on the front page then somewhere inside the daily paper. If it was not the lead story on the evening network news telecasts then it was waiting just off the set, prepared for its cue, always ready to spring forward, if only in the dreadful, banal litany of the weekly body count.

Had the war reached fruition a few years earlier, before I was old enough to take part, I might have had the time and, perhaps, the wisdom to see it as so many in the late sixties did and turn away from the pointless, hopeless policy of a bankrupt government. Had it continued longer as a (relatively speaking) low-intensity advisory war with no regular American combat outfits on the ground—just another distant Cold War brushfire fought largely by proxies—I might have chosen to pursue my education at a small liberal arts college in Maine. What turned the key for me was the approach of my senior year in high school just as the first U.S. ground troops arrived in the war zone and changed the conflict's nature once and for all. The diary I kept during high school recorded the exact moment when I decided to go to war: "July 13, 1965: 'It's an American war'—CBS on Vietnam, now that 3,000 combat infantry (1st Division) have gone in."

I still remember that correspondent's blunt judgment and the creepy feeling that my life had slipped into sympathetic harmony with history. Although a week or more had passed since I had decided to forgo college for a uniform, my real journey to the war began at the dinner table that evening. It may even be that I understood, in some vague and undefined a way, that Vietnam was destined to be the defining event of my generation, just as the Depression and the Civil War had been for generations gone before.

———

In most respects I was an utterly nondescript teenager. I avoided school dances, seldom dated, had no steady girlfriend, and by and large was less than crazy about rock and roll. Except for Bob Dylan's electric work, it struck me as pleasant but superficial background music, and I much preferred "serious" folk artists like Ed McCurdy, Ramblin' Jack Elliot, Oscar Brand and Ian and Sylvia. But I had many friends and my diaries indicate a lot of social activity, from Easter weekend bicycle hikes, to occasional visits to a farm owned by a friend's mother in rural Virginia, to pool and sledding parties as the weather allowed. I supported civil rights, thought the Klan and the Birchers despicable, and considered myself a Kennedy-Johnson liberal. In one respect, however, I was considerably different from my friends. There was, to my knowledge, no one else in my class who wanted to go to war.

As far back as I could remember, war had been a theme in my life. My father's stories about the Pacific struck me as exotic and thrilling rather than cautionary. There was also television fare like *Victory at Sea*, *The Big Picture* (a shamelessly propagandistic Army production, each episode of which opened with the firing of an atomic cannon and the ensuing mushroom cloud, enough fireworks to thrill any kid in the fifties) and Walter Cronkite's *Air Power*. At an age when most kids were barely past Dr. Seuss and Winnie the Pooh, my father was reading me excerpts from British Colonel Arthur Fremantle's diary of a visit to the Confederacy in 1863, and *The American Iliad*, an anthology of first-person Civil War accounts. Before I was through junior high school I had chewed my way through Bruce Catton's *Army of the Potomac* trilogy, Liddell Hart's *Strategy*, Douglas Southall Freeman's *Lee's Lieutenants*, Martin Russ's *The Last Parallel*, and Glen Ross's wonderful novel of the Korean War, *The Last Campaign*. Ross had served as a machine-gunner in the 7th Cavalry during the first year of the Korean War, and later on that came to mean a lot to me. The mysteriously evocative gray and lonely landscapes of his book entranced me, and in reading it I slowly came to realize that combat, like pain (with which I had only the most limited acquaintance) and sex (with which I had no acquaintance at all), could not be experienced secondhand, no matter how vivid the pictures, prose, or sound effects. I wanted to know what war felt like, what it did to those on the line. A field manual for Marine rifle squads, which I ordered from the Government Printing Office, showed how to assault a fortified building, but it didn't explain how it felt to send a 40-millimeter grenade crashing through a window or step into a room emptying a load of bullets from an M-14 on automatic fire. I had to know what war was like, how shooting at and being shot at by other human beings would affect me, and what it would feel like to live in Death's presence. So when Vietnam became a real war, I had to go to war.

3

February 1967

THE FLIGHT CARRYING NEW RECRUITS AND RETURNING personnel from Oakland to Vietnam began with a late start, "because the engines were falling off or something," the crew chief said. At three in the morning we made a short refueling stop outside Anchorage, Alaska, where our thin khakis felt like tissue paper. At an air force base outside Tokyo we crowded into a snack bar and paid no attention to the arrival of a flight going the other way. On the Starlifter out of Yokota, the seats faced backwards toward a view of lashed-down duffel bags and the bored crew chief wearing an intercom headset. At the American air base at Bien Hoa, just north of Saigon, the ramp hummed open, and I looked out into the night. To one side of the ramp stood a shadowy figure holding a rifle, butt perched on his right hip and muzzle aimed toward the sky. A thick, soupy tide of warm air flowed into the cabin like a wet wall, steaming any remaining creases out of my khakis.

We shook ourselves into a file, trudged down the ramp, and veered toward five dark green Army buses. Suddenly, two Phantom fighter jets thundered down the runway and rose into the night with a brutal roar. The sound shuddered the air and overflowed the senses, vibrating in my chest. I could only see the pale, intense blue flames spouting from the jets' exhaust but the throaty howl was cosmic and angry. It's going on somewhere out there, I thought. I had reached the war.

Two days later, when my name was called out for assignment to the 1st Cavalry Division (Airmobile), I was ecstatic. The 1st Air Cav was already *the* elite unit in Vietnam, surpassing even the Green Berets for sheer frontline charisma. The men of the division were, by and large, suffused with the spirit of the cavalry. They were the cavalry of the sky, no matter that their military occupational specialties were the usual ones: light-weapons infantryman, ordnance specialist, combat photographer. The divisional shoulder patch alone was enough to set them apart from the rest of the doggies. It was bigger than any other patch in the armed forces, a great golden shield slashed diagonally by a black stripe, above which was an embroidered black horse's head. The cavalrymen felt they could afford a little extra swagger.

When I arrived, the Cav was operating in northern Binh Dinh Province, between Qui Nhon and the border with Quang Ngai Province to the north. Farther north lay I (pronounced "Eye") Corps, the bailiwick of the Marines. Binh Dinh had been a trouble spot for as long as anyone could remember. The French never had any luck there, and the South Vietnamese could fly their flag with any modicum of safety only along Route One and its towns. Operation Pershing in Binh Dinh meant long, sweaty patrols through the rice paddies, villages, and jungled slopes along with occasional outbreaks of fighting. It was a war of small skirmishes and lethal booby traps interspersed with occasional full-fledged battles that pushed the enemy out of the major villages and into the forests.

The enemy in Binh Dinh was the 3rd North Vietnam Army Division (NVA), comprising the 18th and 22nd NVA regiments and elements of the 2nd Viet Cong (VC) Regiment, for a total of perhaps 3,000 to 4,000 North Vietnamese regulars and Viet Cong main force troops plus an unknown number of local militia forces. How much that meant to the average GI is open to debate. When I asked who we were actually fighting, one old-timer said, "Oh, you know, sometimes it's the 'Yellow Star' Division and others it's a bunch of local gooks out in a fuckin' paddy."

Landing Zone (LZ) English was a sprawl of dilapidated wood-slats-and-tarp shacks protected by weatherworn gray-green sandbags. Here and there, a shallow trench cut across the terrain, looking as if those who built it had given up halfway through the task. Up a hill across the LZ sat a flight or two of Huey helicopters, like tethered beasts—prehistoric and anxious to be released from their bonds. Antennae stuck up all around like thin blades of grass. Several yards away, across the oiled dirt road, was a high, thick berm of earth, on the other side of which were stored thousands of artillery shells, high explosive smoke-marking rounds, mortar shells, helicopter rockets, cases of grenades, bullets, Claymore mines, trip flares, and everything else that explodes, burns, or in any way causes death and destruction through the violent ignition of chemical compounds.

I instinctively sat a certain distance from the five men I was with, close enough to be taken for one of them, yet far enough away so that in my own mind I was a detached observer. Being an observer justified my presence on LZ English without demanding any particular belief or point of view from me. I thought of myself as both observer and participant, and lent equal weight to each.

From where I sat, I could see the boonies in every direction, a vibrant green sweep of paddies—oddly angled plots of water and rice shoots—interspersed with clumps and rows of scrub brush and palms. Here and there were clusters of trees, high, thick hedges, and gray, thatch-roofed huts. People wearing broad, flattened, white hats walked along the paddy dikes or stood up to their knees in the paddy muck,. Working among them were the first water buffalo I had ever seen.

4

Nui Mieu
MARCH 12, 1967

"Let's go hunt Charlie," Sergeant Tatman said.

It sounded unreal, like a line from a movie script. I looked down into the ravine. "There?" I wondered. I was sure I saw Steve Pleasant's quick grimace, probably because he would be the point man for the first patrol into a new sector. Even I could see that the ravine, a defile choked with brush, would be a nightmare if the VC were in it. Pleasant was my first buddy in the company, the one who showed me everything from arranging a poncho liner, stringing out a trip flare, and attaching a claymore, to the finer points of patrolling, pulling point, and taking night guard duty. He knew how to be careful.

He stepped off, leading the platoon along what looked like a narrow animal track. He walked calmly and appeared to be more interested in watching his footing than in searching for signs of the enemy. I thought about booby traps—punji stakes dipped in manure, "toe-poppers," man-trap pits lined with spears—Vietnam's peculiar bad dream. Pleasant was worried about stumbling or tripping, about losing his feet entirely, maybe losing his life. It would only take one grenade attached to a thin, nigh-invisible wire strung across the path. The enemy we sought fought us through devices such as these more often than open battles.

    I soon grew bored with patrols like this. What I had come here to experience happened at Tan An village.

5

Tan An Village
MARCH 20, 1967

THE HUEYS SET US DOWN ON WHITE SAND. OUR FEET SANK into it and the rotor blades sent it swirling into the air. It stung our eyes and infiltrated our weapons, teeth, and clothes. We dashed to the banks of a lazy creek. To the north lay a thin tree line and, beyond that, another, larger dustbowl. To the west, visible from the LZ only as a thicker mass of trees and banana plants, stood the village of Tan An. I had enlisted because I wanted to know what it was like to be in a battle. This was going to be it.

My platoon, the 2nd, moved to the north, sweeping any villages we found along the way. 1st Platoon's men entered a sweet potato field and a large plot of the distinctive two-decker grave mounds to the left, while overhead, two gunships careened about at high speed, looking for something to shoot at. Suddenly, an onslaught hit the company with devastating force. In a few seconds, the firing built up from a staccato rattling to a snarling, crackling roar. One of 1st Platoon's gunners was dead, its lieutenant mortally wounded, and a half-dozen others were shot before there was time for anyone to even think about reacting. We flattened ourselves onto the ground, frantically pulled the quick release snaps on our rucksacks, and scuttled toward the nearest available cover. The men inside the graveyard when the shooting erupted had their choice of the high-mounded tombs, but elsewhere the ground was flat and completely open. Now that I was truly at war and earning my combat pay, I had no idea what to do. It frightened me, this ignorance, much more than the bullet swarm did.

In the village, a sudden puff of gray-black smoke threw up a mixture of smashed thatch and splintered wood. Although men were lying down, firing, and occasionally making short dashes in one direction or another across the front, most of the enemy fire went well over our heads. I found myself feeling detached, as if I were not actually an active part of the fighting.

Two gunships came in for a strike, roaring low overhead, and fired several rockets into the village. Smoke billowed up above the skyline, and hunks of thatch and trees cartwheeled into the air. Someone went down twenty yards to my left. Our platoon leader and a couple other guys bent over the prostrate form and yelled for a medic. The captain called a check fire and the gunships pulled out.

When word came for the platoon to pull back to the ditch, the men along the line crawled a short distance to the rear, then turned around to cover the others. I made it about ten yards before facing about just in time to see the sand spurt up in front of me where a bullet struck. Even with having been little more than an observer, the excitement and tension of the battle had drained me physically. My arms shrieked with the strain of hauling myself along.

When it was again my turn to move, I stood up and ran for the mound behind me, but then realized I was a good thirty yards in front of the rest of men. The sergeant yelled for me to come back. Almost blinded by green tracers whipping past my face, I hit the ground hard. My next dash carried me into a ditch.

Dusk settled across the sand and nightfall approached. I was told to help move the wounded man. It was too dark to identify him, but I heard him moaning every few seconds. We handed him over to four guys who disappeared toward Mortar Platoon with him and I trotted back along the ditch to my squad. There I learned I had been carrying Steve Pleasant, wounded twice in the head by the gunships.

Across the graveyard, 1st Platoon was still shooting up the village and firing at the silhouettes occasionally visible against the orange glare from the burning hooches. I got separated from my platoon and found them again lying in a shallow ditch. All our food, almost all our water, and all but three entrenching tools were somewhere out in the darkness where we had dropped our rucksacks and no one wanted to go wandering around looking for them. We shared the tools, excavating prone shelters where we could huddle beneath the bullets and shrapnel flying over our heads.

Just as soon as we were dug in, we were told to move closer to the Mortar Platoon. The small-arms fire had largely died down, although now and then an enemy burst would send us flopping back into the holes we had dug. After a while, we quit digging and rested, one person sitting on the floor of the hole while the other remained erect and on watch.

The first of the medevac birds flew in, sandblasting everyone in the vicinity and taking out the seriously injured, including Pleasant. A kilometer to the east, gunships prepped a landing zone. Even at that distance, several rounds of red tracer soared over us.

Then the artillery fire suddenly stopped. I didn't think much of it until word came to get into a hole and stay there: Spooky was on the way. Spooky, a run-of-the-mill two-engine transport plane converted into a fantastic aerial gun platform mounted with rapid-fire Gatling guns, droned mournfully overhead in slow circles, looking like a dark cross in the night sky. After seven or eight passes, the crew was sure of the target. A thin stream of red tracers squirted down toward the village. Then a harsh, snap-crackling buzz-saw sound started, a noise that would make the limpest hair stand straight up and salute. The stream moved back and forth for a moment, as if a giant hose of crimson water played down on the village, cascading among the shattered palms and smoldering huts. Around and around the dark cross flew, spewing thousands of bullets. And then the plane simply turned and left.

We dug in for a third time. I couldn't sleep. The day's fighting had worn me out and I was thirsty. I was walking about looking for a canteen when I came upon the 1st Sergeant seated on an ammo box.

"Private Smith, where's your shirt?" he demanded.

I was too dumbfounded to answer.

"You're not wearing your shirt, private," the Sergeant said. "Malaria control. Sleeves rolled down and buttons buttoned. Now get back to your position and put your shirt on."

———

In the morning we swept the village. We saw about a dozen dead enemy troops and heard an occasional shot in the distance. We found a pile of civilian bodies and one still-living baby. We kept going. I assumed the villagers that were left would take care of them. From twenty yards away I watched a couple of men lift a poncho holding 1st Platoon's dead machine-gunner and turn away toward the company perimeter. There was a strange silence around me, broken only by the soft hissing of the platoon's two radios.

Inside the village were concrete bunkers, the first indication of how serious the enemy resistance had been. Despite the intensity of the fighting, most of the guys had still assumed we were tangling with Viet Cong.

In the afternoon we made another air assault on a nearby village, gingerly negotiated a narrow bamboo bridge over a slimy canal, and marched toward Charlie Company. Dusk was already approaching the plains so the captain wanted to find a good, strong perimeter site quickly. The march was a blur of frantic images: a group of Third Platoon's men running a Brahma bull from its burning shed and then scattering like actors in a silent movie when the bull charged through the gate without waiting for it to be opened, sending timbers and men flying in every direction; Walls and Leonard inviting me to share in some small, extremely sweet bananas they found growing next to a smoldering, rocketblasted house; a long file of tired GIs slogging along the slippery, crumbling paddy dike that led south from the village, their boots and pants covered with grey mud.

For several days we patrolled and marched about the plains and paddies, slowly working our way toward the mountains to the west. We learned that the company as a whole was up for the Presidential Unit Citation, the equivalent of a group Distinguished Service Cross. A prisoner had revealed that most of the 22nd NVA Regiment's 7th Battalion had been waiting for us at Tan An. According to the prisoner, the unit had been thirty minutes away from setting a U-shaped ambush when the company had walked in on them. Had we been half an hour later, the low hill would have been occupied, and we may well have been slaughtered in the open. Word came down that not only had Pleasant died, but that the bullets that killed him had come from one of the American gunships during the aborted strike.

During all that time, I never fired a shot. Not one.

6

Duster Hill above LZ Uplift
MAY 5, 1967

THE LANDSCAPE SPREADING AWAY IN EVERY DIRECTION WAS SO familiar that most of us in the security squad on Duster Hill gave it only a short glance. Even I, as fascinated by maps and terrain as I was, paid more attention to the transistor radio Bangarter had brought along. For once the An Khe station had some good rock music instead of "Polka Party" or interviews with notables passing through the division's base camp. The Blues Magoos were playing a tune I remembered from the year before, a hard blaster with plenty of electricity surging through it.

"Somebody's working out over there," Bangarter said.

It took me a moment for my eyes to adjust, but then I saw them: two Chinook gunships, the Guns-a-Go-Go birds, circling above a large valley on the northwest side of the massif. One turned into a shallow dive and small, indistinct smudges appeared behind it. Several seconds later we heard the rattle of machineguns and the faint roar of rockets.

I thought about how odd it was to be watching these gunships rocketing and strafing in the distance, while *We Ain't*

Got Nothin' Yet played in the background. Then I forgot about the music and everything else.

One of the gunships had lumbered into position to begin its hot pass when it seemed to come to a halt in mid-air. Then the forward part of the craft turned from a glinting, silvery dot to a mushrooming burst of orange flame. The fire blew through the bird before anyone had time to call out, so that some of the men who hadn't been watching still puttered about the hillcrest. The bird fell, turning slowly end over end, leaving behind a trail of splotchy smoke, until the flames covered it completely and it went out of sight behind an intervening ridge. A second later a rolling tower of flame shot up. Still no sound reached the hill. Finally, thick smoke replaced the flame, I heard a quick whoof, and several seconds later the sound of the crash, a distant roar of impact and explosion.

By then everyone on the hill realized what had happened, but the shock left us momentarily incapable of action, or even speech. Then everyone talked at once, shouting and swearing.

Ten minutes later, far below on Uplift, the rest of my platoon left the bunkers and headed for the landing zone's helicopter pad where six Hueys were revving up. They boarded and headed east for the valley.

Two hours later my detail was riding in from the hill, all six men crammed aboard a mechanical mule, just as the platoon returned, Rolf Beyer with it.

"Bad?" I asked him.

"Are you kiddin'? There was nine guys on that bird, and, Jesus, they all burned to a crisp, man. One of 'em, musta been the pilot, looked like glass or somethin' melted right down over his face, and we had to sit around with these bodies while the EOD guys looked for all the ammo to blow it up in place. Then we had to carry the bodies to a medevac bird."

Beyer had a backs-against-the-wall look, as though what he

had been through had taken him to the very edge of something.

7

Tiger Mountains
MAY 19, 1967

THE PLATOON ENTERED THE DEFILE THE CREEK HAD CUT INTO the slopes of the basin's north side. A steep, heavily-forested razorback ridge rose to our left just before the creek turned ninety-degrees. Without any room to maneuver, we felt hemmed in. Lieutenant Hanson halted the platoon and formed it into a narrow, elongated perimeter at the creek's angle. Rather than set outposts on the slopes overshadowing the creek, he sent out several mini-patrols to establish security.

Peewee Kreitz and I were directed to scout the crest of the ridge to the left. We scrambled through a rocky clearing that extended twenty yards up the slope and entered the forest. Stopping for a moment to let my eyesight adjust to the sudden gloom, I slung my grenade launcher across my shoulders and drew my .45.

We walked to the crest where we found a well-cleared and well-used path, fully three feet from side to side. Peewee rolled his eyes to indicate how flaky he thought our position was: two GIs with a rifle and a pistol between them, snooping along a fresh enemy speed trail.

Thirty yards along the crest we halted, worried we might

run into one of the other patrols. Instead of heading back, though, we decided to have a cigarette and use up a little more time. Peewee sat facing downslope, his back to me so that we had the path covered in both directions. The forest was silent and cool. Getting away from people, even for just a few minutes, was a novelty. I couldn't remember the last time I had been with only one other person, much less by myself. Sometimes I could pretend I was alone, like when I was in a bunker and the other guys were outside, or on guard at night while the others were asleep. But that wasn't the same. I always felt their presence, whether through sandbag walls or by their muffled breathing and turning in their sleep. So despite our lack of weaponry and the possibility that we might be caught and pinned down by a hostile force, I smoked casually and unhurriedly, stretching out the minutes before we turned back to the platoon.

Lt. Hanson appeared only mildly interested in our report of the trail. He told us to find a spot along the creek and chow down. I dumped my gear next to a large boulder, sat down against it, and heated water for cocoa. When the water was hot, I added the cocoa mix to it, then two packets of sugar and two packets of cream.

Rodney Hester yelled an alarm and Robinson's machine gun suddenly clattered to life, its sound intensified dramatically within the narrow defile of the creek. I hunched over and tensed, waiting for a return blast of shots from the ridge, and continued stirring my cocoa. When it was hot I rested against the boulder and drank my cocoa as the other recon patrols re-entered the ravine. They strengthened the platoon, but the position remained shallow—nowhere more than ten feet across.

Despite our indefensible position and the enemy's appearance, I felt no sense of urgency or apprehension, and I could see that few of the others did, either. Sergeant Tatman sat several yards upstream eating a C-rations fudge bar. Wilus, across the stream from Tatman, dozed against a fallen tree trunk. Downstream, Rob peered over the sights of his gun toward the ridge crest, but he looked like a dog lying in the shade on a hot day. The gooks'll have to walk down here and tweak our noses to get a rise out of us, I thought. No one's going to go out of his way to start a fight. If Rob's burst of fire was enough merely to give them pause and persuade them to keep out of sight, that would be okay.

I turned to find Michael Reynolds kneeling next to me. Reynolds, a gangly West Virginian who wore a gold earring in one ear, was an ammo bearer-turned RTO. The next thing I knew, he was reaming me out. "Smith, you dumb fuck, are you tryin' to get killed? There's a fuckin' gook up there, and you sittin' here drinkin' your goddamn cocoa! You'd better learn!" With that he turned and walked back to the CP (platoon command post).

Reynolds was right, I thought. Sitting here stirring cocoa when a gook was up the hill was not too bright. You can't just ignore shots because they don't sound like incoming.

At the same time, I thought, there was something gloriously defiant about stirring cocoa in the midst of a skirmish, something ballsy and American. It was a supreme gesture of contempt and arrogance, and an affirmation of my self-confidence. I could already imagine the stories. "An' fuckin' Smith, sittin' there, stirrin' his damn cocoa while Rob's blasting away...." There was the clean beauty of insanity about it. I understood how a general at the Battle of Gettysburg could joke about having his sandwich sprayed with gravel thrown up by a plunging cannon shot.

8

An Khe Bridge
MID-JUNE 1967

Beyer was stoned off his ass after the second joint. He sat against the concrete wall of the bunker, giggling, trying to tell me a joke and not making much sense. It was hard to understand any of what Beyer said, but I listened intently just the same, amazed at the effect the marijuana was having on my friend. Now and then Beyer stopped talking and stared with a faint, happy smile playing across his lips, apparently content and sure I was enjoying the story as much as he had.

At that moment a C-130 transport up from Cam Ranh Bay, Tuy Hoa and Qui Nhon droned in for a landing on the old airstrip, which was only a quarter-mile from the bridge and just on the other side of the Green Line. The pilot misjudged something. With a sudden blaze of fire and a rolling eruption of thick, black smoke, the plane crunched its undercarriage and spread itself in pieces along half the length of the runway. I hit the ground when I saw the flash reflect off the walls of the hooches across the road. A thunderous roar arrived seconds later. Like a character in a cartoon, my jaw dropped and my eyes popped open. I threw my arms over my head and pressed my face hard against the gravel next to the bunker, willing the screeches and bangs and crashes to stop. As the uproar lessened I heard Beyer mumbling.

"Oh, man. Oh, Christ. What a scene! This is, …really, I mean, …what the hell?"

We stood up, slowly realizing the enemy had nothing to do with this. I stood speechless in horror. Clenching my jaw muscles over and over, I watched the flames crackling into the sky. Whatever had happened, the plane was destroyed, and all aboard were dead.

Late in the evening, after the flames were out, the new lieutenant, Robert Alekna, stopped by, but there wasn't much to say. He stood next to the bunker with Beyer, Peewee, Small, and me for a few minutes and then continued on his way to the position across the bridge.

9

An Khe
MID JUNE, 1967

"What is it you get out of this shit?" Beyer asked. "Glory? You figure you're doin' more than all your friends back in college? You figure you're doin' something really great, something really wild?"

He had a point.

"Okay, so I'm proud, even happy, to be doing this shit," I said, "getting shot at, humping my nuts off in the heat, bein' rained on, goin' on flaky ambushes, sleeping in mud like a worm. But I ain't lookin' for a lot of God-and-country bullshit at the end of it. You know why I dig it? Because it's the dirtiest, stinking-est, filthiest fuckin' job goin'. And I'm makin' it, doin' it. It ain't glory, it's just the opposite, sort of anti-glory. It's shit from start to finish, and it all comes down to death and blood. But by God, I'm gettin' through it, and that's something most people won't ever be able to say."

10

An Khe, LZ English
JUNE 19, 1967

I HAD NEVER LIKED FLYING, EXCEPT IN THE HUEYS, AND THIS trip did nothing to cure me of my distrust of all fixed-wing aircraft. Gaining altitude in a trembling, jolting fashion, the plane felt like some great fish wallowing heavily through the sea. It slipped and pitched toward the Crazy Horse area and I spent the entire flight sweating, convinced up until the last seconds of descent onto the airstrip at English that the plane would throw itself into aerial acrobatics and dive into the nearest ridgeline. Memories of the C-130 explosion at An Khe, were still vivid in my mind.

LZ English was not the same place I remembered from early April. All along the western sector of the base I saw evidence of an ammo dump explosion. At the edge of the strip sat two smashed Hueys, their tail booms and propellers missing entirely, their metal carcasses torn and twisted and full of jagged holes. The ground was littered with torn sandbags, shell casings, bent engineer stakes, and splintered logs and crates. Everything had been thrown about, blown from within the dump's high earthen ramparts. From where the company formed up to wait for the Chinooks to take it to LZ Uplift, I saw the bunker—or what remained of it—that I had occupied in April, when Beyer joined the company. The explosion had shivered the bunker flat, blowing many of the sandbags off, and jumbling up those that remained. It didn't look like a fighting position anymore, and I wondered what had happened to the men assigned to it when the dump went up.

No more reefers from the kids across the fence, I thought. Probably no more kids across the fence, period.

11

Van Thien Village
JUNE 21-23, 1967

CHOPPERS TOOK US FROM LZ UPLIFT TO THE CREST OF A HIGH ridge to the east of the Suoi Ca Valley and delivered us, chopper-load by chopper-load, into an appalling, suffocating heat. Even on a fifteen-hundred foot mountain, there was not even a breeze. No one walked around, no one dug in, no one moved. An entire company, immobile, driven to earth. Lt. Alekna yelled for Doc Yee to get some salt pills out to the men and to goddamn well make sure the men swallowed them, he didn't want to have to call in a medevac for heat casualties.

When Alekna announced a patrol, we staggered to our feet, dragged our fighting gear about us, and headed downhill toward the woods. We would be grateful for the shade, but we knew every step would have to be matched by one uphill.

Four hundred yards down we made the forest and tottered into the shade of the spindly trees, coiled into a haphazard perimeter, threw off our gear, and sprawled. Immediately Alekna sent Craig and a grumbling Peewee out to scout.

I worked my back against the trunk of a gnarled, twisted sapling until I was comfortable, listening to the diminishing crunching and crackling where Craig and Peewee had disappeared from view. Away to the south, out of sight through the trees, a spotter chopper clattered about.

Distant guns rumbled, their reports muted and dull in the thick, hideous air. No one noticed them consciously, but then a flight of shells came wailing in overhead, low, as if paralleling the slope. We tensed until the shells were well past and had detonated with a loud crash, far down the mountainside. Whoever was doing the shooting, from Uplift or maybe Crystal, was just barely putting the rounds over the ridgecrest above us.

Again we heard the vague, faraway thunder and the rapidly approaching whooshing. I lay to one side, resting my head against the warm, crunchy leaves and sticks next to the tree. This time the shells made a staccato blast on the ridge crest and sent smoke and dust drifting against the sky. Alekna was already on the horn to Captain Stauffer, demanding an instant halt to the fire mission.

Stauffer complied and we relaxed, but then Stauffer was back on the air warning that a spotter chopper had seen some enemy troops near the platoon's location and did Alekna have the platoon together or were his security patrols still out? Before Alekna could answer, a short, heavy string of shots rattled through the forest somewhere downhill.

I jerked myself into a firmer position against my tree, bringing my '79 up to where I could close its breech and fire it in one smooth motion. "Ain't incoming," I said, glancing over at Johnston.

The squad leader was shaking his head slowly. He looked up the slope over his shoulder. "Ain't a 'sixteen, Two-Six. Ain't an AK either."

From off to the left Schebendach called out, "Sir, that's a Thompson, swear to God. Ain't nothin' else sounds like a Thompson."

I felt the platoon snap tight, like a muscle that had

spasmed. The hope that Peewee or Sergeant Craig were merely reconning by fire was gone. No one in the company, maybe no one in the entire 1st Cav, carried a Thompson. Few of them had ever even seen one outside of movies, TV, and comic books.

"All right," Alekna barked, loud enough for everyone in the perimeter to hear him distinctly, "Keep it cool, and don't be firin' off unless you know what's what! You're liable to hit Peewee and Sergeant Craig!"

Alekna looked down at Sellars, sitting next to him with the radio. He lifted the handset with a helpless gesture.

"Well, God damn!" Alekna snapped. "He didn't take his radio with him?"

"Said he didn't need it, sir," Sellers said.

Alekna stared at Craig's radioman for a second, then turned and put his hands on his hips. "Peewee! Two-Five!" he bellowed. "Can you hear me? Get back up here!"

Nothing stirred in the woods below.

"Peewee! Get up here now!" the lieutenant hollered. *"Now!"*

Alekna stood erect, his leanness exaggerated. His dirty yellow hair was plastered across his forehead and his face was wired into a tight, thin-lipped, demanding stare, like some kind of god of the forest.

Johnston leaped to his feet and about-faced in one ballet-like motion. "Shitfire, sir! Give 'em another yell, I – "

"Peewee! Two-Five!"

We heard a faint voice, then a loud snap as a branch broke. Peewee staggered up from the forest, panting heavily, his face white and streaked with sweat and grime. "Fuckin' tryin' to get our ass blowed off," was his breathless greeting. He trudged unsteadily, sounding like a climber on Everest without his oxygen bottle. Craig followed a few yards behind, like a man trying to walk a white line.

"Sir – "

"Take five, then get 'em saddled up and ready to move, Two-Five." Alekna said. There was no other greeting, no joshing, no 'that-was-a-close-one-wasn't-it?'

We waited long enough for Peewee to catch his breath and swallow a salt tablet while Doc Yee hovered over him. He reported that the shots the men had heard were not aimed at him and Craig, although they sounded as if they were fired from less than fifty yards away.

"Take it straight to the crest, Mines," Alekna said, and then he chuckled wearily. "Oh, Hell, just get us up there the easiest way, I don't care."

———

We fell into file and left the trees, dreading the sun's renewed assault but now dreading the forest and the mysterious Thompson more.

A zombie procession, I thought, glancing at the strung-out platoon where it was switchbacking uphill. There were no flankers out; no one so much as looked from side to side. The men marched with their legs only, as if the upper halves of their bodies were wooden racks for hanging pistol belts and helmets and slings on. The only sounds were boots softly scuffing through the thick grass and against the earth and rocks, heavy breathing, and the clacking of ammo bandoleers.

Mines reached the crest and turned right along it. I looked up, estimating how many more steps before I would be there, too.

Pupupupupup!

The men on the crest swung around while I continued to stare up at them, my mind telling me that someone was firing in my direction from the forest below. It wouldn't register. I was too tired, too fed up with the heat and the dreary agony of the hike and the strain of the interlude at the edge of the forest, and the reactions just weren't there. No one dove for cover, or even jumped at the sudden incoming.

Karl Small, directly in front of me, looked down toward the trees. "Get off it, man," he mumbled, and kept climbing.

I pushed myself the last several yards to the summit where the men at the top were shouting and pointing. To the east I heard choppers and the whining moan of jets.

The scene below was like a diorama, all plastic palm trees and plaster terrain and little blinking light bulbs, with a metallic soundtrack to go with it. At the base of the mountain lay what remained of the village of Van Thien: a smoking, flaming maze of trees and hedges and blazing hooches. Evidently, the NVA had left the boonies and occupied the village. Someone had discovered them and was doing their best to wipe them up before the day was out, knowing they would disappear overnight no matter how tightly the village was ringed.

A Huey gunship swept toward the village at a shallow angle, its miniguns peppering a long hedgerow leading toward the mountain. The NVA had broken out from the village along the hedge. Hounded by the chopper, they reached the temporary protection of a large clump of trees before dashing for the main forest. The chopper's red tracers spun and bounced, splashing the clump of trees with quick smudges of smoke. Then it pulled up and banked sharply to the south. Immediately, a SuperSabre howled down and dropped a full load of silvery napalm canisters onto the trees. The clump disappeared in a horrendous billow of flame and black smoke.

The men on the crest exclaimed and cheered, laughing and calling to one another, "Bringin' smoke on them fuckers, boy!

Look at that shit!" Then one of the several gunships in the air swung past us, near enough for the men to see that the doorgunner on their side had his helmet's sun visor up. They waved and shouted, and the gunner tossed back a casual, relaxed salute.

Alekna, holding the handset to his ear, called to the platoon. "All right, this is the deal: they think they're pushing the gooks into a corner. We're up here to call in artillery from Uplift. We can see everything from here, like we're on top of a map."

I dumped my gear next to my pack and stood up to stretch. Just how big an operation was going on here? I wondered. And what does the sniper in the forest have to do with it? The only possibility that made sense to me was that it had been a signal, perhaps a warning, which meant that Peewee and Craig must have been close to something, a camp, or a body of troops, or a weapons cache. The spotter had seen them, though we had gotten no report on how many there were or what they were up to. I had no idea how the NVA on the western side of the mountain fit in with the battalion on the east, but I was sure there was a connection. The fighting in the village isn't even the half of this deal, I thought. No one knows what the hell is going to turn up on this one. It gave me the jitters.

The fighting in the village eased and the only signs of the struggle now were thin plumes of smoke rising lazily from smoldering rubble and brush. Now and then shots would crack, or a grenade would go off. When that happened, some of us would stroll over to the side of the perimeter to take a look down the mountain, but nothing much appeared to be going on. All that was certain was that a good number of the North Vietnamese remained inside the village and that the battle for it might resume in the morning, unless, of course, as was probable, the enemy crept away in the darkness.

With nightfall, the Phu My Valley was black. We stood at

the edge of what seemed to be a measureless void. The night wind brought the scent of smoke, but Van Thien's fires had died down, probably because there was little left to burn. We heard occasional scattered shots and the odd grenade burst, but attributed that to jumpy listening posts and ignored them. Once, in what must have been an acoustical freak, I distinctly heard a human voice from the vicinity of the village.

Then we heard a monotonous drone: Spooky. The men who were not on guard, and who still possessed the energy after the rigors of the day, felt their way across to the east side of the summit. The drone stilled us, as it must have the men below. By the time we were able to spot it, the black cross was circling tightly over the village at about three thousand feet, more or less safe from what anti-aircraft capability the troops below were likely to have. It circled again and again, as if the pilot had lost interest in getting somewhere and had chosen to spend the evening in orbit. The drone was steady, a dull roar in the night, seldom changing in pitch or volume. It made us uneasy. Even I, who had seen Spooky in action before and knew what to expect, began to feel a creeping anxiety—why doesn't he do something? I knew that the eerily disquieting drone was part of the tactic, but I was impatient nonetheless. It might have been meant to unnerve the enemy, but it played with my mind, too.

When the first flare popped from the darkness into glaring yellow-white light, the village and its environs, as well as the mountaintop, were outlined in stark, harsh light. Where moments before there had been complete darkness, now I could see the men on the perimeter, the little piles of equipment and foxholes, and the brush, thick grass, and stones in the path along the crest. As each flare descended it swayed from side to side, sending shadows scuttling back and forth in a jerky, hand-cranked manner. Each faded, another took its place, and the scene repeated.

As if called forth by the light, the men met in small groups, waiting for the climax, and it came suddenly. A flare sputtered out and the night went black. Before anyone's eyes had adjusted, a thin line of red beads appeared below the flying cross, floating straight down in a line, one after the other, almost lightly. The tiny dots of fire were unimpressive after the flares and the drone—until the sound came. It sent a current of tension snapping through us. For seconds at a time, the sky was filled with the evil buzz-saw snarl of the guns, a whining, urgent sound that made hair stand up and take notice. I can feel it, I thought, right into my god-damned skull! It felt its way into bones and teeth and soul, producing a mixture of ecstasy and deep dread. It was like the smell of dead humans or incoming rounds—an experience that from the first made itself a niche in my mind, a corner from which it could never be excavated.

There was a continual muttering about the perimeter, the men speaking but making little effort to be understood. This wasn't the same as watching gunships working out, or joking about a pair of jets laying down napalm on a target. The men shook their heads and said things like "Spooky, man ...," and "Cuttin' loose," and "Looka that shit, man," but no one was listening. The words merely surfaced between bursts and drifted off, or were drowned by the next roar.

It stopped without ceremony. The tracers simply failed to appear after a burst. For several moments no one dared suggest that Spooky was done, but then I could hear it—the drone was no longer circling but was drifting south and I knew it was over. The mountain fell into darkness again. A wave of shock lay over the company.

"Ain't no one ever told me about that shit," Beyer said, his voice sounding flat.

Mines told of an incident when the company had made a night march to another battalion's support and Spooky was working over a village they had to walk past. "Couldn't even lie down and pretend you were safe that time," he told us. "Jus' had to keep on walkin', tryin' not to think about it too much."

"Kept Charlie's head down, though," Johnston put in. "Y'can say that much."

Mines shrugged it off. "Yeah, but that's about all. Unless the gooks is out in the open, that's all Spooky'll do, just keep 'em down for a while."

Which means the North Vietnamese are still down the hill, I thought. Maybe they're shook up, maybe Spooky even caught some of them, but if they sat tight in their bunkers, they're there. Spooky, for all his horror, was little more effective against a well-entrenched force than a lawnmower against crabgrass. Slow them down a little, that's all, so they will still be there to fight again in the morning, or bug out around the southern foot of the mountain.

———

My platoon didn't walk off of the mountain the next day, but 1st and Third did. If they didn't run into the enemy, it was a close thing, resulting from a combination of the enemy's speed in evacuating the village and withdrawing into the Suoi Ca, and the continued intense heat of the day, which led Stauffer to cancel their mission and order them back up the hill.

"Found all sorts of shit down there," 1st Platoon's leader reported. "Got a bunch of bandages, all bloody. You could see where they were goin'. We could follow the trail real easy, just by pickin' up the stuff they dropped."

Then, in the valley to the west, the spotter choppers caught a number of NVA in the open, prompting a series of air strikes, artillery barrages, ARA attacks and an air assault that lasted all day and virtually tore the whole valley apart. One sergeant who had been here for eleven months said that it was the biggest demonstration of US firepower he had ever seen.

With all that, though, the area was still full of NVA.

We finally set up a perimeter in napalmed rice paddies at the edge of the flat valley floor. The mountain to the northeast was crawling with NVA. Spotter choppers saw them and jets blasted them. Twice, the big bombs were close enough to send rocks and dirt flying all over my platoon.

With the approach of darkness the mountain took on a fearful aspect. The final jet strike of the day had been against its lower slopes, and now the black wall seemed to rise from a huge glowing brazier. A light evening breeze brought with it the pleasant autumnal odor of smoldering leaves, but I could not appreciate it.

The side of the mountain facing us was said to be infested with North Vietnamese fleeing north. That idea bit the dust, though, when Lake reported that a spotter pilot had seen mortar positions and a howitzer. "They're dug in like they plan to stick around for awhile. They aren't running."

Even though we already had flares, Johnston told me to go over to the C.P. and pick up more. "Things may get bad tonight, y'know? We're to put out two lines of flares, maybe more."

I was hoisting a box of flares to my shoulder when I heard Captain Stauffer say, "This is the worst position I've ever been in."

Coming from Stauffer, that stopped me cold.

"They're everywhere," Stauffer said. "The FAC's been catching them all the way from here to the Suoi Ca today, and all up and down that mountain. One of 'em called the woods up there 'one big bunker complex.'"

"Those air strikes must have taken care of them," I heard someone say.

"I doubt it," Stauffer answered. "They're probably still

there, plenty of 'em. I'm just betting that the air strikes fucked 'em up enough so they won't be in any shape to want to hit us tonight. The whole situation's really fluid."

In other words, I thought, no one has any idea what's going on.

The evening passed with no more air strikes, but it didn't help our nerves any when an artillery spotter round dropped within 50 meters of our perimeter's southern edge and, later, when the listening post cut loose at "movement." As jittery as we were, every sound was a mortal threat.

After all that, nothing happened.

———

Charlie was there last night, though. We started another patrol in the morning but were called back within half an hour to be lifted out. On the way back, while I was protecting the flank, I passed one of the craters where our mortar had dropped a round the night before. There, about 250 meters in front of my hole, in the fresh, black mud, were two well-defined Ho Chi Minh sandal tracks.

12

LZ Dog
LATE JUNE 1967

THE MOVIE WAS A HOPELESSLY AWFUL COUNTRY-WESTERN, AN atrocity of bad acting, an amateurish script, not much plot, and midway through a steady drizzle began. But something about the movie, dreadful as it was, affected the three of us despite our normal lack of self-pity and homesickness. We sat in the light rain, drinking our beer slowly, until our hair was plastered down and our fatigues were soaked through, engrossed in the trials of a rising young Nashville star fully as much as if we were watching a movie about ourselves. The singer was being screwed over by an unscrupulous agent and an assortment of conniving businessmen and Beyer, Schebendach and I saw in that our own situation. It made us see how our energies, abilities, and enthusiasms were being exploited by the Army brass who seldom, if ever, walked through rice paddies.

But it was more than that. We had not allowed ourselves to break down for too long a time. The plastic, absurd movie reminded us how far we were from home and how long it would be before we returned. Beyer was the first to begin crying, but shortly Schebendach and I were also weeping silently, our tears indistinguishable from the rain on our faces. We sniffed noisily now and then, hopelessly maudlin. We drew stares from the men around us—three sopping wet, drunk GIs sitting in the drizzle—but something about the intensity of our interest in the movie kept anyone from cracking wise or laughing.

We had cheered when the singer overcame all the obstacles in his path and made it big—it was a guaranteed all-American film, after all—and declared blubberingly that it was a tremendous movie, something that most of the men around us thought it most definitely was not. Schebendach began to whistle one of the singer's tunes and I sat with my head down to my knees, mumbling again and again, "Jesus, that was good. Christ, that was a good movie." Beyer put his arms around both our shoulders and after a little while we said we ought to be getting back to our bunker, someone had to relieve Peewee on guard.

I thought about my girlfriend and wished there were some way she could be with me just then. I wanted her to know about this, to understand how desperate everything was, how the war was changing me, burying my old self under so many experiences of blood and fear and sadness. I wondered if I would be recognizable whenever I returned home, or if my friends would whisper to each other, "My God, Mark's really changed. You'd hardly know he's the same guy."

"Hey," Beyer said. "Let's go, man."

I nodded and dropped my nearly-empty beer can into the mud. We walked slowly across the chopper pad, narrowly avoiding the Hueys in the pitch darkness, oblivious to the night and the rain.

Beyer was singing to himself, making one of the movie's songs his own. I was surprised to find that despite his rough-hewn speaking voice, Beyer sang very well, very clearly and smoothly.

"Oh, I'm the Jersey rebel," he sang, his accent turning the word into 'Joisey.' "I got things to do and things to say in my own way."

By the time we reached the bunker, I was weeping again.

13

An Hoa and An Quang
28 JUNE 1967

THE CHOPPERS SET US DOWN ON SAND DUNES BETWEEN THE village of An Hoa and the South China Sea. We exploded out of the slicks, blown around by the propwash and sand-blasted at the same time, formed a thin perimeter, and waited for the rest of the company. The other three platoons swooped in from LZ English in one huge flight, 20-odd Hueys delicately maneuvering their way onto the sand—the epitome of the airmobile concept.

Artillery began crunching into the area beyond the rise between us and the village, close enough to throw a few shards at us. We started plodding at an angle to the south of the village, which was still hidden by the dunes to the front. Now and then we could hear bursts of rifle and machine-gun fire at the north end of the village.

Topping the rise, I saw a broad strip of land connecting the dunes with the village. On both sides of the strip were rice paddies and, to the south, another lake. I began to work along the south side of the strip where the rice paddies merged with the solid ground, feeling sick. This was how Tan An had started

—a large open space with a company advancing across it on a village and a battalion of NVA waiting for us. Sgt. Mortenson yelled for me to stop and turn around. The company was going to set up for the night where the dunes rose up from the solid corridor across from the village. We were close enough that the artillery was becoming a nuisance. One ugly frag came whispering in to land with a heavy thud a few feet behind us. The scrap-metal whizzing around was ours, not theirs.

We moved to a high point on the dunes where we could observe the village from its northern junction with the dunes all the way south to where they petered out across the corridor. The northern half was smoking heavily.

We dug a deep, wide hole at the edge of the 30-foot drop that marked the dunes' limit and sat back to watch. The small-arms rattle was continuous now and we instinctively ducked when a fine whitter of rounds tracked overhead. Not thinking that whoever was shooting at us, intentionally or unintentionally, might lower his sights a little, I decided to write a letter. Beyer and I snapped pictures of each other so that we could send them home as photos taken under fire, though our relaxed poses gave no sign of it.

All during the afternoon, two gunships had been orbiting around, followed by two Chinook Guns-a-Go-Go. Five more gunships and ARA choppers arrived and they all went to work tearing things up. The two Go-Go ships fired short, heavy bursts from their fifties, loosed several rockets, and a part of the village erupted in smoke and flashes and streaks of red. The gunships followed. Occasionally, return fire flashed up to meet the birds.

A troop ship from 1/9 Cavalry landed on the strip of land south of the village sealing that exit off. At the same time, a platoon of tanks and dusters swept up to the northern end of the village. As darkness approached, we slid down the steep slope, advanced into the dirt field, and set out trip flares and Claymores.

With the darkness, the gunships and the small-arms fire quit and the artillery at Uplift and Ollie took over. All night long, the 105s, 155s and eight-inchers blasted the village from one end to the other. Mortars targeted a large stucco house a few score meters beyond until a white phosphorous round caved in the roof. The windows and doors were filled with fleeing enemy. Every so often, tracers from 1/9 Cav's blocking unit would slice into the village or go caroming off above the palms to burn out harmlessly. At three a.m. I awoke to find the whole place lit up by artillery flares and then fell back asleep.

Morning dawned and we sat in our holes for quite some time. I shared some of the fruit my parents had sent while we waited for something to happen. The artillery was still lazily working over the village.

Robinson's machine gun suddenly opened up way over to the left. I ran up to the CP where the view to the south was open and watched, stupefied, as Robinson closed in on some tiny figures who appeared to be wading in the lake a good 300 meters away. They went down. A gunship took over after receiving the report, plastered the area with rockets and machine-gun fire, and then took up patrolling the area for any more escapees from the village.

I saw someone walking barely 100 meters to our right front. I punched Beyer and exclaimed that we had a gook out there. Beyer looked, threw his rifle up to his shoulder and snapped off several rounds. The man went down. I leaped over to Jones's hole and directed his gun's fire until he was pounding the gook's hiding spot. Then I popped a couple of grenades into the grassy field he was lying in. He never rose, so we assumed he was dead.

We were still excited about this when I noticed several people just on our side of the village. I again alerted everybody and was about to open fire when Jones yelled at me not to shoot because he could see they were women. We held fire, though I was annoyed they weren't NVA so I could have some action.

An old man came walking toward us, heading directly for our CP. Mortenson ordered Petersen to nail him with the machine-gun. Everybody was crowding over to see the man die. Many thought it unnecessary to shoot him since he was obviously unarmed and scared. Don't shoot him, he's an old bastard, knock him down, let him go, Christ, he's not going to matter, get him, no, he's down!

Petersen finally connected. A slug smashed the man's leg and he collapsed into a low hedge along the trail. We watched, half in amazement and half in anguish, as he struggled to his feet and continued toward us. Petersen pulled the trigger again, and again the old man went down.

None of us could believe it when he once more arose and, with a look of sad resignation on his ancient face, turned and began staggering back to the village. By this time, Mortenson was the only one who was excited about shooting him. The rest of us were sickened. Petersen's gun rattled some more and the man pitched forward. This time he stayed there. We filtered back to our holes.

A young woman trotted toward us near where Beyer, Jones and I had killed our lone man. Nobody was about to shoot at her and she made it to 3rd Platoon's line without incident.

A flight of Skyraiders roared in and dumped canisters of napalm on the northern end of An Hoa. The red fire splashed up to turn into thick gouts of black smoke. Some of the canisters hit the paddies and only half ignited. The water splashed up amid the smoke and fire and everyone was excited.

We started moving north to support D Company. More airstrikes were called in. Each time a bomb exploded, we went into a collective crouch until the metal ceased buzzing and thudding around us. Capt. Stauffer managed to get us into a line at the edge of the dunes where we waited while the dusters went to work knocking off treetops, which might hold snipers. Occasionally, there was a short spatter of rifle fire from far down the village where 1/9's troops were catching escapees. Then Lt. Alekna waved his arm and we plunged down the bank, through sharp-leaved brush, to the first trees of the village.

The line went to pot immediately. It didn't matter. Most of us were past masters of village search-and-destroy-missions so we knew what to do. Grenades were thrown into bunkers, tunnels, wells. Van Weeks tossed one into a small hole and nearly hit SantaMaria as the blast went right out the hole on the other side of the mound. The hooches went up in flames as we applied cigarette lighters to the brittle thatch. In the area where the rocketing, bombing and shelling had been concentrated, there was nothing left to burn or blow up. It was possible to walk several-score meters on flattened walls or smashed palms without touching the ground.

We moved across small open breaks and held up. I went over to a bunker and prepared to throw in a grenade. 1st, I hollered to see if anyone was inside. Mortenson told me to go ahead and blow it but I waited. A woman and three small kids crawled out. I shot Mortenson a dark look and then tossed in the grenade.

We decided to eat lunch. The tank commanders sprayed tree-tops with their grease guns as insurance against snipers. We found an old woman sitting in the dirt. She seemed unhurt until we turned her around and saw a quarter-sized hole in her back. Doc Yee disgusted us by refusing to help her. Medevac was also refused. We tried to ignore her. The worms were eating the intestines of a man a few meters away. I spooned sliced peaches from a can.

Some jets came in and put more napalm down in front of

us. A few gunships also performed during the break. The small stable in front of us began to stink as the bodies of three cows bloated in the heat. We laughed and joked and poked around the ruins until the tank engines roared up and we were told to keep on pushing ahead.

Eight or nine children came running out of a bunker and headed toward us. It was obvious they were just trying to get out of our way and we shouted for the tank to hold fire. It didn't. A beehive round left the children looking like so many plastic dolls someone had knifed up and tossed into the ash dump.

A woman, weeping, brought her child to us. The child was bleeding from a head wound and its little finger was torn up, but Doc Yee refused to help. It was a toss-up whether we would shoot the enemy next or him.

The sweep now began to dissolve into a mass of squad-size groups going after this or that bomb shelter. Some shelters did not need to be checked—the tanks had ground over them and they were flattened. Eleven women and kids swarmed out of one bunker. One was an infant, probably born during the fight; its eyes, nose, ears, and mouth were obscured by dozens of flies.

A cow stood with half of its shoulder gone. Sergeant Craig shot it six times before it blinked. Small fired once more and the poor beast collapsed.

Mortenson came upon a box of small pink paper fans and had his picture taken cooling himself amidst the rubble.

A new man in 1st Platoon blasted a bunker with a grenade. A head and weapon appeared in the doorway. Mortenson got hysterical until the man put three rounds into the figure and it fell back inside.

We finally arrived at 1/9 Cav's line and threw ourselves down on the dirt, drinking the last of our water. Word came down to turn turn around, go back through the village, and smash everything that was smashable. We got out our entrenching tools and slowly moved back to the north end. Nothing escaped. We knocked over the few upright walls, burned the people's rice baskets, and even knocked holes in the small clay pots. Where the village narrowed, everybody came back together and followed the armored vehicles onto the dunes. I noticed one last hooch that had not been burned and lit the thatch. Mine was the last one to be set on fire before the company ascended the sandy hill to set up for the night.

From the dunes, we could see the whole length of the desolate village, a long strip of grayish-green topped off by fingers of orange flame and thin streams of dark smoke. A quiet crackling was the only sound amid the confusion of feeding and arranging the company in a defensive perimeter.

An Hoa village was still in ruins in January 1968 when my company flew over it for the last time before leaving for Eye Corps. From as far away as the 506 Valley, it could be seen from the air as a brown smudge on a green horizon, the hundreds of bomb and shell craters still visible. The ashes and blackened logs appeared to have been washed or carried away, but the only signs of life were the green tops of the palms.

14

to LZ Horvath

JULY 22, 1967

MORE HELICOPTER FLIGHTS, MORE FRUITLESS PATROLS, A HUT burned in a backwater fold of a ridge, a false alarm by a scout dog atop a thickly-forested hill south of Hoai An, and after three days we found ourselves back on the place we called Miami Beach.

By nine a.m. the next day the long company file entered a narrow passage at the base of the ridge. A clear stream flowed swiftly between the vertical walls of the ravine, cutting a narrow, shallow channel through the gray sand. Rounded and weathered boulders—small-grained hunks of rock five and six feet in diameter—reminded me of the scenery in Cowboys and Indians shows I had watched as a child. It was a place of delicate, finely-tuned beauty, and the scuffling of many combat boots against the sand and rooks complemented rather than intruded on the serenity of the defile.

By afternoon we had marched in the heat all day, up to a ridgecrest and down to the first narrow reaches of paddies, overgrown with mats of aquatic weeds. The air was still and thick; the heat trampled our spirits. Now and then a man stopped, shifted his load slightly, took a deep breath, and closed his eyes tightly for a second before moving on, slogging unsteadily.

We headed for LZ Horvath to organize a position for the night. The hill had no bunkers, trenches, or enemy positions on it, just interlocking masses of thorn bushes through which we tripped and stumbled and fell. The platoon line fell apart into straggling groups of men trying to find the paths of least resistance through the thickets.

Almost everyone on the hill was arguing with everyone else. The squad leaders snarled orders with abnormal harshness and the men replied in kind, telling the squad leaders what they could do with the order. Alekna told Mortenson to get his goddamned half of the platoon straightened out. Spurlock told Alekna that he was sick and tired of the asshole captain and his stupid ideas. Beyer announced to all within range that he hated the Army, the war, the hill he was on, and the weather.

We reached Horvath and fell down in a heap along its sector of the company perimeter. Knowing that chow and water were already on the way, we drained our canteens greedily. The ground was soft, so digging in was not difficult, but despite that, it took longer than usual for the holes to be finished and the trip flares and Claymores to be run out. The day, having started so pleasantly in the cool ravine at the base of the ridge, had turned out to be such a broiling horror that we were determined to take it easy and use every possible spare moment to lie in the shade.

At dusk new orders came down.

"We can't put up hooches tonight," Alekna reported, "and the ones that're up will hafta come down. At three o'clock in the morning we're marching out of here. There's gonna be an Arclight—a B-52 strike—up there," he gestured at the mountains around the northern edge of the basin—"at six, and we hafta be outta here and at least three kilometers away. Gettin' up at three and humpin' is the only way we can do it. There's supposed to be a battalion of NVA up there."

We sat by our holes making bitter comments about "the idiots running this whole thing" and "that dumb bastard," who in most cases meant Capt. Kelly, although he was in no way responsible.

We started guard at eight p.m., an hour earlier than usual, in an effort to get as much sleep as possible in the eight hours available. I figured that, assuming nothing untoward happened overnight, each man would be able to get about two and a half hours of sleep.

Sometime after midnight Rogers radioed from his listening post (LP) that he could hear what sounded like a squad-sized body of men crawling through the woods. Again the platoon was alerted and we dragged ourselves awake and to the holes. Rogers was convinced he was hearing the real thing and not making anything up, and at last Alekna and Capt. Kelly gave in. "Have your men throw grenades and then get back here as quickly as you can," they told him. Unfortunately, they didn't tell the men along the perimeter. The sudden roar of grenades and sharp flashes of light took us by surprise, and then a trip flare popped illuminating a face.

"Gooks!" Peewee yelled. "Hit 'em!"

I snapped shut my '79 and raised it to my shoulder.

"Stop!" Alekna hollered, running forward from the platoon CP. "Don't shoot! It's Rogers comin' in!"

The face reappeared in the flare's light. I opened the breech of the '79 and lowered it.

"God, that was close," Peewee breathed.

My hands shook as I set the grenade launcher onto the hole's parapet, covered my face, and leaned forward against the rim of the hole. Rogers and his men jogged into the perimeter, breathing heavily. They knew what I knew: I had almost killed them.

15

Night March

JULY 23, 1967

WE WERE UP AT THREE AND MARCHING. FIFTEEN MINUTES outside the perimeter, I knew we were going in the wrong direction. Whoever Alekna had pulling point was leading the company much too far to the left—to the east—to hope to reach the open paddies, which was the first march objective.

"We're goin' the wrong way, Mines," I said. "We oughtta be going more to the right."

"You sure?"

"Hell, yes. I don't need a compass to know when everything's fucked up."

Mines walked forward, returned shortly, and tapped me on the shoulder.

"Lieutenant wants you to come up and lead."

After a quick compass check and a word with Alekna, I stepped off, turning the file sharply to the right and advancing toward the open paddies. I felt a thrill of pride: it was the first night march since I had joined the company, and I was leading it. I thought of all the times I had gone night-hiking through the woods around home, through fog and rain and snow, until I had developed an easy sense of direction, and the ability always to go where I wanted to, even on the blackest nights. After twenty minutes I passed through a belt of palms and came to the edge of the paddies.

On into the night, southeast now, away from Horvath and the basin and the coming Arclight. The march wasn't difficult and it was a good deal cooler than any daytime hump could have been. At dawn we were well away from the basin, marching quietly down a dirt road through the center of a village. Many of the inhabitants were up and around, working over cooking fires and beginning the day's labor. I was pleased to see their surprised glances as I strode past them. We did it this time, I thought. They never expect us to go humping around at night, and this time we did it.

The order to halt came after another kilometer, and the platoon leaders arranged their commands in a broad circle across dry, stubbled paddies between the dirt road and the river to the east. With no further instructions, we relaxed, ate, and tried to nap in the sunlight, which grew in intensity by the minute. As for the Arclight we had marched to escape —nothing.

In the evening I dug a hole, put up a poncho hooch, and arranged my sleeping spot. In the near-dark I could hear Beyer singing, "Joisey Rebel."

I started to speak, but a sound I had never heard before stopped me. The sky above the eastern Tiger Mountains began to hum with a grinding, whining reverberation of descending scales, a grisly, multi-toned nose-dive roar that made me think of a heavy truck's gears being shifted down suddenly. The Arclight.

Wildly-hued glows of lurid color pulsated up from the beach side of the mountains. In seconds the flashes advanced to the nearer slopes in full view of the perimeter. Like strings of unearthly flashbulbs, the sticks of bombs rippled and flared across the ridges and into the hidden ravines, casting weird split-second shadows into a sky already clogged with rolling towers of smoke and dust.

Gunships, artillery, even jet strikes were nothing near to this. The final bombs from the third and last B-52 plunged down, detonated in brilliant reds and yellows and oranges, and ripped up more tons of earth and shattered rocks and trees. The mountains seemed to have grown luminescent, as if they were on the verge of erupting catastrophically all by themselves.

Then the a-rhythmic, beating, pounding waves of concussion reached me, swatting lightly, playfully, and making the material of my clothes jump and quiver with a life of their own. A mélange of cracks and booms and thuds and earth-deep rumblings smote the perimeter and shook the sandy ground—the sound of the mountains themselves breaking apart and crumbling violently into their valleys.

The tumbling echoes still thundered away into the night and the mountains darkened. Here and there remnants of the forest burned, red-yellow flames dim through the clouds of pulverized debris covering the range. Around me I could hear muffled exclamations: "Sonuvabitch!" "Jesus fuckin' Christ!" "Bringin' smoke!" The voices sounded subdued and stricken. "Arclight." The code name brought up images of hellish power, of bolts of crashing energy storming across the sky and through the earth with the rage of a thousand blast furnaces gone mad.

After a while, a mysterious fog drifted onto the perimeter, thickening slowly until the outlines of trees and hooches a few yards away became indistinct and fuzzy and were finally hidden altogether. It had a strangely musty odor to it and I realized with a start that this was no ordinary manifestation of the weather. No, I was breathing the mountains themselves, the bits of wasted bark and stone and earth and leaves and Godalmighty, who knew but that it was flesh and blood and bone, too and I was breathing it, inhaling whatever ghastly refuse the bombing had rendered to dust.

A gagging sensation uncoiled from my gut. I wiped my hands across my pants. The fog seemed to take forever to drift across the perimeter and continue south, thinning slowly. Watching the fog disappear, flowing through the night like a bank of ectoplasmic vapor, a filthy ghost of sorts, I felt a violent shudder gust through me from my toes to my neck. I wiped off my hands again and spat into the dirt. I felt violated, as if the mist were more than should be expected of us, even in a war.

16

North Tiger Mountains
AUGUST 15, 1967

"C'mon, Smith," Sgt. Campbell said, "take that hooch down."

I hadn't fired my launcher for weeks. Without breaking my stride I snapped shut the breech, pleased with the hollow, solid clink it made, pushed off the safety, and raised the stock to my shoulder. Stopping for only a second, I guesstimated the range ... a hundred yards now ... and pulled the trigger, punching the explosive shell squarely into the center of the thatched roof. Almost before the smoke of the explosion blew away, a circle of small, jumping red flames was eating at the dry palm fronds. I ejected the empty cartridge and raised my weapon over my head, brandishing it like a Plains Indian waving a Winchester in triumph.

We destroyed a lot that day. No orders were issued, no word was passed down through the chain of command, but the brief shooting match was taken as some kind of signal, a sort of cue, by the spread-out elements of the company. Detonations sounded from the left where Third Platoon was sweeping quickly toward a cluster of hooches; its leftmost flank squad, skirting the very base of the mountains through thick brush, now and then opened up with rifle fire, cautiously spraying possible hiding places in its path. There were fewer hooches in front of the rest of the company, but the grenadiers were busy anyway, methodically blowing in roofs and walls. There were more and more explosions, sharp and crunching from the '79s, heavy and dull from the frags thrown into bunkers, and the men were shouting "Go get your own bunker!" and "Watch it, for Christ's sake, you want to get blown up?" and always, minute by minute, "Fire in the hole! … Fire in the hole! … Fire in the hole!" … *Fwhump!* Always that last call, the litany of search and destroy.

Fuqua and I teamed up and worked a section of the valley by ourselves, sometimes running into others from the platoon, but more often isolated from the rest. I was eager to find a bunker so I could use the white phosphorus grenade I had been carrying since the end of June. I found one next to an already smoldering hooch where the hills edged closer, forming a neck between the upper and lower halves of the valley. While Fuqua stood to one side with his rifle aimed at the hole in the caked earth, I straightened the cotter pin and called a warning. I was about to pull and throw when Spurlock appeared through a clump of trees behind me.

"Don't throw it in there, Smith. It's already been blown."

I had noticed the blackened clay around the hole, but I was up for using the phosphorous now. "Oh, hell, Sarge, no telling when that was done. Might have been a week ago. Who knows what's inside?"

Spurlock shook his head in a low sweeping motion. "Oh, go ahead, throw it. I don't care. Just do it and let's go."

The pearly white smoke gushed from the hole after the soft, almost quiet explosion. I stood a few feet from the stomach-wrenching fumes, staring at the hole they streamed up from. The rising column was not alone; across the width and breadth of the valley there were pillars rolling toward the sky. Mine was unique, though, its brilliance contrasting sharply against the greasy, thin blackness of the others. The phosphorus's virginal whiteness gave no indication of its rotten-sweet-brimstone stench, while the darker columns smelled of autumn leaves and campfires by the Appalachian Trail.

17

Hoai An Valley
LATE AUGUST 1967

THE OLD MAN AGREED TO POLE THE COMPANY ACROSS THE KIM Son at the rate of fifty piastres a boatload, which struck me as an embarrassment. Here we were, a company of airmobile infantry, theoretically the most technologically advanced fighting men in history, able to leap high mountains with a single flight of Hueys, now forced to shell out our own cash so an old farmer would take us from one bank of a not-very-wide river to the other. Were it not for the farmer and his boat, I thought, we'd be stuck right here.

We clumped aboard the ancient gray scow and sat down clumsily along the gunwales and the keel. Bunched together, bemused sweet-sour expressions on our faces, we looked like anything but warriors, projecting gun barrels and dangling grenades notwithstanding. The Boy Scouts go for a boat ride, I mused.

At the bow, one of Three-Six's men was sawing away at a homemade one-string Vietnamese violin he had picked up. Probably he had found it in the village they had cordoned earlier that day. The notes he produced were slurred and discordant, unrelated to one another. It certainly wasn't music, but I found it curiously affecting. The fellow stroked the instrument softly and the notes were faint and distant. I felt a deep sadness creep over me, a sudden rending loneliness that seemed to incorporate my entire war experience and sink deep into me.

Doubts had beset me before—after Tan An, after An Hoa—but never like this. Before, I had wondered about specific situations. Was it right to risk killing civilians in pursuit of the enemy? Was it wrong to refuse a medevac to a wounded old lady, or to deliberately fire on a man who might or might not be armed? But the remote strains from the violin let loose an immense doubt: was I losing more than I was gaining by this experience? Was knowledge of pain and death and degradation worth the cynicism, callousness, and bitterness that went with it? I had learned much and done much, things none of my friends would ever know or do. So what? Was it worth anything? Does a laboratory guinea pig end up any the wiser after the experiments on it are done, when it is cancerous or deformed or incapable of bearing young?

18

Tiger Mountains
AUG. 30, 1967

"What happened up there, man? Did you actually see the gooks?"

"Ran right into 'em, about six of 'em, standing, lounging around the trail. Didn't even see us until Blackhat fired at 'em. Man, we turned around and hauled ass then!"

"Shit," I said. "By the time it got back to where I was, it was 'a hundred gooks up there gettin' ready to ambush us.'"

"Well," Beyer said, "however many there are, they know we're here and we know they're there."

I knew we would be going back up that hill. After the gunships, after the artillery, after the jet strikes everyone was hoping for, we would form up again and walk through the streambed and turn left up the path. I felt a new sensation. If the heavy supporting fires were off target, or if they were not heavy enough, then the gooks would be there, sure as shit, and it would be the first time I had ever gone forward knowing without a doubt that a fight would take place.

Up from the creekbed, past a new bomb crater that still stank of high explosive, up to the spot where the gully led away to the left, and then the small clump of bushes on the right of the path. Any second now, I thought. Just any second, it's going to happen.

The platoon halted and I knelt, swallowing and then running my teeth over my lower lip, wondering what the holdup was, and wishing we would move forward and get it over with. I was about to ask why they—

Bap! ... Bap!

Two shots, then silence and the men crouched lower, tense, almost vibrating in the suddenly supercharged atmosphere. Neither shot sounded like incoming; there was no crackling to them.

"Recon by fire," Van Weeks muttered.

I shook my head. No, it wasn't recon. Wood wouldn't fire just two single shots. He'd blow the bushes apart with half a magazine on full automatic if he were reconning. Something was wrong.

I frowned and turned to face Van Weeks. The ammo bearer's expression was a frightened blank. He was worried; his comment about recon by fire had been a statement of hope more than anything else. We stared at each other for a few taut seconds.

With the rustle of shifting bodies and turning heads, word was passed back along the path: "Wood got hit."

The whispered report said Wood had halted the platoon in order to check out a side path ascending the ridge to the left. He had walked up the path to within his own body's length of a North Vietnamese bunker. The bunker's occupant fired one shot, apparently striking Wood in the chest. Wood, falling, instinctively fired a return shot, which went straight up through the trees.

"He's right in front of the gook and no one can get to him! He's ten yards away from the other guys up there!"

We were to advance until we met the enemy and then pull back to the perimeter at Horvath for the night. That's what the orders said, but now the orders were out the window. No one would be pulling back until Wood was recovered.

The fact that Wood seemed to be still alive filled me with dread. Alive, Wood could be used as bait to draw other GIs forward, where they could be blown away. We would have to try. Wood might be dying, might already be dead, but as long as it was possible that he might be breathing, it was imperative for the men in the platoon to reach him.

It took two tries to reach Wood, but then with enough covering fire, a group brought him back, unconscious and barely alive. He died as we were getting him into the medevac sling.

Night fell.

"Gimme six men to carry Wood."

I held back, not relishing the idea of carrying Wood's corpse down the dark streambed, but at the same time not wishing to shirk the responsibility. Wood had been a friend, after all. Beyer made up my mind for me.

"C'mon, Smitty, let's go ahead and get it done."

A hand appeared to take my '79 and I stepped to the left side of the litter. In the dark it was hard to tell how it was arranged, and I had to grope in search of a handhold. My hand brushed something cold and limp and I drew it back with distaste. But then I found one of the canvas loops and the six pallbearers were ready to start.

The streambed was a jagged, treacherous agony for mind and body. Every step was the wrong one. I lost count of the number of boulders and limbs I cracked into. I could not see anything—not Wood, not the men in front of me, not even my free hand when I lifted it to my face. I could only hear the stumbling and scuffling and muttering before and behind me.

There was no way to gauge the platoon's progress through the streambed. When my carrying arm felt as if it were finally giving way and separating from my shoulder I clutched toward a nearby sound and asked for a relief. It was Van Weeks.

"Fuck no, I just got off it."

I forced myself along, straining to the limit of my strength each time Wood had to be lifted slightly to clear a branch or a rock, until my entire right arm was numb and my fingers were locked into the canvas loop as if frozen to it.

"Hold up," Farmer said, touching me on the back and handing me the weapons he was carrying. "Here, take these. I'll carry for awhile."

I released my grip and stepped away.

The platoon passed out of the streambed and on to the brushy sand flats, just as Uplift's artillery opened up with illumination rounds over the ridge. A murmur of relief rose among the men.

"C'mon," Sgt. Campbell said wearily, "let's get to the perimeter and not be takin' a break now."

No one seemed to have his own weapon. Alekna was carrying Rob's machine gun. Rob had my '79. The ammo box Farmer had given me belonged to one of Third Platoon's gun teams. Letts was going all around the company looking for the owners of three helmets he had wound up with. The company seemed to have passed through a giant blender on its flounder through the streambed, with everyone too beaten down to notice. I thought it would not be too much of a surprise if the still form on the litter turned out to be a dead North Vietnamese instead of Wood.

19

LZ Horvath
THE NEXT DAY

We were grateful when the division commander, General Tolson, came over to our section of the perimeter after he was done conferring with the captain and the battalion staff. He stopped when he came to the listening post group.

"I understand that you were the men on point yesterday," he said. We looked down, nodding. "Well, I think you did a pretty good job up there."

I frowned. We got our ass kicked and Wood got killed and that ain't good any time. I wondered if the general really knew what had happened yesterday.

"Is there anything you men need? Anything at all? You know, clothes, equipment, ammo? Let me know and I'll see that S-4 gets it to you."

"Yes, sir." It was Van Weeks and the general turned to face him. "We need pants, sir. Pants!" Van Weeks spun around and bent over forward. A gasp went up from the men standing by. Van Weeks's pants had rotted entirely away from the belt in back to the fly in front, and his buttocks were staring the general in the face.

I closed my eyes. It was the stockade for Van Weeks. You simply don't go around mooning major generals.

But the division commander roared with laughter. "Okay! Okay! Pants it is! I'll see to it that S-4 gets a complete resupply of clothing out here this afternoon."

The general walked back to the landing pad, waving to the men as he boarded his chopper, still laughing to himself and shaking his head.

20

September 1967

A GREAT CHANGE TOOK PLACE WITH THE ARRIVAL OF CAPTAIN Bonthuis. Captain Kelly, the rumor went, had come to the war with a fiery eagerness to mix it up with the enemy, to lead men into battle. In contrast, Bonthuis seemed to embrace the role of Reluctant Soldier. Suddenly we had a captain who slouched when he stood, looked morose all the time, and griped about his mother-in-law.

Morale in the company became measurable for the first time in weeks.

21

LZ Horvath Basin
MID-SEPTEMBER 1967

THE PLATOON, ALONG WITH THE COMPANY C.P, WERE choppered to the mouth of a small stream running from the Dam Tra-O to the ocean. Captain Bonthius led us due west to the entrance of the LZ Horvath basin and set us to work looking for a mass grave holding fifty bodies a *chieu hoi* [defector] had spoken of two days previously. As usual the *chieu hoi's* story proved inaccurate. We found only three single tombs in a narrow field between the creek and a brushy hill. Deveau and I volunteered to begin disinterring the occupants to check for booby-traps.

The earth was soft and in fifteen minutes I scraped the soil from the top of a gray wooden coffin three feet down. I pried the lid off to reveal a slightly-decomposed corpse. That the man was a war victim was obvious: his skull was half-shattered, with a jagged hole more than an inch in diameter above the left eye.

The second grave was different. Like many others that dotted the landscape around villages, it was more than just a simple elongated mound. At its base it was nearly circular, two feet high and flat on top, and was surmounted by a second, slightly smaller replica of the first part.

"This ain't no NVA," I said. "This is just some villager. You can tell by the way it's built – a big mound, then a little one on top."

"Well, it's awfully fresh. Maybe the people in the village downstream buried the gooks."

That made sense, I thought, and I bent to the task of digging it up. A few minutes later, something gave way beneath the thrust of my entrenching tool. Alekna was fumbling with his camera, setting the exposure and checking the distance and depth of field.

The body was not in a coffin. A thick cotton wrapping was all that protected it from the earth. A strong cord was tied around the waist. I extended the pick portion of my entrenching tool, slid it under the cord and began tugging slowly and firmly. Alekna made a last hurried check of his camera settings and I wrenched the corpse free and held it up at arm's length. The cord hung from the pick and both ends of the body sagged toward the hole.

Click.

"Smith," Small said, "the North Carolina Vulture."

They laughed at this and I was pleased. That's good, I thought. It had a rhythm to it—the North Carolina Vulture. When we got back to the company, I would have to put that on my helmet cover.

The third body was more than half-rotted, being little more than a skeleton, a grimy specimen so old that no stench rose from the pit. I dredged up the skull and provided the men with some morbid entertainment by carrying it around on the end of a stick.

Mortenson told me to throw "that damned disgusting thing" away, I sure as hell wasn't dragging a filthy skull around.

I kept it on the stick long enough for Alekna to take one last snapshot of me, grinning madly, shirt open and sweat-dark, a cigarette butt in one hand and the skull on a stick in the other, with Hester leering over my shoulder and the sharp peaks of the Tiger Mountains in the background.

22

LZ Pony
LATE OCTOBER 1967

ON THE THIRD DAY OF OUR STAY ON LZ PONY, 2ND PLATOON'S leader took a patrol into the small side valley. A spotter plane was flying high overhead, little more than a slowmoving silvery dot in the sky, as the platoon, with me near its tail, marched from the LZ perimeter and advanced through a scrub-covered strip of flatland. As the point man led the file well into a line of uncultivated paddies we heard the faraway, muffled kettle drum sound of the eight-inchers on Uplift being fired.

The rising wail of large caliber shells took us by surprise. The wail became a shrieking metallic howl and two eight-inch projectiles fell and exploded with a roar not one hundred yards in front of us. A shower of evilly splintered steel whipped past us. Hunkering down, I listened as one particularly large chunk hummed almost soothingly over my head, so close that the hum was more a felt vibration than one I heard. It splashed heavily into the water a few feet behind me. I turned to find the man in back of me staring at me, lips half open with a bubble of spit across his mouth and his right shirtsleeve liberally sprinkled with paddy water.

The next pair of shells was already whining but we were

thrashing wildly toward the dubious protection of the banks around the paddy, throwing ourselves into the water, hunting desperately for a niche in the earth large enough to fit ourselves into. Someone yelled that the shells had landed closer than before and then the platoon leader, who had been talking frantically into the radio handset, told everyone to run for it. I lunged onto the bank of the paddy and charged in Pony's general direction, swerving only to avoid trees and running over whatever else was in my way. The third salvo was already inbound.

The shells blew up the better part of the paddy but we had moved so quickly that not one of us was caught by the blasts or the shrapnel. In fact, only one man had been injured: during his dash for safer ground he had been stung badly in the chest by a bee.

The shelling had been a mistake. The spotter plane pilot had noticed a file of armed men outside Pony. He had not been informed about our patrol, so he assumed he was seeing NVA and put in a call to Uplift. The pilot realized his mistake when he saw the men running helter-skelter for Pony instead of deeper into the valley.

Jotting a few figures on the back of an envelope, I realized that I had come under fire from friendly forces almost as often as I had from the enemy, and, as a matter of fact, the friendlies had often come closer to sapping me than had the NVA and VC. Somehow this discovery tickled me and engaged my sense of the absurd.

23

Outpost Harry
DECEMBER 2, 1967

I COUNTED NINE BODIES ON THE BARBED WIRE JUST OFF THE northern corner of the outpost. They were the usual color. The streaks of dried blood were pinkish, diluted by the early morning sprinkle. Not one of the dead was clothed in more than a pair of gray cotton shorts. It did not seem possible that they had actually knocked over Harry, these small, half-nude men, wearing underpants, carrying satchel charges and rocket launchers, crawling through the slick, cold mud and the tangled wire. My mind whirled. How could the ARVNs possibly lose, sitting behind the wire and the broad ditch, protected by bunkers and crisscrossing bands of automatic weapons fire, able to call on all the artillery in An Khe for support? Truly it was mind-boggling. Even a company of brand new basic trainees could have held the outpost, I thought. The ARVN soldiers hadn't been asleep, the nine enemy bodies well outside the bunker circle confirmed that, so what was it? What was the secret of this war? It was ridiculous, the idea of loin-clothed savages giving a beating to well-armed, supported, and dug-in troops.

24

XYZ Ring [An Khe]
MID-DECEMBER 1967

THE PLATOON WALKED THROUGH THE COOL, DAMP DARKNESS toward a circular cluster of hooches named Ba Thach 2. We tensed once when a dog barked at us unexpectedly, but met Captain Bonthuis and the rest of the company. Campbell and the other platoon leaders conferred with Bonthuis before initiating the cordon of the hamlet.

Following a lane overhung by trees and bordered by high, thorny hedges that led around the perimeter of the village, the platoon wound its way to the eastern side. No sound or light came from within the broad circle of hedge, but I was sure the villagers were awake and wondering what the crazy GIs from the An Khe camp were up to at four-thirty in the morning.

Campbell led us east across a slowly rising meadow and then back toward the north, halting for a map check when two hooches grew out of the darkness ahead.

"Gotta spread out north and south. Each squad'll split in two and set up about thirty to fifty meters apart. You know the rules: no one goes in or out of the village once we're in position. If someone won't stop, shoot 'em."

Pop pop pop pop!

"Goddammit," Campbell hollered toward the village, "this is Two-Six! Two-Six! Now knock that shit off!"

One of 1st Platoon's radiomen called. "Thought you were gooks, over," he said.

Fifteen minutes later a water buffalo was machine-gunned when it advanced curiously on one of Third Platoon's positions. I tried not to laugh too loudly when I heard about it. Shooting at one another, shooting the local water buffalo, yelling back and forth—the whole mission was screwed up. That is, I thought, everything is proceeding as smoothly as anyone familiar with things would expect. There came a scuffling from within the hooch.

A woman inside was talking quietly. Moments later a bright yellow glow lit up the cracks around the door of the hooch. The squad members perked up at this: the light meant a fire, and a fire meant warmth on this chilly morning.

Small led the way into the dimly-lit, shadowy room. The woman was stirring something over a charcoal fire and behind her, in the far corner, a kerosene lamp burned. To the right, through a narrow foyer, I could make out several forms curled on a pallet bed. The woman took slight notice of the GIs, as if their presence was in no way peculiar, but she was a little hesitant, thoughtful, it seemed to me.

"Hey, mama-san, what you cookin' up?" Kreitz demanded, peering over the woman's shoulder and wrinkling his nose. "Damn, it sure ain't for me!"

I was surprised to find myself annoyed with Kreitz for poking fun at the old woman and her meal. There was no reason for it anymore. For how many decades had this woman followed this morning routine? And for how many years had her mother done so before her? Were we the first unexpected guests she had received? No, probably not. Probably the French and the Japanese and again the French had been in her kitchen in years past. Who knows? Maybe even the Chinese had barged in on one of her more distant ancestors. There was no point in bugging her; she would know exactly how to react, what expression to wear, the correct way of standing to exude deference, etc.

"Peewee," I said, "leave the old bitch alone. All she's tryin' to do is fix breakfast for her old man."

25

Tiger Mountains
JANUARY 8, 1968

WHILE THE GREATER PART OF THE COMPANY MOVED IN A MORE or less direct line down from the ridge toward the beach, my platoon left the summit in a northwesterly direction, following the ridge toward the higher peaks. We were in no great hurry and Sergeant Campbell halted us frequently for rest breaks. My men were in an unusually heady mood, which they expressed with such volume that Campbell had to pass the word back for me to keep down the noise.

"Fuqua, tell those guys to shut up, will ya?"

"Hey, Smitty says to shut up."

A mumbled but clearly audible "Ah, fuck Smith" came back. I sat up abruptly.

"Okay, fine, but shut the fuck up!"

Fuqua smiled. "You sound tough."

I shook my head and grinned.

"Shit, you know what this place is like," I said. "Remember Wood getting it over there, across the valley? The new dudes don't know all that. They think they know what's happening, but they haven't seen any of it, yet. Man, this is one place where I just don't like to fuck off."

Fuqua nodded and folded his arms over his knees.

I poked at an exposed root with my foot. "It took me a long time to get used to this shit and to feel like I knew what was goin' on. Hell, anyone can get shot at. I guess it wasn't 'til those villages on the beach that I really felt like, … like I was a part of all this ,… like I really felt it."

Both of us were silent for a moment. Mention of the beach villages never failed to cast a pall over conversation.

"Movin'," the word came back.

"Movin'," I said, standing to adjust my gear.

"Movin'."

26

LZ Ollie
MID-JANUARY 1968

THE DMZ WAS COMING UNGLUED—THAT MUCH WAS CLEAR TO me. Why else would the whole division be displacing in that direction? For years elements of the First Cavalry had been used as fire brigades, quick reaction forces for the innumerable hot spots that cropped up from month to month. Over the past year battalions from the division had seen duty in the western highlands near Dak To, north of Binh Dinh province near Duc Pho, far to the south around Phan Thiet, and to the north again, beyond Duc Pho, in the Chu Lai area. Two months previously only three of the nine infantry battalions organic to the division had been operating in the First Cav's official area of responsibility; the rest were scattered far and wide across the countryside of Vietnam. Up to now, none of the division's detachments had been of more than brigade size. So it followed, in my mind, that if the entire division were moving to the Demilitarized Zone, then something terrible must be happening. I felt certain that some sort of climax was approaching. At the same time, my tour was almost over. I had only one month left before I would be flying home, and suddenly things were falling into place. I could feel it in the way the men received the order to prepare to move north, in the way they soberly listened to the instructions the captain and the platoon leader handed down. I could see it in the quietness of the men as they packed extra magazines of ammunition, tried on the new flak jackets, and packed away the sand bags and gas masks they were issued. Fifteen magazines, not twenty, was the normal basic load. No one ever carried sandbags or gas masks or flak jackets. It meant that something big and important was coming. With the order to move north, the many months spent patrolling and skirmishing and ambushing in Binh Dinh province were transformed into nothing more than an extended, live-fire training exercise.

27

Phu Cat Air Force Base
MID-JANUARY 1968

Last night in Binh Dinh Province before moving north to Quang Tri.

Aside from seeing to it that we stayed within the area designated for the company, Captain Bonthuis allowed us to set up for the night as we wished. We erected a city of poncho tents, clustered in small groups, or walked away in the direction of the base exchange, our pockets stuffed with scrip for cases of Cokes and beer. Lieutenant Zuccarelli, who had been brought in to replace Lt. Alekna, and Sgt. Campbell left us to our own devices. They, like the men, were sure we were being sent north straight into hell's backyard, and they thought it best to allow us one last undisturbed evening.

 I joked with Doc and Andy and the rest, but as the dusk thickened I felt more and more like being alone. I figured my last month would probably be exciting enough, fifteen kilometers from the DMZ and all, but I would just as soon stay where I was, even if it meant another trip into that goddamned Hoai An Valley. The DMZ, hell, that was a whole different war, one you read about in the papers, nothing like the one around Bong Son and Phu My. It was the fucking Marines' fault—they couldn't handle all the trouble they had stirred up and now they needed help, just like at Duc Pho, when the brigade had to fly up so a Marine regiment could move farther north.

28

LZ El Paso to Camp Evans
JANUARY 17, 1968

A TRUCK CONVOY WAS A NOVELTY FOR A UNIT THAT USUALLY employed flocks of helicopters. We enjoyed ourselves immensely as the long line of deuce-and-a-half trucks and jeeps and other vehicles wound north along Route One toward Hue City, passing through what looked to me like a stateside Marine base. On every side there was evidence of the Americans: the road itself was lined with sturdy chain link fences, the dirt tracks running off at odd intervals were well-graded and oiled, and American jeeps and trucks were everywhere. The dull-brown hills a mile to the west of the highway were so bare that vehicles ascending or descending their slopes stood out sharply. It was easy to make out the American positions on them from the sandbags and aerials and dirt roads. I wondered if the road north from Chu Lai was one long base camp devoid of Vietnamese, save those hired by the Americans. In places, the palms and ragged-leaved banana trees appeared grotesquely out of place, and seemed to be made smaller by the profusion of barbed wire and English-language signs and military symbols. When a Vietnamese vehicle drove past, heading south, its unmilitary hues—for some reason most of the ramshackle buses were painted sea-blue—looked alien in its own homeland.

The convoy reached the outskirts of Hue City, a tight warren of tin-sided or stucco houses, one after the other, jammed together so closely that one began before the previous structure ended. The streets were crowded with all the types I had come to recognize: old wizened men wearing pith helmets; crones with rusty, ground-down teeth and faces like stirred butterscotch pudding; youths of indeterminate age, all wearing gray or gray-blue shorts; young women with smooth faces full of resentment and pride; slick dudes riding motorscooters and wearing patent leather shoes; and here and there an ARVN toting an old M-2 carbine, a baseball cap on his head, smiling up at the GIs in the trucks and waving as from a great distance.

29

The Tet Offensive

January 29, 1968

SOME DOZEN OR MORE MILES SOUTH OF QUANG TRI, THE trucks turned left from the highway and plowed their way along a track of fine, white dust, so that within the mile everyone appeared to have been covered with flour. We sat and made faces at one another and tried to keep our mouths closed so the dust wouldn't coat our teeth and tongues.

We soon passed into a maze of low, sparsely-vegetated hills. The region was a vast graveyard. Upon each hump of ground, it seemed, stood an ornate, gracefully-constructed stone tomb. Each grave mound was surrounded by a horseshoe of stone wall, so that in effect each tomb was like a miniature fortress. I had heard, or read somewhere, that outside Hue there were the grave sites of the Vietnamese emperors, and presumably of other, lesser members of royalty. I guessed that I was seeing them now. The graves gave the area a Chinese atmosphere, but the truth was that they all looked pretty old and worn out.

Sgt. Campbell gathered the squad leaders and unfolded his map. "This is where we're goin'." He pointed to a low knob half a dozen miles to the south, just north of a large stream running toward the coast. "It's the Tet truce. We can't move anywhere except by platoons, one at a time. So it's gonna take four lifts to get us out to the boonies."

By the time the platoon landed on a narrow hilltop, the dry grass and brush were on fire, ignited by the rockets and tracer bullets fired by the escorting gunships. Shimmering blue smoke circled the steep slopes. To the south, I could see the defile of a large stream and through the smoke to the east, two ARA birds rocketing hooches that stood where the stream left the hills.

We crossed a deep ravine and climbed another steep slope of loose rock to a rise slightly higher than the one we had landed on. As dusk approached, the high mountains darkened in the west, and to the east, toward the sea, the plains turned a dull, deathly gray.

Mortenson lumbered from position to position just before it was fully dark, bearing the latest, and most ominous-sounding, directive from Captain Bonthuis: there would be no poncho hooches allowed, and the ones already set up would have to be taken down. He didn't want the enemy spotting the silhouettes and zeroing in the perimeter for mortar fire. If it rained, that was too bad.

It rained, but it was no more than a nagging, misty drizzle. We pulled our ponchos over us, and those who were on guard put up the hoods on their parkas and were thankful for the sweaters they had been issued. Cupping a cigarette between my knees, I silently swore at Mortenson, as if the dangers prompting the no-hooches order were all his fault. Twenty more days of this shit. Three more weeks.

January 30, 1968, morning

There was no talk of a truce when the company stirred into wakefulness in the morning. The orders were to pack up and be ready for an air assault—a big one. The whole battalion was going somewhere. Exactly where was not known, even by Captain Bonthuis. Word filtered down that maps of the new area of operations wouldn't be issued until the troops were actually on the ground. I noticed no one was talking about one platoon moving at a time, but the thought made little impression on me. I assumed the higher-ups were spooked about all those NVA said to be massing across the DMZ.

We were in the air by eight a.m., ridge-skipping north through the foothills, flying within a few hundred feet of the ground, swooping through the narrow, twisting valleys, and then gaining altitude in order to clear the next dun-colored ridgeline. There seemed to be no point to it, unless it was to avoid anti-aircraft fire.

We reached a broad river valley and banked in formation, rising swiftly, beating away from the sun, and gaining altitude until I thought it must be possible to see most of the way to Laos over the pilot's shoulders. Below us, the only level ground was the river floodplain, which was at most several hundred meters wide. Everywhere else the land stood on end. The mountains went on and on in dark blue rows, ridge upon ridge, to the north, south, and west.

The valley of the Thach Han broadened directly west of the new landing zone. In the middle of the plain were the ruins of the abandoned Ba Long Special Forces camp, a dusty triangle of decrepit bunkers and trenches, a dirt track, and several dark bomb craters. Beyond the deserted camp there rose layer upon layer of green and blue mountains, extending all the way to the A Shau Valley and Laos. The Thach Han ran due west. Everyone in the company knew it started only twenty-five miles away at the Marine Combat Base at Khe Sanh.

To the north, somewhere beyond the hills, was Route Nine, the highway from Dong Ha, near the coast on Route One, to

Laos, just down the road from Khe Sanh. Along Route Nine were towns and camps familiar to the American public: Cam Lo, Camp Carroll, The Rockpile, and Mutter's Ridge. It seemed to me that LZ Cindy was in as bad a spot as possible. The Thach Han valley disturbed me. Lying as it did on a line from Khe Sanh to Quang Tri, the valley was an obvious infiltration route for the NVA If the Marines at Khe Sanh were overrun or withdrew, the NVA would have an open road to Cindy.

As the sun lowered toward the horizon, the ragged mountains stood out sharply in silhouette, casting long shadows across the Ba Long Valley. Sergeant Campbell took Bedford and me aside for a short talk. "This place just don't seem right to me," he said. "There's something fishy about it. Stickin' the whole battalion way out here halfway to Laos, an' no one else anywhere around—I don't like it at all. There's too much wrong about it."

"You know what they said," I said, almost under my breath. "Four or five divisions of NVA around the border, probably getting ready to come across. That was four days ago. Maybe they're already on their way."

The blast of a grenade shook me awake at two a.m. I heard Zucarelli and Andy whisper something about "possible movement in that high grass," and then someone hand-popped a flare and tossed it into the ravine. The soaking, dew-covered grass glistened in the yellow glare. I noticed that the outside of my poncho liner was wet and chilly. I put my helmet on, but nothing else happened, and the only sounds were whispers.

I rolled onto my back and tried to go back to sleep. Maybe the gooks were probing, maybe they weren't, but I wasn't going to stay awake all night unless something really bad started. If those NVA divisions wanted to fuck with us, they'd have to hurry. It'd be light in four hours or less.

Meanwhile, the men on battalion radio watch, listening to

the traffic on the brigade net, were hearing more messages than they thought usual for such an hour—code names they'd never heard of, unfamiliar coordinates well outside the area covered by their maps, and excited voices. Something odd was happening somewhere.

Falling asleep on the dew-covered hill above my Company CP, I didn't realize it, but the war was changing. Campbell was right about one thing—something fishy was going on. Thirty miles to the east the night was collapsing in flashes and rattles and booms as the towns and bases along RouteOne became the victims of a deluge of enemy rockets and mortar shells and bullets. Already khaki-clad men armed with Chinese-made rifles and Czech rocket launchers were in the streets of Quang Tri City, the provincial capital. LZ Jane was being struck fiercely along its perimeter; casualties were above the two-dozen mark and climbing steadily. Away to the south, on the banks of the Perfume River, Hue was being swamped by a massive North Vietnamese force. Unaware of these events, the battalion on LZ Cindy slept uneasily.

January 31, 1968

During the early morning of January 31 we learned only that three of the Cavalry Division's landing zones near Quang Tri were rocketed and mortared; one base reported one man killed and over forty wounded. We were ordered to build bunkers with thick walls, preferably three sandbags thick. No one realized that the night's attacks on the three landing zones were but a minute segment of a countrywide offensive. All we knew was that if the damned gooks were able to smash up three bases in one night way out near Route One, then they would certainly be able to raise the devil with a jumbly, hilly battalion perimeter halfway up the valley to Khe Sanh. We went to work building thick-walled bunkers.

Then we were told to hold everything: the whole battalion was lifting out, heading to the flatlands around Quang Tri City. Lt. Zuccarelli pointed at a dashed line on the map between the highway and the railway and said that the battalion would go into a regular linear defense when it landed. The ARVNs were in a big fight, the North Vietnamese were trying to withdraw, and the battalion was going to try to block the routes to Quang Tri City's southeast. Then he said that on their way east the helicopters would be flying over a village a company-size force of North Vietnamese was known to be occupying. We should have recognized that last message as a warning: the Cavalry just did not ignore a known company of North Vietnamese, not unless something really ugly was happening somewhere else.

There was no circling this time, no seemingly endless flying about, waiting for the landing zone prep to be finished. The pilots dropped from cruising altitude without ceremony, diving closer and closer to the earth in a direct line. Below me the low gray hills gave way to flatlands and paddies. Off to the right I spotted a church at the end of a paved avenue of large statues. The French must have done that, I thought, a church out in the middle of the boonies.

We crossed railroad tracks and below was a field of sand crawling with GIs trying to organize themselves into platoon formations. Some hooches burned fiercely, orange flames glowing in contrast to the overall grayness.

The pilots lifted barely above a last tree line, then lowered quickly toward a paddy, scooting just feet above the surface and then abruptly whirled and pulled the noses of the birds up, landing hard atop an embankment.

I hurled myself from the chopper, had time only to register the fact that I was standing on Route One when it seemed as if every officer and non-com was yelling at everyone else – Do this, Do that, Get here, Move your ass, goddamnit, this way!

Zuccarelli was waving his arms toward where Small was regrouping his squad and then there was a soft, powerful *Whooomp!* from behind me. A bubble chopper lay in the paddy across the highway, a ball of flame rising and rolling skyward. To the north, beyond a line of trees a half mile away, came the rattle and crackle of small-fire. I trotted as best I could toward Zuccarelli, who was leading the platoon in a ragged line toward a dirt track that led west from the highway. At the junction of the track and the highway Captain Bonthuis was giving orders and talking on both the company and battalion nets at once. Someone yelled that another bird had gone down. A sudden tower of smoke rose to the northwest in the direction of the railroad.

Choppers filled the sky. The ones that had brought us in increased power and rose, turning away to the south, while a line of gunships pounded the area to the north, one bird after another, rockets, grenades and mini-guns blazing. The whole world was blowing up—two birds down, a hell of a fight underway, things snapping and banging and crashing. Walker's gun team was on the other side of the track, keeping pace, but everyone else I saw was from another platoon. Where was Kreitz? Where was Sergeant Campbell and Doc and Andy? What the fuckin' hell was goin' on?

"Get down, get down!" someone howled from behind me. "They're comin' this way! Get down! They're comin' across the paddies!"

We dove into the paddy on the left side of the track. I tried to keep from plummeting all the way to the slope, tried to dig my heels into the bank and at the same time twist around to where I could see the gooks coming across the paddies at us, *oh, fuck!* Everything all screwed up, no organization, trying to make my way past some of 1st Platoon's riflemen who hugged the bank, staring over the edge. And where the fuck was that dumb-ass lieutenant?

The bank gave way and I said to hell with it and slogged through the muck, keeping my back bent so that my head was below the top of the bank, and found Zuccarelli who was scared white, neopolitan complexion erased from his features.

"Smith! Where's Small? Where's Two-Five? Can you see them?"

I didn't know who the lieutenant meant by "them," the gooks or the rest of the platoon, but I had had enough and blew a cork instead of answering the questions. I threw myself sideways against the bank and pulled the quick release snap on my pack, wriggling out of it while managing to hold onto my rifle and the handset.

I pulled myself up to where I could peer out across the broad paddy to the north, toward the trees where the sounds of firing continued and the gunship rockets and grenades exploded. I heard yelling all around me. "Where're them gooks?" "Get down!" "Here they come!" "What the hell's goin' on?"

I slumped back down from the edge of the bank. There weren't any gooks out there, that much was obvious. With all the firepower the gunships were putting into those trees—must've been a village up there—the gooks sure as shit weren't comin' out into the open.

———

We spent that first night in a battalion line defense, a unique experience for us, our being used to company-size perimeters. Line defenses were, in our view, obsolete, Korean War tactics not fit for a war without fronts. If we were using conventional tactics, something had come badly unglued. We just spread out along the length of a wide paddy dike, no rear security, every other man awake, flares and artillery, and Spooky's miniguns crashing and rattling and whistling and buzzing all night long. We were told that a full battalion of North Vietnamese was in the village to our front, separated from us only by a broad sweep of rice paddies. Then, during the night, a bridge only five hundred yards down the road behind us was attacked. We had no friendlies in that direction, not even an outpost, and we had no communications with the South Vietnamese on the bridge, and therefore no idea what the situation was there. For all we could tell, all the North Vietnamese in the world were charging toward us from the rear. Bright yellow flashes and sharp gunshots and explosions were our only information.

February 1, 1968

Then the Quang Tri dawn came, slow, soft, and heavy with fog. The word that morning was that the North Vietnamese were moving south from the village and might blunder into the battalion line unwittingly. This seemed unlikely. Even the dumbest North Vietnamese weren't going to cross three-quarters of a mile of open, flat, coverless rice paddies if they could help it, even in the fog. And the lack of small-arms fire told us that no one was trying very hard to make the North Viets do anything they didn't want to do. So instead of kneeling in our sandy holes and looking alert, ready for fearful combat, the men of Alpha Company stood talking in small groups, drinking water from the paddies, and wishing someone would tell us just what in hell was going on.

Late in the morning, seven Marines from a pacification team in the village across the highway gave us our first information. As they had it, a full regiment of North Vietnamese had moved through the villages to our north heading for the mountains to our southwest. They had left behind a company to delay pursuit and that was what the ARVN were tangling with. We didn't learn until later that the regiment had attacked

Quang Tri City and been thrown out and that was why it was making for the hills.

The Marines were fascinated by our helicopters. One of them had been in Vietnam for fifteen months and had never seen a single gunship and suddenly choppers were all over the place, strafing and rocketing and generally raising hell. One of them whispered to me that there sure were a lot of strange-looking aircraft around. Later in the day the Marines went through us when they wanted a medevac for an ARVN who had been lightly wounded down at the bridge. They were completely amazed at the ease with which we called one and got it to them.

The only thing ominous the Marines had to say was that Da Nang was overrun and that the opposing forces were fighting in the streets. It turned out it was Hue, but we didn't know that. Being completely in the dark as to what was going on outside our immediate area, we were willing to believe whatever we heard.

Around one p.m. some artillery began to drop several kilometers off to the north-east where the coastal sand dunes began. I borrowed Lt. Zuccarelli's binoculars and focused on the impact area just in time to see at least a company's-worth of men moving south about four kilometers away. While I watched, artillery began to fall but they kept walking through the shellbursts. I told Captain Bontuis who said they'd check into it. I never heard anything more about it and all I could figure out was that I witnessed a Viet Cong or an NVA unit withdrawing from Quang Tri.

We were told to pack up and be ready to be lifted out around five p.m. for a short move about 1500 meters south along Route One, almost an equal distance south of the ARVN-protected bridge. My slick was so crowded I had to lodge myself on the floor with Zuccarelli holding an arm around my chest and Anderson hanging on to my legs to keep me from rolling out into the ether. Below us a village beyond the tracks was in flames.

The villages we swept during the first days of fighting gave us the creeps. We had seen very few refugees along Route One, but the villages all seemed deserted. We never saw more than a half dozen people at any one time, and many of the villages were completely vacant. They weren't all blown apart—in fact many of them seemed to have been untouched by the war—but they were silent and empty.

A few villages had been shattered. We saw one from a helicopter during the second day of the offensive. Most of the roofs were gone, and others were burning. The village was orange and black and gray. One of the black spots appeared to be a woman, but it was hard to be sure.

February 5, 1968

The company dug in for the night in a sand flat on the west side of the railroad tracks. The sand was terraced in spots, sloping gently toward a stretch of rice paddies. Clumps of stiff-leaved scrub provided a modicum of concealment for the foxholes. The nearest bamboo was an easy two hundred yards away across the tracks, and small parties from the platoons now and then left the perimeter, armed with machetes, to cut poles for their poncho huts.

I walked out on my own and soon was in a tiny, hedged-in clearing, apparently a once-used sweet potato patch. I finished my task—poles in one hand and machete in the other and a .45 at my hip—and realized I was alone. In the eleven months I had been in Vietnam I had never been as isolated as I was in that field. Even late at night, on guard or listening post duty, there had always been friends a few inches away. But in the sweet potato field I was out of sight and sound of the company or any bamboo-chopping groups. I dropped the poles and machete and lit a cigarette. The only sounds were muffled detonations from the one-oh-fives at Jane, many kilometers to the south-southwest and for the first time in my life I felt claustrophobic. The hedges cut my horizons to a matter of feet. If I were to meet a Viet Cong or NVA soldier, I would not have a chance. I might die here in a sandy sweet potato patch. I stubbed out my cigarette and hurried back.

Our battalion base camp, named LZ Sharon, sprawled over a low hill across some paddies from the large church and nunnery I had seen from the air. We were mortared on two of the three nights we were on Sharon, each time just at ten o'clock in the evening. Not being used to incoming mortars, we took no special precautions. We lay in our bunkers, satisfied we were safe, as the fifteen or twenty shells crunched in. The first night, we didn't even bother to reach outside to wake the lieutenant. Being mortared was an exciting novelty that somehow, in our eyes, didn't relate seriously to us. We wrote home about the mortars as if they were some athletic event. The first ten days of the offensive, the wildest ten days South Vietnam had ever been through, the extent of our action was being mortared at night.

30

Quang Tri to Danang
FEBRUARY 11, 1968

IT WAS TIME TO GO. I SLUNG MY RIFLE AND TURNED TO WALK UP the easy slope past the self-propelled guns. Five of us slopped along a muddy road until we found a deuce-and-a-half at battalion headquarters to drive us to the airstrip at the Marine combat base north of Quang Tri City.

I caught glimpses of gray streets and people and when the driver turned onto Route One, I strained to see down the road, searching for the block of huts the platoon had occupied on outpost duty the day the fighting at Hay Lang began, but all the shops and houses looked the same.

The driver let us off in front of a hanger-like building, told us to wait for a plane to An Khe, gunned the engine and rattled away through the gray, wet afternoon, heading back to LZ Sharon and the war. There were no planes that day so we ate dinner in the Seabees' mess hall and made a makeshift camp in a passenger terminal for the night.

Next morning we caught a plane to Da Nang. I peeked out one of the ports as the plane swept off the ground and got a lingering view of Quang Tri. In the distance I thought I made out the church. Goodbye, I mouthed silently. Take it easy, guys. Faces surrounded me: Beyer, Gundolf, Schebe, Sellers, Rob, Tatman, Mines, all the men who were dead or wounded or already gone home on schedule. Despite their memory, something of them was being torn raggedly away, as if I were a snake whose skin was shedding before its time, so that its peeling off seemed unnatural and painful. Goodbye, I thought, and I shuddered suddenly, as a flurry of emotions swept through me. Embarrassed, I turned away from the others, shaking and crying. The plane was in sunlight, flying somewhere east of Hue over the South China Sea, when I regained control.

We collected around a two-story frame building at the edge of the freight-loading section of the Da Nang base. Someone bummed a copy of the latest *Stars & Stripes* and we gathered around to see what the news was. Hue was still an almighty horror, getting worse by the day from the look of it, and fighting continued in Saigon. But that was all secondary to the lead story, the fall of the Lang Vei Special Forces Camp, a small, fortified outpost adjacent to Laos a few miles down the road from Khe Sanh: for the first time in the war, the North Vietnamese had employed tanks.

I was seized by a vision of the North Vietnamese Army, an unconventional force made up of stolid, hard-marching little men, transformed overnight into a clanking juggernaut of steel and iron and high-velocity cannon. In my mind a long column of khaki-clad soldiers, bedecked with red and yellowstarred flags, rumbled through the Ba Long Valley toward Quang Tri and my battalion. Worse, I imagined enemy tanks rolling south, squashing all that got in their way. I looked up from the paper and glanced across the runways half-expecting to see the treaded brutes appearing from among the clutter of barracks and quonset huts in the distance. Not only was the tempo of the war changing, I thought, but something else was happening to it, something indefinable that only someone who was used to it could pick up. The whole scheme of things, which I had come to know and appreciate, was unravelling now, and a great transformation was taking place.

31

An Khe
FEBRUARY 12, 1968

THE BATTALION BARRACKS AT AN KHE WERE SO CROWDED I had to sleep on the floor between bunks. After an early formation, I got some clean stateside fatigues out of my footlocker and went down to the USO and hung out with some guys I knew. I went to the PX and bought things to shave and wash. It felt great after being grubby for three weeks up north. I helped paint the barracks for an hour in the afternoon, then got some stuff sewn on my shirt and got a haircut.

I was sitting in the Enlisted Men's Club having a beer when I got the news: the company's luck ran out last night. They got in some shit near the church below Sharon and suffered fourteen casualties. It wasn't until the next day I learned who.

The wounded included John Ulloa, William Anderson, Stephen Bellville, Michael Kilfoile, Venie Cato, and Doc Campbell.

Those that died were:
James "Nick" Fuqua, Bartow, Florida
Rodney Cantohos, Waipahu, Hawaii
Ernest Davidove, China Lake, California
Roger Sipp, Hanna City, Illinois

Hobart Rollins, Washington College, Tennessee
James Albertini, Attleboro, Massachusetts
Timothy Thomas, Hawthorne, California
William Williams, Fayetteville, NC (died of his wounds on March 15)

It was the worst fighting my platoon had experienced in eleven months and I was sitting in the rear, enjoying a beer. I should have been there, sharing it with them, perhaps even doing some good for them.

I should have been there.

THE RETURN
MARK M. SMITH

32

Why I Went Back

MY REASONS FOR GOING TO VIETNAM THE FIRST TIME WERE reasonably straightforward. I had been brought up on military history. I understood that combat could not be experienced secondhand. I felt intuitively that Vietnam was going to be the major event for my generation. I wanted to do something other than continue going to classes. I wanted something dramatic to happen in my life, which to that time, if only to me, had been mundane.

In retrospect I am surprised by the lack of reaction to my decision to go to war. My family never raised objections, even to my going back. I think they understood my stubbornness once my mind was made up, and that before I had announced my intentions, I had thought things through and reached a conclusion not likely to be shaken. Some of my friends wondered about it, but none—even those who were not pleased with the war—tried to talk me out of it or even challenged my reasoning. One friend did ask why I wasn't going to officer candidate school or becoming a paratrooper or going into the Special Forces, but that was it.

The $64,000 question, of course, is why I went back.

I knew I was going to return even before I came home from my first tour. For more than eleven months my unit had pursued a generally small-scale war of isolated skirmishes, the occasional deadly booby-trap, and hours upon hours of fruitless patrolling hither and yon, and only a few incidents that achieved the level of "battle." Then, two weeks before I was scheduled to go to the rear to begin processing for home, the Tet Offensive broke out and the war turned upside down. All of a sudden it was rock-around-the-clock. It seemed there was fighting going on somewhere in the vicinity all day long, and when there wasn't any fighting, we were finding evidence of it: enemy bodies, equipment, gear, guns and rockets, burned villages and smashed bunkers, trenches and mortar pits, and fresh blood. And just as it was blowing up, my tour ended and I left.

I had always assumed an American victory, if only because the possibility that we might be defeated was too remote for words. Americans did not lose wars, it was that simple. Sitting by the airstrip at Da Nang, I had imagined North Vietnamese tanks appearing suddenly from among the hangers across the tarmac, and then imagined the enemy's tanks entering Saigon and winning the war. The image stayed with me. I felt that we hadn't seen anything yet.

A day later, my platoon—the microcosm for the average infantryman—was shattered. Out of perhaps two-dozen men, eight died and eight more were wounded. I felt I had ratted out.

A couple of mornings later I was sitting on a stump not far from the barracks, smoking a cigarette and trying to hide from the day's work details, and I suddenly understood that I wasn't done with the war. It wasn't so much a matter of thinking, it was just there in my head, the knowledge that in some way at some time I'd be back. Or perhaps it was even subtler—the eerie feeling that I was simply not ready to leave something that was getting a lot more interesting.

There were times toward the end of that first tour when I recognized that the war had become a home, a familiar place and experience, one in which I had come to feel comfortable. Where I served was like a hometown with its set of discrete neighborhoods, like the Hoai An and Soui Ca valleys, where you couldn't buy enemy contact; the Tiger Mountains, where you couldn't avoid it; lodgings such as Landing Zone Pony, which always had the best hot chow; and the Bong Son bridge, where we built a huge bunker and put up a sign designating it "Desolation Row." There was the goofy barbershop-whorehouse near the Ha Tay Special Forces Camp, where the only music was the soundtrack to *Cabaret* and one of the girls was half-French and looked like a petite Barbra Streisand. And there was the small pocket beach on the South China Sea where the guys used their air mattresses as surfboards.

All it took was about seven months of aimless, seemingly pointless garrison duty in West Berlin, and I was eager to transfer back to the war. In addition, my relationship with a woman at home, parlous to begin with—we had met only a week before I went into the Army—was imploding, and another woman, for whom I had carried a terrible torch in high school, had broken off our friendship.

But what was really at work was simple: I missed it. As Bill Knapp, my West Berlin roommate, put it, it was "our kick."

Vietnam was, in author Michael Herr's words, a place "where no drama had to be invented, ever." We enjoyed freedoms such as none of our peers at home would ever know. Even if we weren't eager to kill people, we were conscious that we had the absolute freedom to do so. We had the freedom to rob graves, to burn whole villages, to call in artillery on abandoned churches, to order jets to bomb and napalm homes, and no one was going to question us about it. We were allowed an arrogance that went beyond anything one might experience back home. One World War II observer said that British troops walk the earth as if they own it, while Americans walk the earth as if they don't give a damn who owns it. In Vietnam, I never had to analyze the thought. We were surrounded by and suffused with a variety of horrible, nearly hysterical dangers, so that even the most peaceful moments acquired a certain soft, spooky glow. Looking back, we were like the Hardy Boys on a perilous quest, Boy Scouts on a camping trip that would turn deadly in a split second, and the losers of this game lost for keeps. We weren't just risking some bucks at the track or in Vegas, or the trauma of a divorce, or a pink slip at work, we were risking our entire selves, day in and day out for weeks and months at a time. It was a life with all the edges straight razors, and you weren't going to slip more than a couple of times before it was all over. And the net effect was of a frighteningly seductive lover—a Mrs. Robinson who might abruptly turn into Sil from *Species*, and you hoped you'd be lucky enough to enjoy her sensual favors and be out of the house before things got ugly. We were rubbing up against the real thing, and I think many of us felt the same nerve-wracking frisson of fear and attraction that some people in the Roaring Twenties did when they had the opportunity to hobnob with a gangster. As Bo Diddley sang, "I'm just twenty-two an' I don't mind dyin'." We were supremely arrogant.

 Hiking down a mountain one afternoon toward the end of my first tour—the path so steep the helmet worn by the guy in front of me was occasionally right next to my boot, holding onto branches and saplings and vines just to stay upright, each of us carrying fifty, sixty or more pounds—I realized that all the irritations and irks that had bothered me in the past were gone, and I was utterly comfortable. In a sense, I felt I had become an inhabitant rather than a visitor. The war was all mine now. From surviving it, I had begun to thrive in it. I was, to put it bluntly, good at it—I was a pro. I could take the monsoon rains and the mud and the supernatural heat and humidity and the hours of guard duty at night and the moments of real terror when I felt more alive than I had ever felt before.

In West Berlin I was just marching in place, slowly reaching the point where I could not resist the temptation to return to the war, and when it happened, three of us volunteered to go back the same week. We had our reasons and rationalizations, but I think it came down to the simple fact that we didn't know who we were away from it. In addition, this was 1968. There had been the North Korean capture of the Pueblo, the Tet Offensive and then the May Offensive and then the Third Wave in South Vietnam, the assassination of King and the subsequent riots, the assassination of Bobby Kennedy, the student occupation of Columbia University, the Chicago convention riots, the Russian invasion of Czechoslovakia, Johnson's abdication and the re-emergence of Nixon. It was a chaotic year and Vietnam seemed like a coherent, black-and-white contrast, a place where I knew who I was and what was expected of me and what I might be called upon to pay. With all that was going on around the world, it seemed insane for me to be biding my time in a garrison 110 miles behind the Iron Curtain, attending pointless classes during duty hours and then going out and getting drunk every night.

What made my decision to go back a little more complex, however, was my increasingly avid anti-war stance. While I was home in the late winter and spring of '68, I had marched in an anti-draft parade and attended an SDS (Students for a Democratic Society) rally at the University of North Carolina and a major anti-war rally at Duke University. All my best friends from high school were longhairs and we listened to Frank Zappa and The Doors and Country Joe McDonald and the Jefferson Airplane and, of course, Bob Dylan. Yet not one of them tried to talk me out of going back and neither did my parents.

Part of it was the feeling that I had joined the Army solely because of the war. Getting into it was the only reason I enlisted and now I felt like a sailor on the beach. There was a war still going on, and as a young sergeant and a veteran of a year of combat operations, it was the natural place for me to be. It made sense, notwithstanding my anti-war attitude, that I should be in it. My personal desire for the intensity and the excitement of combat won out over my moral and political predilections.

There was also a unit loyalty at work. The 1st Air Cavalry was an authentic elite. Herr referred to it bluntly as "the best of our divisions," while another historian noted its "uncanny" willingness to fight the enemy. My company, which was part of the 5th "Black Knights" Cavalry Regiment, had a lineage stretching back to the pre-Civil War years. It had led a doomed charge in 1862, trying to prevent a Confederate breakthrough during one battle, and it was present at Appomattox when its pre-war commander, Robert E. Lee, surrendered. The division had a unique aura about it. Some Army units had an air of the mundane, but not the Cav. In the end, part of me just wanted to feel that little bit more special. I knew that as a volunteer for combat I was part of a small minority among that relatively small group of people who served in the Army infantry in Vietnam. Now, by voluntarily returning, I was making myself part of an even smaller group, the incorrigibles, the ones who had the nerve to push the odds even further. I wanted to see how far I could take them.

THE WAR IN THE JUNGLE
MARK M. SMITH

33

The Dream

IT TOOK ME A LONG TIME TO KNOW HOW TO DESCRIBE, EVEN TO myself, the spring and summer of 1969. At first I thought of it as a chaotic bloodbath, a torrid, dirty, almost abstract red splash. Later I imagined a treadmill through a gloomy blue-green mist across a swampy expanse of blood, surrounded by immense trees straight out of Conrad, with weary men trying to trudge along the moving belt to reach safety somewhere in the distance. Now and then one of the men would stumble off and disappear soundlessly into the lurid murk, but the others were too crushed and numb to take notice.

During my first couple of weeks as a civilian the same dream would wake me every night, sometimes several times a night. Once I woke on the floor next to my bed, at five in the morning, wondering what I was doing there. In the dream I was lying in a deep bomb crater with a buddy, when a hidden North Vietnamese soldier cracked a bullet into his head. I crawled across broken ground and tangled brush to the next crater, and there was another of my buddies there. The same thing happened. I kept crawling, slithering my way from one crater to the next, knowing that if I remained with the last man to die, the sniper would get me next. I did not wake screaming or gasping for breath. I just woke up and the dream was gone, waiting to come back the next night or the night after that. Very patient dream.

34

The Month Everybody Got Shot
FEBRUARY 1969

I ARRIVED AT QUAN LOI, ABOUT 90 MILES NORTH OF SAIGON, in late January 1969, and was assigned to C Company of 2/7 Cavalry. The unit was notorious among American elements for its ancestry. In 1876 it had been led into the valley of the Little Big Horn by George A. Custer and everyone knew what had happened there. In 1965 it had marched into the Ia Drang Valley and suffered roughly 75 percent casualties. Its history hung over the battalion like a shroud.

When he discovered I was a second-tour trooper, Pappy, a real old-timer who had been with the battalion in the Ia Drang, plied me with beer while the rest of the new guys slept outside. I was disappointed not to have been assigned back to 1/5 Cavalry, but after visiting its orderly room and discovering that no one I had served with was left, I accepted my new home.

At the beginning of February the battalion was transferred from Quan Loi to Bien Hoa. Our platoon leader was Lieutenant Welton, a classic FNG (fucking new guy) who was gung-ho, and intolerant of the experience of veterans or of the normal lapses of discipline. On the morning of February 5, we got our gear together and the birds were loaded up and we took off. The platoon totaled thirty-three men. We were going into the area known as War Zone D.

Of the eight NCOs and one officer, Staff Sergeant Marvin Hasenak, who was my platoon sergeant; Sergeant Larry Merrill, who was in charge of one of the machine-guns; and I were the only combat veterans in the platoon. Hasenak, from Abilene, Texas, was tough and fair. I called him "the Marlboro Man," admired his leadership style, and modeled my own after it.

I was the squad leader of the second squad. Bob Kaehl, from Long Island, N.Y., was my assistant squad leader, and Danny Dodd, from West Virginia, was close to Bob. I trusted them implicitly. John McQue, from California, Mike Hozey, from Georgia, Richard Graham, Phil Powell, Frank Goytia, from somewhere in the Southwest, and Jearl "Red" Bartee, from Texas, made up the rest of the squad. I didn't get the names of anyone else, just the names of the other squad leaders, Marvin and Lt. Welton. It didn't seem possible that one year before most of these guys weren't even in the army. Now they were the same as Beyer, Fuqua, or I had been – privates and specialists—and I was a squad leader, a sergeant, and the oldest veteran in the platoon.

―――

February 10, 1969

Third Platoon took point. We entered a clearing and I saw the situation. There were a few paths running down to a small stream. Streams meant water and the streams were all downhill, so I faced uphill. A grenade came flying down, a few shots were fired, the column whipped around uphill, and just like that we were in a firefight.

Lt. Welton's platoon popped red smoke to mark our position but the HueyCobra pilots thought it was meant to mark the target so they sent two rockets right on the red smoke. I was standing up smoking a cigarette and talking to Bartee and Lt. Welton who were crouching in front of me when shrapnel started flying by us. Nothing happened to me but both of them were wounded, along with a third of the platoon—ten wounded, three very seriously. Spec4 Robert L. Howell, from Deputy, Indiana, took a rocket splinter through his helmet and died later that day. I remember Howell for the defiantly non-regulation holster he wore—a Wild West holster complete with bullet loops. Five out of the six men in 1st squad got hit and two from Gun Squad, three from mine (Bartee, John McQue, and Richard Graham) and one from Woollard's 3d squad.

Everyone was applying field dressings as fast as they could and I ran back about 75 yards to get help. At the same time, Pappy and some of the guys were crashing along the trail. I collided with them and led them back. Bartee yelled that there was movement off to the right so I ripped off twenty rounds. At that moment, I just wanted to *shoot something*. Hasenak told me to calm down.

After we had evacuated the men wounded in the Huey-Cobra rocket strike, we returned to a grassy field where Marvin told me I was now the platoon sergeant, Danny Dodd was RTO (radiotelephone operator), and Lyn Thompson was senior radio man. In the morning we began moving about a thousand yards to the east, toward where there had been an Arclight the day before. Third Platoon was last in line. Up ahead the men found a trail running across our line of march. Then they saw some NVA maybe thirty yards away up the trail. There was a smattering of gunfire. At the same time, there were suddenly more NVA on the other side, meaning we had split some unit, right and left. First Platoon moved south and it and Second engaged in a firefight to the south.

First and Second needed more grenades so we passed them down the line. I got off the trail toward the jungle and found Pappy sitting on a jerry can of water, just looking around. He was so in control. "Sounds like a B-40 to me (a rocket)," he said and I thought, if Pappy can do it, so can I.

We found two grave mounds and a termite hill, formed a perimeter around the grave mounds and dug in. All of a sudden we heard two savage blasts, one to the east and one to the north. I thought it was incoming mortars but then a few AK-47's opened up to the north and everything came unstitched. I was protected from the blast by the grave mound but when a spray of small-arms fire came from right in front of me, maybe 35 yards away, I got on top of the grave mound and opened fire. Others did the same. After a minute or two the enemy fled down the trail and disappeared. Hasenak told the men to get up and move out. Everyone just lay there, stunned, and stared at him. I lost my temper completely and bellowed, "Get on your goddam feet and move!" They stared at me, and for a second I felt I had made a complete ass of myself. Then they all got to their feet and began moving forward.

Two bodies were lying right in front of the anthill. Doc Cooley and Hasenak jumped right out to them and as soon as I fired a few more bursts, I followed. Dodd and Groves were dead. Nino had a slug in his leg. Woollard's left arm was a mess, twisted and shattered from shoulder to hand, and his left side was leaking intestines from a small hole. Hasenak patched Woollard up and Doc and I made a stretcher for him. There was not a lot of blood but he was already dying. I put Doc by his head and I took a position by his feet. We were about a hundred and fifty yards away from the perimeter. I had a hell of a time with Woollard because he was convulsing so I had a hard time holding on. I eventually managed to return to the CP and I was so sad. It was too much.

Marvin got things together, back down the trail, and now I had two rifles across my back from the dead guys and one or two bandoliers from the wounded or dead guys. I took charge of the point. It was not far, maybe 75 yards between the perimeter and the CP but everything I saw, I fired at. I saw movement and I cranked off a bunch of shots. Finally we got back to the CP. The shooting had stopped but not the casualties. Lt. Maddox was killed by one of the gunships he was trying to guide in.

We gathered around the perimeter and set up for the night. We had two gun crews, one squad and the CP: Marvin, Bob Kaehl, Milt Thompson, Doc Cooley and me.

Sergeant Ronald L. Groves from Evansville, Indiana; Sergeant Russell D. Woollard from Shamrock, Texas; my radioman, Specialist Danny J. Dodd, from St Albans, West Virginia; and Lieutenant Robert B. Maddox, the company's forward observer had all been killed.

I hoped the place would cool off. As Dodd would have said, "we're so bunched up, one ass-chewing will get us all."

February 15, 1969

The company came to a ravine, 3rd Platoon pulling point. On the other side the point man reported back that he could see a slung hammock, and maybe a hut, and that it appeared someone was in the hammock. Automatic fire broke out and we all dove for cover. Sgt. Hasenak called for me to bring the rest of the platoon forward and Capt. Meager called for 3/6 to swing out to the right and try to maneuver onto the enemy's flank. I led the rest of the platoon down to the bottom of a slope where we could spread out.

We were firing up toward the enemy position and they

were burning rounds just over our heads. I looked up when some leaves started falling around me, and just a couple of inches up the sapling I was next to, a little hole appeared as a bullet passed through it.

Then 2/6 got blasted, someone reported that the enemy had fire lanes cut, the lieutenant was down and screaming—shot in the groin—and no one over there was maneuvering any longer. We kept up our fire and I think some 1/6 guys were tossing grenades forward. After a while Meager told Hasenak to pull us back to the near edge of the ravine by the big tree trunk.

Hasenak passed the word for the guys to get moving, and he, I, and our RTOs kept up a base of fire to give them some cover. Finally he and I were alone and decided it was time to go. We came to our feet, firing our rifles one-handed on full automatic, like immense pistols, something out of *Butch Cassidy and the Sundance Kid.* Then we turned and started dashing up the slope. To our amazement, some of the guys we had sent back were crawling. They were in the beaten zone of enemy fire and they were just inching along. Hasenak and I literally leaped over them and told them to get the lead out and *move!*

As we straightened the platoon into a line along the lip of the ravine, someone yelled for help to carry wounded, so I moved to the right and found 2/6 being brought out in a poncho. I took hold of one edge and six of us started stumbling along under sporadic machine-gun fire, just hoping the bullets wouldn't hit any of us. We tried to set him down to get a better grip once, but as soon as we did, he screamed awfully, so we picked him back up and finally got him to the collection point behind the line.

Several other wounded were there, including John McQue, who had been slightly wounded in the rocketing on February 10th, senior RTO Lynd Thompson, and Rick Shaw, who wore glasses like Coke bottles but was a good gun-crew member. He was hit by a bullet in his high school class ring, and his finger was pretty mangled. I went back to the line and was standing by a tree trunk when another burst gusted in.

I helped carry Thompson back to the collection point when he took two bullets, one in the left arm and the other in the left thigh. Some green tracer came in near the wounded from directly off our right flank, which indicated the enemy was trying to flank us. I told some of the guys to keep their eyes open and started back to the line.

Lt. Kendall told me to sit down in front of everyone and throw smokes for the gunships. I didn't have my weapon, but I went about 10 yards down into the ravine and sat there with a "shoot me" sign on my forehead. I didn't realize it at the time, but the enemy gun was kicking up dirt in front of me and hitting people behind me. But I kept throwing out smoke as Kendall had ordered. For some reason he kept calling me "Doc" (perhaps my lack of a weapon led him to think I was a medic).

At that point the whole company began pulling back to where the mortar platoon was clearing an LZ and the fight wound down for us. We could hear where another company was in action to our left front some distance off, but for us the day's action was over.

February 16, 1969

We finally reached the 24-hour Tet truce. It was what it took to get there that hurt.

On February 10th the company lost one killed and twelve wounded. On the 11th, it was four killed and one wounded. On the 15th we walked head-on into a bunker complex and lost two more killed and twelve more wounded. We were all nervous, jumpy, and generally slowed down. We couldn't get anyone medevacked before 9 p.m. and three of the guys couldn't get taken out until the morning. We were using trip flares to guide in last night's medevacs and the scene the wavering, brilliant yellow glare lit up was like something out of Dante.

I could not believe how quickly the casualties mounted up. Our number of men hit had risen from a couple of men in 2nd platoon to seven or eight to twelve to fifteen, which included two killed, one of whom we had to wait until this morning to recover. Capt. Meager, the CO, took a slight scalp wound, but he was still out there.

I was definitely shaky.

February 22-23, 1969

We spotted some *chogis* [farmers] to the north. We veered up a low hill and at the same time, Hasenak took half the platoon toward the *chogis*. Only they were not *chogis*, they were two VC, shooting. Hasenak, McCance, Kaehl, Doc Cooley, and Griggs were all hit —by just two VC. We were up the hill and the radio wasn't working because a bullet had hit it. We could hear "3/6, 3/6!" from two hundred yards out in the paddy.

We didn't know about the VC and didn't understand why Hasenak was yelling, so we went back down the hill and waited at the edge of the paddies. Hasenak was wounded in the chin and wrist and Griggs had been killed. For the moment, the platoon was leaderless: there was no medic, no radio, and no squad leader. Without a radio, Hasenak had had to shout to get help. All of a sudden, a Loach swept in and gunned the two VC down. I don't know how they knew. Our part of the platoon was helping recover the wounded and calling a medevac. Suddenly I was the platoon leader and Mac was the platoon sergeant. Lee Collins and Calloway were the two radiomen.

At the beginning of the month the company had 141 men. By the end of the month we had 86 left.

35

War Zone C

From the air, War Zone C was a vast, nondescript, nearly-flat tract of thick forest, a yellow-brown-green tangle broken here and there by elongated fields of short grass, a couple of narrow dirt roads the maps said were "provincial highways," the slight creases of streambeds and, to one side, the bold defile of the Saigon River, meandering south toward its namesake, the southern capital. To the north—undefined but always a vivid presence—lay the boundary with Cambodia, "the border," across which one imagined the enemy hidden in his sanctuary, planning new offensives.

With a decrease in altitude the landscape changed for the worse. The area looked as if it had been shot point-blank with a huge riot gun and then run through a mangle before being spread back out. Each acre had its complement of holes: small holes where mortar shells and rockets had clawed at the vegetation, larger holes where artillery shells of various calibers had torn into the hardwood canopy, entire square kilometers of holes where B-52 bomber strikes, called "arc lights," had shattered the trees and earth with thousands of tons of explosives. There were holes filled with stagnant water, mosquito-rich and whitish with mud; holes overlapping other holes (the war was nothing new here); holes with beautiful starry patterns of dirt and mud splashed out from them; long lines of holes and compact galaxies of holes. We took cover in the holes, ambushed from them, air assaulted into them, received our supplies through them, and evacuated our dead and wounded from them. Where no holes existed, or where they were not sufficiently large, one seven-and-a-half-ton "daisy cutter" bomb would blow out a huge gap in the forest, large enough to admit at least one and sometimes two troop-carrying Huey helicopters.

In other parts of Vietnam, it was usually possible to find some terrain that was relatively unmolested, but not in War Zone C. That stretch of ragged, churned-up land seemed to embody the war's most pitiless aspects. It was utterly evil in appearance, even for a war zone.

Alongside the river the bottomland was muddy and stinking. There were thick clumps of bamboo and every joint of every stalk was spiked. No one lasted very long without acquiring ripped fatigues and scratches that could quickly erupt into jungle rot, 'the creepin' crud,'—bleeding, pus-leaking skin ulcers on the arms and legs and face. There were crawling creatures—scorpions, poisonous bamboo vipers, centipedes and stinging red ants. After a while, War Zone C scared the hell out of me, all by itself.

At times the war seemed to have involved, not two sides, but four: American soldiers fought North Vietnamese soldiers and American airpower fought the forest. Sometimes the distinctions grew muddled. More than a few Americans were killed or wounded by "friendly" bomb splinters, fiery globs of napalm, and rocket fragments, or misdirected cannon shells, grenades, or machine-gun bullets. Whose side the jets and armed helicopters were on at any given moment could never be taken for granted.

During the summer monsoon, every evening brought violent thunderstorms. We couldn't come in out of the rain. We could only lie or stand where we were and pray that we were charged right, and no bolt would come down and fry us. Some afternoons as we plodded through the forest, the sky would suddenly turn apocalyptic, all black turmoil, with gusts of wind tearing at the trees, straight out of the Old Testament.

On nights when the rain cascaded down and I figured I was learning what it would be like to live under Niagara, incredible lapses of security would take place. Instead of remaining faithfully on guard, eyes peeled and ears cocked for the enemy's approach, we would leave our positions and huddle together, forgetting noise and light discipline, passing around cigarettes and grumbling out loud, totally fed up, "If the gooks wanna come out on a night like this, they can have my ass." It never seemed to matter how tightly I built my hooch for the night, or how carefully I laid out my poncho liner inside, in the morning I would get up damp and chilly and mud-streaked, dirty and feeling ornery and forsaken. And that night, or the next, the same thing would happen again.

War Zone C was a shattered, drenched land that seemed to thrive on blast and fire and concussion. There were times when I believed it consciously hated me. If the North Vietnamese and my own supporting aircraft didn't get me, War Zone C would.

36

May 1969

IN EARLY MAY 1969 I RETURNED FROM A WEEK OF R&R IN Australia to Quan Loi, my battalion's supply base, which sprawled across a broad, low whaleback of a ridge about sixty-five miles due north of Saigon. When I had left in late April, the battalion had received orders to leave its lazy security operations around division headquarters to the south and move some twenty miles to the west to War Zone C. The rumors that filtered down to us were ugly. "Guys are getting shot up there every day," they said. "The gooks are using Claymores like they're goin' outta style."

I was glad to see the familiar rust-red dirt and the shaded rows of single-story, wood-frame barracks and offices and faded, dusty wall tents among the rubber trees to each side of the airstrip. It felt good to be on my way back to the company, but my good cheer paled quickly. There were men at Quan Loi that should have been out in the field but were there recovering from wounds. Their presence confirmed what I had already heard: the company was involved in some serious fighting.

Before I'd left, the rifle squad I led had been seven men strong: my assistant squad leader, a grenadier, four riflemen, and me. Now two of the riflemen and I were the only ones left unscarred. My assistant and two riflemen had sustained a neck wound, a broken shoulder, and a pair of shattered legs among them. John, the grenadier, was dead. At about the time he was being blown down by an enemy Claymore, I was picking up a couple rolls of snapshots from a pharmacy in Sydney. Now the pictures of him—John staring coolly at the camera, with cigarette smoke slightly hazing his features; John scooping a mixture of peanut butter and jelly from a C-ration can—were eerie and unsettling. That first evening in Quan Loi, several of us sat around in the barracks, looking at my photos over beer and grass, talking quietly about the guys who had been sent to the evacuation hospital in Bien Hoa, or to graves registration. I gave a couple of snaps to one of John's buddies to send home to his folks. In time the photos I took—of John and many others—became an album of the wounded and the dead.

In the orderly room after chow that evening, a lieutenant named Houx offered me a short briefing. More than thirty of the company's men, or about a quarter of its field strength had been hit while I was gone. The Mortar Platoon had been wrecked, its already short roster nearly halved when a single enemy shell pitched in one night, blasted a foxhole head-on, and killed six men in one ghastly moment. Houx, no alarmist, tapped the map of the area of operations and said, "It's pretty bad out there."

The next day I flew twenty miles to the southwest to the field headquarters and operations base of the 2nd Battalion, 7th Cavalry, of the 1st Air Cavalry Division, an open patch of ground called Landing Zone Jamie.

LZ Jamie sat astride an unkempt dirt road fifteen miles south of the Cambodian border and half that distance west of the Saigon River. It was placed so as to interdict the enemy's supply and infiltration routes south toward the great Michelin rubber plantation, the Iron Triangle and Saigon. It was a forlorn hope, if it were ever taken seriously: 500 troops to cover an area of about 150 square miles, all of it cloaked in dense forest and bamboo.

In the morning I waited for a flight to be laid on. When the bird came in, I stood aside while cases of C-rations, containers of hot chow and five-gallon cans of water were handed aboard. I fitted myself atop the pile, the pilot increased power, and we took off. I watched Jamie disappear behind the trees as the nose of the Huey veered to the east and aimed for the company's position and my platoon.

37

1st Platoon

WITHIN EACH INFANTRY COMPANY IN VIETNAM THE PLATOON was the microcosm, the home away from home. It was what the GI depended on, socially and professionally, the framework to which he most thoroughly related. A member of any given platoon would tell an outsider that he belonged to, say, Charlie Company, but he might be a virtual stranger to the men in Charlie's other three platoons. So the platoon was the microcosm and 3rd Platoon was mine. Since I had joined it in mid-January, I had served as its senior squad leader, its platoon sergeant and, for one week, its platoon leader. Third Platoon was family, a damned tight family, after all it had been through: fifty percent losses in February, more later on. Those of us who were still in the field were close. Despite Zone C's grisly reputation, I was glad to be back. When the chopper pilot set down in the anonymous clearing among the trees, I jumped out and greeted the men. We laughed and yelled back and forth over the clatter of the Huey, they asking me how I had made out in Sydney, I telling them how good it felt to be back, it really did, and how the hell were things?

"Well," they said when the chopper had left and we could converse without bellowing, "Well ... shit."

There was John, dead, and the other guys, wounded, and when you got right down to it, things were pretty lousy all the way around. I was glad I was returning as platoon sergeant instead of squad leader.

John "Mac" McAndrews was still there. He had taken over as platoon sergeant while I was gone. Mac looked like Clark Gable without the jug-handle ears. He had inscribed the word "Ruffles" on his helmet's camouflage cover, and would say only that it was a reference to his wife in Indiana. I was always suggesting some lewd meaning, but he would just shake his head and laugh, "Sometime I'll tell you, Smitty." He was my closest friend in a world where making friends was a risk.

And there was my boss, Lt. Jim Frank. There had been times when Frank and I could hardly stand to be around one another except on official platoon business, but now I was happy to see him. the Company CP was in the woods a few yards away. I made my way over and reported in to Capt. Meager. Seeing him was almost as good as seeing Mac and Frank.

I almost missed it when he addressed me as Staff Sergeant Smith; I had been promoted while I was gone. Suddenly I was one of the ranking enlisted men in the company and all of twenty years old. We shook hands, and Meager gave me my new stripes in the form of a black collar pin, and then told me I was, as of that moment, transferred to 1st Platoon. A buck sergeant was running the show there and Meager wanted someone with more rank and experience to take over. Had I not been so dumbstruck, I might have laughed. The idea of leaving one platoon for another was inconceivable. It just wasn't done. But here it was, I was being told to get the lead out and meet my new subordinates, the company was setting out on its day's hike in fifteen minutes and 1st Platoon was to lead the way. I knew nothing I could say would deter Meager. There wasn't even time for me to hop back over to 3rd to say goodbye. Instead, I hurried to 1st Platoon's section of perimeter and met its acting leader, a trim, pinch-faced blond guy named Roy Stern, who looked like a Depression farmer in a Dorothea Lange photograph. There was barely time for us to say hello and for me to meet the squad leaders and radiomen. "Saddle up and move out, into the forest," I told them. "Whoever's got the point, follow such-and-such a compass azimuth and take it slow and easy. Let's go. Pass the word back. Movin'."

For the next two weeks the company worked its way south along the axis of a small stream, then southeast along a larger creek, and finally east, upstream along the Saigon River's right bank. Those two relatively easy weeks gave me time to become familiar with the people in my charge. Day by day I learned who was who.

Roy Stern, Floyd Rogers and John Ropp were my squad leaders, leaders by example, physical and strongly built. Floyd's thick mustache, glasses and shock of heavy brown hair gave him an intellectual appearance, as if he were a college physics instructor who had suddenly found himself lugging around a rifle and heavy rucksack. Ropp was all country, oval-faced, sandy-haired, and just a touch on the beery side. In an obscure reference to a Bob Dylan song, I thought of him as "Rock-a-day Johnny." Bart Beatty, radioman, looked like an amiable suburbanite who might have been more at home with a briefcase and an off-the-rack suit than with a PRC-25 field radio on his back and a steel helmet on his head. Joel Smith, junior radioman, was very young looking and decidedly irreverent.

If anyone in the platoon ended up keeping me sane through that summer, it was the medic, Mike Bodnar, from western Massachusetts. A remarkably even-tempered fellow, he appeared on the supply chopper late one afternoon, returning from Quan Loi, where he had been nursing a seriously infected hand. Before we had time to meet formally, a firefight erupted not far away when 3rd Platoon, leaving the company perimeter for overnight ambush duty, blundered into a small gang of the enemy. Mike and I dug a hole together when things quieted down, got around to saying hello and exchanging names, and were buddies from that moment on. An enlistee like me, Mike refused to carry any sort of weapon. His dedication to the platoon was such that, later on, when lightly wounded twice within twenty-four hours, he refused to be evacuated. There were times when his words, and once his actions, kept me from falling apart entirely or getting myself blown away.

Through Mike I came to know others: Gunner Charlie Hamilton, whose rugged features made him look like an understudy for Fess Parker's role as Davy Crockett, was as mild-mannered as anyone in the platoon and ran his crew with a minimum of fuss or furor; Tom Vinciguerra, a moon-faced guy from Baltimore, whose helmet bore the finest decorations in the company (he carried a set of felt-tip pens to touch it up now and then) and whose Teflon frying pan often helped us outwit the makers of C-rations; Johnny Velez from New York City, whose folks mailed him large cans of steak and chicken and potatoes that all went into Tom's pan; Howie "Stretch" Anderson, a tall string-bean from Oakland whose blond mustache forever threatened to creep into his mouth from both flanks; Ray Simonetti, self-styled "Flower Child in the Nam," it said so right on his helmet; "Stubby" Hoffman, who talked like a sawed-off James Cagney and humped one of the heavy M-60 machineguns; Gene Fuller, a nervous-looking, shy Philadelphian and occasional point man; John Routt, a quiet, always proficient African-American.

There were others, of course, then and later on during the summer: Terry Ammons, a jovial good ol' boy from Waycross, Georgia; Rick Schneider, an oddly normal Pennsylvanian who supplanted Roy as platoon sergeant and kept us straight on LZ Jamie when we were too stoned to navigate efficiently; "Bub" Stites, memorable as the only person I ever knew who got hit with napalm and survived; Bob Hackney from Wisconsin, who seemed familiar with every rock and roll song written since the days of Bill Haley and the Comets, when warfare in Southeast Asia was already an old story; Frank Barrientes, a Mexican-American from Texas on whom bandoliers of machine-gun bullets looked perfectly natural; Bill Cox, whose sheer energy and toughness made him Ropp's obvious choice as assistant squad leader.

Sooner or later I came to know everyone in my platoon as individuals. I learned about their homes, their cars, their girlfriends and their often aggravating, occasionally delightful idiosyncrasies. As I was to find out, however, the platoon leader navigated that sinister demarcation where friends and buddies and other human beings were referred to as "field strength," "effectives," "bodies," and "your people, dammit, Sergeant Smith."

38

Along the Saigon River

ALTHOUGH NO ONE IN THE COMPANY WAS KILLED OR WOUNDED during those two weeks along the creeks and the Saigon River, the skirmishes were nerve-racking, and the short but noisy engagements drew fears closer to the surface. One evening, 3rd Platoon left the company's perimeter and almost before Lt. Frank's last man had faded away into the dusk, a torrent of shots cascaded out of the forest. Bullets crackled past us, people cursed and yelled warnings, and for a second I thought we were under direct attack. I had been sitting at the edge of an immense bomb crater, writing home about my promotion, and after a few seconds I could see that it was not quite "balls to the wall" time. Determined to remain cool, I slid a few feet down into the crater and continued scribbling: "Wow, all sorts of firing just started...." It did not occur to me that I was doing anything peculiar, but then Bart was barking at me to get farther down, bullets were damned near taking my head off. I skidded a few feet deeper but continued to write until the gunfire sputtered and died away almost as quickly as it had started. The small group of enemy soldiers Frank's platoon had stumbled into was gone and our artillery was already ranging in, but suddenly I grew frightened, grabbed an entrenching tool and began to dig like a gopher.

I did a lot of crosswords those days. At every free moment, in perimeter or during a hike, I whipped out my paperback of puzzles and went at them. What I wanted was distraction—from the heat and skyrocketing humidity, from the bugs, from the exhaustion of hauling around sixty or more pounds of assorted gear all day long, and, most of all, from the unbroken anxiety that never quite let go. What else was there to do when you got the word to take five, except to look around at the nearly opaque vegetation and wonder if the enemy might be about to light you up? Sit back against the rucksack, open the book and hide in it, Zone C doesn't exist, and what's a two-letter word for the Egyptian sun god? I spent little time agonizing over clues but, when stumped, immediately peeked at the answer page and filled in the blocks correctly. Whenever I took too long to determine a word, my mind would wander back to the reality around me, my part in it, and the low-grade terror that inhabited me just below the surface, always right there, emerging from what had become too many months of experience.

During another skirmish, I threw myself down behind a large termite mound and instead of using my rifle, pulled my camera from its pouch on the side of my pack and began taking snaps of the guys as they spread out and found cover. I had always imagined the enemy hiding during the day to avoid our ubiquitous planes and choppers and then cautiously creeping about at night, slinking along the narrow trails in single file. The evidence that gangs of them were parading around at high noon shook me up. This was not the enemy I thought I knew. How far away were they? Were they just inside that far tree line, waiting to see what we would do?

Once, miles away from anything resembling civilization, we heard a rooster crow.

Third Platoon was up ahead, spread out on line through an old napalm burn, patches of light underbrush and new, bright green grass, sparring slowly with a team of North Vietnamese. The shooting was scattered, a staccato mixture of the flat *Pow!* of a single shot, the hysterical *Brrraaaap!* of automatic fire, and once or twice the abrupt metallic crash of a grenade. Meager ordered me to split 1st Platoon and bring it forward to extend 3rd's flanks to the right and left, just in case the enemy might be swinging more troops in from one or both sides. I gave my directions to my squad leaders, then went jogging forward, passing Meager and his CP group, and wondering, as always, if this was the wrong time to be up and about when there was shooting under way.

When I came up behind Lt. Frank and 3rd Platoon, I glanced to the left to see if Roy Stern was bringing the rear half of my platoon forward in that direction, and for a moment, unexpectedly, it all looked like a movie, and I forgot about the danger and just stopped to look. Roy and his people came jogging forward across a grassy clearing, moving briskly, almost at a slow trot, well dispersed and perfectly aligned, rifles held high, silhouetted against the sun and actually gleaming in the pristine early-morning light, for all the world like a well-drilled squad in a training film. For a split second I was locked into something special, and the war came alive, the image so different from the usual cramped view of men crawling through the dirt or huddling in a hole or stumbling all too slowly through thick bamboo. It was about as thrilling a show as Zone C could offer, and I might have stood there and enjoyed it for a moment longer, but Meager would have hollered at me to get the lead out and tie in with 3rd, damn it.

Being a platoon leader meant I carried the responsibility for two-dozen lives. I had to give the orders: move that way, you go on LP tonight, dig in right there, put the gun in here, move out to the left, follow this azimuth. And every order, however innocuous, might somehow lead to someone's death or injury. I was all too aware of that. I knew that I did not want to come home and have to look back and think that Private So-and-So was dead because I decided he was needed out on the right flank. "Just doing your job" didn't begin to clear it up.

More than that, though, I was ordering people to risk their lives in a war no one believed in any more. In World War II, a soldier might comprehend that risking his life—and possibly giving it up—would in some small way help gain the ultimate victory over a criminal regime that, for the sake of the future, had to be expunged. By May 1969, we all knew that the first American troop withdrawals were in the air, that the negotiations were going on in Paris, and that eventually America would be gone. There would be no victory or defeat and no one in 1st Platoon, I believe, thought his death would matter one way or another. Another body would be just that. I know I could no longer see any point to the war. It was just a great, perilous adventure and "victory" was a word that simply did not apply. I had been through the Tet Offensive in '68, and I believed then that if, after all the prior months of hard fighting, the enemy were able to mount such an extensive, well-coordinated operation, then no matter what we did, the Viet Cong and North Vietnamese would always be out there. We might hurt them once in awhile, but we would never injure them to the point where South Vietnam would be able to stand alone. There were a couple of cranks—a major in battalion, a sergeant in Mortars—who thought we could and should do it, stick it to the enemy until he ran screaming back up the Ho Chi Minh Trail and gave up. But no one seemed to take that sort of thing seriously.

Our rules, however, were the same as if we had been fighting from the beaches of Normandy to the banks of the Rhine: find, fix, and destroy the enemy. That was the infantry's job, we were the infantry, and we tried to do it. And that meant platoon leaders took orders from company commanders, passed the orders on to the men in their platoons, and without a doubt someone was going to end up dead or minus an eye or a testicle or an arm. I hated knowing that if I remained a platoon leader long enough, someone in my care was going to catch it, so there was nothing I desired more than to turn over the platoon to a lieutenant and slip back into harness as platoon sergeant. I was exceedingly happy, therefore, when at the end of my first week in War Zone C, Meager told me a new lieutenant would arrive on the afternoon log-bird.

Line One

First Lieutenant Roche was late of ROTC and a job with an armored cavalry outfit at Fort Meade, Maryland. Unlike the usual run of new platoon leaders, he had gained some practical experience as an officer and might be expected to know his duties. He was athletic, confident, good-natured, and handsome in a blond, California sort of way, and I liked him immediately.

That afternoon we patrolled west a few hundred yards, looking, in vain, for an enemy track. On the other side of a small, sluggish stream we ran into the thickest, dustiest, most impenetrable canebrake I had ever seen. Progress slowed to a near halt, and in the brilliant afternoon sunshine the heat was unreal. Twenty yards into the thicket, every man was reeling, desperately thirsty and worn to a frazzle. Lt. Roche turned us around and aimed for the stream. We sprawled exhausted along its banks, guzzling our water and dipping up more into our canteens. Roche must have swilled a good two quarts. He immediately threw it all up and then had the dry heaves. This was no joke, even when it happened to an FNG (fuckin' new guy). There was no bantering, "Welcome to the 'Nam, sir." He was on the verge of heat exhaustion and he didn't try to joke about it, either. Mike passed around the salt pills and after a rest Roche took us back to the company perimeter. I think he learned a lot in those few minutes along the creek and he was willing to cut short a patrol that might not result in anything more than a request for a medevac chopper to take out heat casualties. He would, I believed, treat us as human beings and not service numbers or lines on a roster.

The air in the bamboo lowland was musty and dank as my platoon led the company away from its perimeter by the field in the early morning, hiking generally parallel to the river but a couple of hundred yards from its banks. On point, rifleman Gene Fuller made his way slowly but efficiently among the trees and clumps of dead bamboo. Behind us extended the long, slim file of men. I was a good hundred yards into the bottomland before the last man in the company had pulled away from the night's position, which was now a dump of half-filled holes and smoldering garbage. The sun was still relatively low and we weren't even sweating yet, when Fuller opened fire from the hip, a long, mad rattle of shots spraying out to the front. I catapulted forward toward a low hump of earth, checked to make sure no one from the platoon had gotten in front of me, snapped my rifle's selector switch to automatic, and ripped off a full magazine. I had not seen the enemy troops Fuller had fired on, but I saw which way he was aiming and tried to shoot in the same direction. Floyd and a couple of the other riflemen joined in, and then Barrientes brought his gun team forward and cranked a belt through his M-60, spewing red tracers off through the bamboo, hot red flashes snapping away among the shadows.

Wide-eyed and breathless, Fuller crawled back and said he

had got the drop on them, spotted three enemy soldiers as they were, in his word, "boppin'" across his front not twenty yards away. No way to tell if he hit any of them—they moved so quickly—but we knew no shots had been returned. Floyd scouted forward and discovered a well-beaten trail leading away from the river, but no sign of blood. I was not surprised. Seeing the enemy at close range, running into him so abruptly, was always a wild shock, and it was never easy to stay calm and take good aim.

Roche moved up to confer and then had the company advance in three parallel platoon files, each about twenty yards apart, with the lead men more or less abreast. Mortar Platoon would be the only reserve. This formation would allow the company to move forward on a relatively broad front following the slim path the enemy had apparently used. By placing the platoons well apart to each flank, we would have some built-in depth, side to side as well as fore and aft, in case we stumbled into an ambush. Meanwhile, battalion dispatched a Loach spotter chopper to aid us by inspecting the forest from above. We requested a gunship team but none was immediately available. Just then, I don't think any of us believed we would catch up with the enemy. They had taken off so precipitately that we figured they were probably close to Cambodia by now and not likely to be a problem for us. It didn't occur to us that they had been on a short walk down to the river and were heading back to their unit's camp. Nonetheless, as the platoon began advancing, battalion's refusal to supply helicopters armed with rockets and grenades irritated me.

My orders were for the squad leaders to proceed at a pace they thought comfortable and to let the flanking platoons—2nd to the left, 3rd to the right—worry about keeping up with us. The path led to a small, rough clearing, beyond which stood an intensely thick, nearly opaque barrier of bamboo. I was relatively certain the enemy had fled the area, but all of us crept forward carefully, acutely aware that we could see nothing past the wall of foliage and that to anyone hidden inside that wall we were completely exposed.

The racket of an automatic weapon from somewhere in the bamboo brought us up short. We all recognized the distinctive staccato rattle of an AK-47, the enemy's standard assault rifle. Roche called to say that the spotter chopper had drawn the fire and the pilot said that the one enemy soldier he could see was not running at all but was acting as if he meant to stay put and fight it out.

Very slowly now, inches at a time, silent, and hunched over, we moved ahead, knowing that this time we were in for it. They were in there waiting for us, and at some spot, just a few yards ahead, they would let us have it. Better to be taken unaware, I felt, with the unexpected blast of shots in your face, than to be walking forward to it this way. A sinking, quavering hollowness spread through my bowels and groin and descended into my legs. I wanted to find Roche and tell him, "Sir, this isn't how it's done. You do not just stroll into a fight like this." I had done this before, up the country on Tiger Mountain, and that evening had ended with us lugging a dead buddy back down the hill.

Now we were into the bamboo, sneaking from sapling to hummock, eyes alert for the nearest cover—a slight fold in the earth, an ancient, smashed bunker a few feet to the right. Then it came—a sudden crackling, snapping sound to the left front. No matter how often I heard it I was never ready. Like a jolt of electricity the sound shot through my body. Down, scuttling behind something, anything at all, wriggling into the dirt and the dead leaves, drawing your legs up, trying to crawl up inside your helmet, you want to push your dogtags aside to get closer to the earth.

I was still alive, I was not bleeding anywhere, and I could think and act. The shots had been aimed at 2nd Platoon, to the left. Two of its men were down and no one was sure if they could be reached without the rescuers ending up shot, too.

Aside from the one burst of fire, the bamboo was utterly silent. Was 2nd Platoon doing anything? Then Floyd said he and Fuller were crawling off to the left on their own. If 2nd was going to vegetate, then the two of them would go after the casualties. Well, more power to them, I thought, but inside I was writing them off. The North Vietnamese would probably get them, too. I felt angry that they had gone off on their own, without so much as a by-your-leave. I stared at the twigs and the branches and the volume control on Joel's radio, waiting for the harsh snapping that would take two of my people away from me.

But no one opened fire and 2nd Platoon came to life on the radio, telling Roche that my men had recovered the casualties and brought them in, and it looked as if the wounds weren't too bad. And now that we had some idea where the enemy troops were positioned, wasn't it time to pull back a little and think things over?

I expected that, having disengaged, Roche would follow standard operating procedure and pull us back a prudent distance so jets or artillery could work over the enemy position. But today the battalion brass were feeling gung-ho. Even before 2nd's wounded were flown out of the clearing, we were being ordered to turn around, get back in there, and do some fighting. From their command-and-control helicopter, up a thousand feet or so, the prospect of an infantry firefight looked just fine.

Roche may have been inexperienced as far as live combat was concerned, but he could add, subtract, and tie his own shoes. Sending us back into the bamboo with no further preparation struck him as a very bad idea. He listened to battalion's get-those-gooks chatter and radioed back that he wasn't having any. No one in the company—his company, now—was going anywhere near the enemy unless something almighty violent was thrown in first. No, no, no, battalion radioed back, no time for a strike, go in there and fight, dammit. Roche stuck to his guns and told them he wasn't budging. Out.

I waited for the lightning to strike. Battalion wasn't likely to stand for that, not from a guy with barely a week in the boonies behind him. Even Meager, as far as I knew, had never flatly rejected an order. So it was with no little sense of awe that I received the order to saddle up and pull back—battalion had given in and agreed to call up an air strike. All I cared about was the fact that Roche had taken a stand because he wanted to keep us alive and whole. It was a new experience for most of us.

Soon two jets moaned up from the south and the FAC (forward air controller) fired a white phosphorous marking rocket into the bamboo. The brilliant white plume of smoke defined the target (or at least what the FAC understood to be the target) with unmistakable clarity. In preparation for the bombing runs and the inevitable shrapnel that would be thrown out across the landscape, we edged behind the trees or huddled against the thicker clumps of brush.

The jets screeched in, visible in blurred, split-second glimpses through the vegetation, diving at a shallow angle and then pulling up sharply as the bombs were toggled free and seemed to wobble in slow motion down to the trees. The sudden howl of the afterburners, as the pilots strove to pull away to a safe distance, mingled with the shocking crashes of the bomb detonations. We tensed and lowered our heads as the ground and air shuddered together, and then the scrap metal whizzed and buzzed past. When a splinter struck against a tree with a loud clack we all flinched. Momentary relief swept through us when a jet's pass ended not in the blast of high explosive, but instead with the round, almost soft *who-o-omph* of napalm, which did not throw shrapnel. We kept our heads up and watched the thick black smoke boil up into view above the trees.

With or without the fragments spinning by us, we loved the air strikes. If they were accurate, then the enemy would be gone, blown to bits or buried, and our advance through the debris would be no more than a peaceful survey of an overturned landscape. That was all that mattered to us. In an intellectual way I could oppose Dow Chemical, but I never felt any remorse when the napalm splashed orange and frightful across the jungle. I wanted the enemy to die so that I wouldn't.

By the time we were ready to creep forward again, the jets had already landed back at Bien Hoa. This time we halted less than twenty yards from the small clearing and the platoon spread out to right and left. The idea was for us, on order, to lay down a base of fire which would serve to keep the enemy's head down while 3rd Platoon swung around to the far right to take the North Vietnamese position in flank. Even if the hostiles remained in position and retained some combat effectiveness after the bombing, my platoon's fire would pin them in place, 3rd's maneuver would lever them out of their holes, and we would clear the area. That was the idea.

Looking ahead through the latticework of green and gray, I could see only deeper, thicker foliage. It looked as if the air strike had been off target. There were no smoking bomb craters, no charred, smoldering tree skeletons.

No time to worry, either. Lt. Frank said 3rd Platoon was ready to go and we opened up. Every weapon in the platoon exploded at once. The forest reverberated with a steady roar of shots punctuated by the weird *thoop* of the grenade launchers and the crash of the shells' detonations. Branches, leaves, and vines jumped and a thin gray fog of gun smoke settled around us. The North Vietnamese would know we were back, but with any luck our fire would keep their heads down. If Frank could then bring 3rd Platoon onto their flank, they would die or be driven out.

Roche yelled for us to cease firing, Frank was ready to move in across our front and we should be careful not to shoot any of his people who might appear up ahead. No sound now but for our stealthy shifting about in the dirt and bamboo debris, some muttered comments, and the soft sigh from Joel's radio handset next to me. We changed magazines in our rifles, stowing the empties in the pockets of our fatigues. Some of us lit cigarettes. Up ahead, the woods were quiet and slightly hazy with the smoke and the dust kicked up by our outburst. No one had fired back at us.

Frank's voice came over the radio, sounding calm and in control. I imagined his men inching across our front, bent over, rifles up, slowly looking from one side to the other. He had nothing much to report—a few unoccupied "spider holes" and an abandoned bunker or two. Perhaps the air strike had done it after all, and the NVA had said the hell with it and pulled out.

Wait a moment, now one of 3rd's men thought he saw some movement, Frank reported his platoon was going to—

"Incoming!"

We flattened ourselves as the first shots crackled from the front. Frank's men, who were now directly ahead of us, answered the initial burst. Then more enemy shots snapped toward us. We could see nothing but the foliage and branches, we could only lie there and hear the dreadful crackle of automatic weapons.

"I've got a line two," Frank said over the radio. "Line two." Radio code for a man wounded in action. I remained on the ground with the side of my helmet pressed against the twigs and dry leaves. More shooting, but still sporadic, as if each side were waiting for the other to open up before replying in turn.

Frank again: "My Five is line two, over."

His "Five" was his platoon sergeant. Mac, I thought.

Staring at Joel I muttered, "Mac.

And then, as if a tap had been wrenched open, the jungle ahead of us blew up in a blaze of enemy shots and sudden, solid blasts, and Frank was on the horn, calling for the company's mortar crew to start firing, he needed support now! The afternoon collapsed in gunfire and blurted, staccato radio messages. I caught something about rockets being fired at 3rd Platoon. From the clearing to the rear came the comforting sound of the company's mortar tube, chunking out shells to try to suppress the enemy fire and Ewing asked Frank how things looked.

"I've got a line one, over," Frank replied.

Line one. Killed-in-action.

If anyone still wondered if the jets had done any good, the racket of enemy gunfire was the answer. Third Platoon wasn't making any progress so it was time for Frank to think about getting the hell out of there. By holding in place and fighting it out, Frank would risk freezing his platoon into position and turning the initiative over to the North Vietnamese, with more friendly casualties the result.

Frank called Roche to say he was sending his men back: "Give us some cover fire if we call for it. Don't mistake us for the enemy. I'll let you know when no one's left out here."

Roche ordered us to spread out to right and left and be prepared to lend a hand with any of 3rd's casualties. I listened to the incoming fire for a second and then threw myself upright and dashed to the right, and slid down behind the same low mound where I had been during the first probe into the bamboo. Joel was right with me and then Roche went running past farther to the right with some of Ropp's people. They halted a few yards away and I turned in that direction just in time to see a burst of smoke appear right in front of them. I didn't hear a thing—sensory overload, I guess—didn't even have time to think to duck, but I knew a rocket had blown up right in front of Roche. He went down as if a wrecking ball had smashed him full in the chest. I howled for Mike, wherever he was, to get over there, but I didn't imagine there would be a lot for him to do. Roche had been decked so violently, I was sure he was dead. My radio call to Ewing was short and simple: "Team Six, this is One-Five. My Six is down. I am now acting as One-Six."

Fuller darted up behind me and hunkered down, looking stunned. I think he said Roche was still alive, but his words made no impression on me. I stared at the thin stream of blood running down his arm. When I told him to get back to the clearing to have the wound dressed and wait for a medevac chopper, he just looked at me blankly. Then he stood up and left the bamboo. It had been a strange tableau, each of us talking to the other and neither of us hearing. What was happening had become so confusing that we were operating on autopilot, going through the motions that had been drilled into us in training and then through months of actual operations. What had begun as a textbook maneuver straight out of the Fort Benning Infantry School – base of fire, maneuvering element, and so on – had devolved in seconds into a rout and there hadn't been time yet to make sense of it.

The firing had slackened as 3rd's men moved back and finally Frank called to say that they were all out. I passed the word for 1st Platoon to withdraw and as I watched to see that everyone was out of the bamboo, the shooting ended. I was still in the thicket when I caught sight of Lt. Frank a few yards away to the left. His mouth was sagging at the edges and there were dark smudges under his eyes. He gazed at me for a second, hardly acknowledging my tired greeting, then muttered, "Mac got it."

You said he'd been wounded, I thought, but then Frank pointed to my left, to the base of a clump of brush at the edge of the clearing and I understood.

Mac was stretched out on a poncho. His hands were raised to each side of his head, as if he had been frozen in the middle of a chin-up. There was a bandage halfway up one arm. For a second I thought with strange clarity that Mac had been sweating a lot, but there was a reddish tint to his soaked black hair, and near the top of his head the hair had been swept apart in a whipped, circular pattern.

A long, drawn-out *No-o-o-o* went through my mind. Frank was telling me what had happened, how Mac had taken a slug in the arm when the enemy first opened fire, how they had just slapped a dressing over the wound when the enemy really turned on the juice, and then a sniper put a bullet through Mac's helmet and he was dead before anyone quite realized he had been hit a second time. Frank's words sank slowly into my understanding.

After sixteen months in the war, after so many deaths, the enormity of this loss jarred me more deeply than I would have imagined possible.

As I wandered back to where Ewing was calling for medevac choppers and trying to organize the company into a defensive perimeter, someone said Roche was asking for me. He was alive, but all I could manage was a nod.

Roche lay on his back in some shade. A huge bandage had been placed across his chest and he was in a lot of pain but nevertheless able to speak. He asked me to take care of the guys, he was sorry to leave them. I tossed off the normal refrain: "Don't sweat it, we'll be okay, don't come back to this shit if you can avoid it, sir." I told him he would be missed, but it was only much later that I realized myself how sincerely I meant it. The medevac bird was on its way in, so I stepped away and left him to the medics.

While Ewing and battalion talked things over, I walked over to where Frank had established 3rd Platoon's CP around a shallow hole in the dirt. Lee Collins and Dave Calloway were with him, and soon Ray Karr, now the only one left from my old squad, joined us. We didn't say much. We just sat there and looked at each other or stared at the ground. I was feeling a bad mix of misery, rage, sadness and confusion. Mac was not supposed to get it. He was supposed to go home at the end of his year and enjoy "ruffling" with his wife, and now I'd never again be able to tease him about what that meant. Calloway was crushed. On and off for three months he had been Mac's radioman and now Mac was dead. We sat there for a long time. No one bothered us, asked us for orders or suggested we get our platoons straightened out. Inside, things were breaking up and crumbling; I had never felt so drained, so resigned and so fed up. There was something wintry about the scene, as if we were so many lousy stumblebums, huddling somewhere up an alley as the first gusts of a frigid night penetrated our rags, too stupefied and numb to heed the warning in the breeze.

———

The company was put back in order presently, by whom I have no idea. After a while the company plodded back to the position it had occupied the night before. With darkness close upon us, the filled holes were cleaned out and made ready for use again, flares and Claymores were set out, guard schedules were established, and poncho hooches raised. We settled down, carrying on with our nightly routines as if nothing much had happened since Fuller led us down into the bottomland so many hours ago.

I walked a few yards away from my platoon sector and ran into Collins. The two of us stood silently in the darkness, talking softly for a little while. I just needed to be with someone who had known Mac, someone who might understand my bitterness, my anger, and my fear. After a time I squashed out my cigarette and returned to my position.

40

Death's Golden Eyes

FOR TWO WEEKS THE WAR IN ZONE C SLIPPED INTO WHAT amounted to a lull. the company spent most of that time as a security force on LZ Jamie, luxuriating in the strong bunkers, conducting occasional short patrols into the surrounding forest, and enjoying three meals a day along with quantities of beer and soft drinks. The nightly rains did not let up, but pulling guard through the dripping dark hours on LZ Jamie was a relief from sitting at the edge of a slimy hole somewhere out in the boonies. One of the guys had a tape player with earphones, so we were able to listen to the Beatles, Cream, and the Butterfield Blues Band.

Some afternoons, when the breeze was right, the scent of death would drift across the perimeter, reminding us that there were bodies decomposing in the woods, tokens of the earlier attack on the landing zone. At night, far away, the horizon would glow with the bright swaying dots of falling flares. There were other landing zones out there, with names like Grant, White, and Ike. The war would surge up against them for a night or two, and we would see the flashes and hear the muted thunders. There were mornings when the rolling tattoo of a B-

52 heavy bomber strike would shake us awake in the black predawn hours. We would watch the distant wall of fire and smoke and wait for the concussion to reach us and make our clothes twitch and jump. If the pre-dawn sky were clear and our eyes were sharp, we could pick out the rapidly moving specks of light far overhead. I always wondered, did the bomber crews feel a part of the war?

My platoon got a new lieutenant, a skinny splint named Ed Kansler, and once again I reverted to platoon sergeant. He was the third lieutenant I had broken in that year and I began to feel like a one-man training school.

After the company left Jamie and returned to the field, the quiet lasted for several days. We air assaulted, patrolled, and ambushed near two abandoned landing zones to the northeast, Rita and Phyllis. Nothing significant occurred, but we were jumpy, for the maneuvering took us beyond the range of much of our supporting artillery. The border with Cambodia was only a few miles away, across which was the enemy high command's headquarters, the near-mythical COSVN ("Coz-vin"), or Central Office for South Vietnam, and I felt as if we had crept out to the end of a very insubstantial limb.

One afternoon, a Huey sporting a brace of whisker-like antennae appeared overhead. It was a signals intelligence bird, we were told, sent up to scan rapidly through radio frequencies in the hope that it would find one used by the enemy and pick up some useful information. The bird orbited around and around. The sky seemed to swallow up the clatter of its prop, which accentuated my sense of isolation. I was glad when it finally clanked off to the south and the forest silence returned.

A ceasefire rumor made the rounds, based only on the report that the battalion chief had ordered all the companies to suspend operations and just stay where they were until further notice. I found myself believing the rumor might pan out, the war might actually be over, and all of us would go home on our feet. I should have known better.

Later that afternoon, I sat on the floor of a Huey, flying through the unnatural haze of atomized Zone C, hurled skyward by yet another B-52 strike. We were headed for an area northwest of LZ Jamie known as the Mustang Trail, allegedly a major North Vietnamese infiltration and supply route from Cambodia south toward the Michelin rubber plantation and the environs of Saigon. We landed in a tiny, grassy clearing and even before the company collected itself we had one casualty—a guy in 2nd Platoon broke his ankle jumping from the skids of his chopper. Lousy omen.

What ensued seems, even now, a demented blur, a grim kaleidoscope, the whole spectrum all at once: four weeks of too much of everything, blood, smoke, shouts and groaning, detonations, flames, green and orange, exhaustion, panic, gunfire, flashes, terrible sounds, total chaos. Before one awful incident could be swallowed and digested, something worse had happened. When the company was not fighting, someone else in the vicinity was. The forest seemed to swarm with troops, ours and theirs, scattered across the terrain like salt and pepper.

From far away the sound of automatic weapons fire was strangely soft, almost soothing in a perverse way. It sounded like dead leaves rustling in an autumn breeze, or like distant surf under an overcast sky. There was hardly a day when a jet strike wasn't going in somewhere in the vicinity. The planes, always in pairs, either bright and silvery or painted in gray and green camouflage colors, sighed in great circles over the land. We could feel the ground jump when the bombs erupted or see the smoke rise from the napalm. More often, the artillery cranked up; the howitzer discharges sounded flat and monotonous, almost apathetic, in the distance. At night, the shells would wail over us like so many freight trains in formation, and the sound would die away and end with a short series of abrupt, unemotional bangs. From time to time someone in the area would call for Spooky and the tracer bullets would pour down from the night sky like red water from a hose.

We were out there hunting the North Vietnamese and, after a while, we realized that they were on the move, too, hunting us, and pretty soon it was all balled up. Retreats turned into unplanned advances. Patrols got lost and floundered through the woods until, more by luck than acute navigation, they stumbled back to the perimeter. Some patrols just found a spot to hide and holed up for a few hours. Very little went right and no one gave a damn. We just wanted to get out of there before the war in Zone C ingested us entirely.

———

I don't know if anything the company did that spring and summer made it into the papers back home. If it did, it was probably masked by phrases like "elements of the 1st Cavalry Division" or "light contact was reported in an area north of Saigon," nothing that would begin to represent what was actually going on along the Mustang Trail. No one back home read about how Stern and I blew up when Kansler got us lost on patrol—Zone C seemed perilous enough when you knew where you were—and how we took the platoon away from him and led it back to the company as quickly as we could thrash our way through the tearing, resistant underbrush. No one was on hand as Delta Company was slowly hacked up, or when a dead North Vietnamese with a gold belt buckle was found in a smashed bunker and suddenly the rumor went round that we were messing with the headquarters of the entire 1st NVA Division, and maybe we hadn't seen anything yet.

It was a hidden war, just us and them, grunts and gooks, wrestling about in a lousy patch of woods a million miles from nowhere, no reporters, no sound-men, no TV cameras, no villagers, damned few of our own brass. What we did never produced names like Khe Sanh and Hue and Hamburger Hill, that insinuated themselves into the language of the sixties. Our war produced no blaring headlines. It just kept grinding ahead, objectiveless, invisible. Despite the frequent uproars, the jets, the artillery, the shots and explosions, the whacking sounds of the helicopters, I thought of it as a strangely silent time, as if I had been strapped aboard a soundless juggernaut. Whenever I was so lucky as to snag a newspaper or catch an Armed Forces Network broadcast, I realized how distant we were from the rest of the world—or from the rest of the war, for that matter—and how everything that was out there was in no way affected by anything we did.

During the great Tet Offensive in 1968, it was possible to see the war as having reached a climax of some sort, and a participant could feel that what he was doing was, at least indirectly, finding its way back to the home folks, and that alone seemed to offer some reason to be a part of it. But now I was in a grubby combat backwater that meant little, made even less sense, and was unlikely to be noticed by anyone fifty miles away, much less on the other side of the planet. When I went to war, I pledged myself to write honest, no-holds-barred letters home, but now I found it difficult to scribble it all down. Just living through it without slipping the tracks was hard enough and I knew there was almost no one in the States who could appreciate what was happening to my life.

So, a certain thrill attached to the idea that we might be up against the headquarters of the 1st NVA Division. That would at least offer us something significant. For the most part our actual assignments were embarrassingly mundane. We might be told to poke through the forest for a "reported rice cache," or perhaps for some "suspicious looking crates" a chopper pilot had spotted. Who wanted to risk becoming a paraplegic, or worse, for the sake of some sacks of rice or some boxes? Reluctant as most of us were—almost all in the company were draftees; as an authentic volunteer I was quite a rarity—we retained a certain pride in our status as soldiers, and given an object worthy of that status, we would, I believe, have tried in good faith to achieve it.

Leaving the company perimeter began to be difficult for me. Within the circle of bunkers, I felt secure, but stepping outside, if only to chop out a field of fire or to urinate, unnerved me. As I put one foot down, I wondered if there would be time to step forward with the other before an enemy Claymore splattered me against the trees, or a storm of machine-gun fire shattered my legs. I couldn't decide what was worse: open forest in which I could better see where I was going—and where the enemy, dug in and waiting, could see me more clearly—or really thick brush and bamboo where I might be hidden, but where I might also might walk into the enemy's sights at such close range that even the most myopic rifleman or gunner could hit me.

A couple of the others saw what was happening to me. More than once, as we inched along through the forest and my fear became an almost physical throbbing, Mike turned to me and said, quietly and gently, "Take it easy, Mark." Meager himself tapped me on the shoulder once as we advanced against entrenched North Vietnamese who had already shot down five of the company's men, and asked, "You're a little 'short' for this, aren't you, One-Five?" He seemed to understand when I muttered, "You better believe it, Six."

For hours at a time I would go through the motions, like I was, in some way, paralyzed but still mobile. There was nothing I could do. Nothing I could do. Nothing I could do. Without the words and actions of the others—Mike and Meager and the rest of the platoon CP group—I don't know how I could have maintained my balance.. There were plenty of options: death of all humane feelings, an emotional ice age, cowardice, psychological breakdown. I had a choice of roads to follow even at the end of the line.

———

There was not much we could rely on. We believed in each other, and a good many of us believed in our immediate leaders, with pardonable restraint in some cases, and I suppose we had faith in our weapons. But from outside the company there came precious little support or sustenance. The music helped. We were as much a product of the sixties as any acid-scrambled hippies and when the Armed Forces Vietnam Network played rock, we listened. Several of the guys carried transistor radios and we occasionally heard songs that seemed to have been written with us in mind, sometimes eerily so. It didn't seem odd that it was during the spring and summer of '69 that we listened to a short, bouncy song by Creedence Clearwater Revival called "Bad Moon Rising" that had grimly appropriate lyrics, like it had been written specifically about Vietnam. There were others equally evocative, like The Beatles' "Get Back." I heard the Stones's "Sympathy for the Devil" that summer. I used to sing to myself at night, it helped keep me awake and alert on guard at the bunker. That started my first night in the boonies, March '67, and the words were there as if they had been locked in a psychic vault just for me. But nobody ever got those black, fathomless nights down more accurately than Dylan in "Visions of Johanna."

American popular culture crept up on us, twisted in a special way to reflect our experience and bleak sensibilities. Sometimes it came back lopsided. Tom Vinciguerra's helmet sported, among other graffiti, a garish peace symbol surrounded by wild flames and below it the caption: "Dow Chemical, we love you."

Several of us inscribed "SDS" (Students for a Democratic Society) on our helmets. Although we knew next to nothing about the organization's actual politics, Students for a Democratic Society was against the war and that was fair enough. Strike fists and Vs for peace were commonplace. Popular in the platoon was an asymmetrical peace symbol, inside of which we wrote "Peace," "Love," and "Sex." Seemed like a reasonable combination to us. A major on the battalion staff once noticed the peace symbol I wore on an old bootlace around my neck and asked me why I was wearing it. "I'd like the war to end, sir."

41

The Grim Landscape

ALWAYS, NORTH VIETNAMESE IN BUNKERS AND TRENCHES, unseen through the bamboo. Second Platoon lost four men wounded in a few seconds and recoiled as if it had stuck its finger into a socket. The rest of us plodded forward to take up a position around two overlapping bomb craters and prepare to go into action. Meager called for helicopter gunships and told the pilots to put their ordnance within fifty yards of us. The pilots called right back and demanded his initials; if there were a bad mistake, they wanted the record to show who had asked for it. Meager didn't hesitate—I'm not sure he knew how to hesitate—and the rockets came pouring down. I was approaching the craters, moving along woodenly, trying to keep it together and not allow the fear to take over. Each long train of loud crashes was followed by the quick, frightening whicker of rocket splinters hailing all around. I felt dazed after the first salvo, barely thought to flinch, just kept moving my feet and keeping my eyes on the boots and rucksack of the guy in front of me, remembering a terrible day back in February, when misdirected rocket fire destroyed a third of my platoon, one dead and ten wounded in a couple of seconds. Now I walked in a weird sort of dumb nonchalance. I felt drugged, all slow and logy, and if the next blast took me with it, well, blame it on Meager, it wasn't my fuckin' fault.

We joined 2nd Platoon for another try after the Hueycobras were done, but on the way into the bamboo, where it was already matted and tangled after the rockets had battered at it, Kansler somehow got the platoon curled around the enemy position. An enemy machine-gunner waited until half of us had passed by and then pulled trigger. Frank Barrientes took one in the mouth and, screaming wetly, ran back to the perimeter at the craters. Mike took off after him to administer first aid. The rest of us lay there and waited to see how bad it was going to get. Kansler called for gunship support and as he shouted instructions, I began to realize how badly matters had become fouled up. Whenever he directed the gunships to fire their rockets more to his left, the warheads detonated that much closer to me and when I called in directions to adjust fire to the right, the impacts were too close to his position. I finally ordered a checkfire until we could figure out how to correct matters without anyone else getting shot. It turned out Kansler and his radioman were speaking on two different radio sets.

Meager was all for close air support so he told Kendall to call for the big stuff—napalm, 500-pounders and 20mm cannon fire from a pair of Super Sabres. I found a huge fallen tree trunk, with just enough room for me to slide in and cower as the most fantastic fireworks display imaginable began. When the jets made their low passes over the forest, they were so close to us the pilots were visible in the cockpits. When the dark green bombs were released and wobbled uncertainly toward the trees, we could almost read the yellow markings before the planes howled away from the blast and shrapnel. Then the forest erupted in lightning-like orange flashes, furious pillars of smoke and dust and pieces of trees, and convulsive, earth-jarring concussions. There was just time for me to draw my head back under the tree trunk before the scrap metal began clattering all around, a sharp metal rain sprinkling across the perimeter. When the gleaming napalm canisters tumbled into the bamboo, we remained in the open, watching the smoking forest turn to fire, chunks of flame curving across the forest canopy, arching away from the central inferno of each pass. Waves of heat bathed our faces each time the jellied gasoline rioted through the bamboo. The cannon fire came as an afterthought, the heavy buzzsaw scream and the sudden stream of hot-pink flashes among the branches to our front.

When the jets wailed away and we went back in, we took it slow and easy. The enemy, we figured, could return to the positions as rapidly as we could advance upon them. When we reached the first bamboo-cluttered remnant of enemy trench, Kansler began firing a 90mm recoilless rifle. The shock of each discharge staggered him, sending spasms through his entire body. Meager sent forward an order for the lieutenant to stop it before he turned his insides to jelly, but Kansler persevered until all the shells were gone. There wasn't anything much at stake now, aside from a few square yards of tattered jungle. Five men had already been shot over it and now this young lieutenant was busy convulsing himself into knots and it was senseless and wasteful. I was frightened, but what affected me then went to a point past fear and frustration, a point on a stark, cold landscape somewhere beyond desolation.

Next morning, we reached a new low.

After a slow and useless mortar barrage, we set out from the perimeter behind Lt. Ewing's 2nd Platoon. Kansler peeled us off to the right, or west, toward some dense bamboo. The maneuver all but doubled the platoon back on itself. At one point I was almost able to reach through the brush and shake the hand of the point man walking by in the opposite direction. A North Vietnamese appeared like a khaki-clad jack-in-the-box and took off deeper into the green labyrinth, cracking off a short wild burst from his rifle and Kansler immediately decided the platoon was pinned down. I had to take charge and swing the rear half of the platoon forward to bring it on line along the edge of the bamboo. I occupied a bomb crater to secure the left flank, from where several of us kept our eyes open to the front, the left and the rear. This patch of acreage obviously held its fair share of enemy troops and I didn't like holding a position that left one flank dangling.

For a few minutes nothing happened. Then there was a sharp crunch to my right, from near the center of the platoon line. When I turned to look there was a bit of gray smoke at the edge of the bamboo and then Howie, eyes wide, came floundering across to the crater, yelling for the medic. Mike took off with a couple of the guys and Howie slid in next to me. A rocket had careened in out of nowhere and burst against a branch directly over Stubby's gun crew. Stubby was badly wounded. Peterson, the ammo bearer, was dead.

The rest of the guys put out a sporadic fire now, shooting up the bamboo generally, more in an effort to keep the enemy from moving in closer than with the hope of actually hitting anyone. Mike sent over word that he was littering Stubby back to the company perimeter; the platoon had lost the second of its gunners in as many days.

When Meager called to tell us a team of HueyCobra gunships was inbound, Kansler and his half of the platoon found shelter in a large abandoned enemy bunker. I pulled my people back a few score yards to the middle of a blast-cleared area, where a crater gave us both protection and a broad field of fire if we needed it. Both halves of the platoon were soon tossing out smoke-marking grenades, swathing the area in drifting violet, yellow and red vapors. When they showed up, the gunship pilots began pounding the bamboo with long ripple fires of rockets and whining bursts of mini-gun fire.

After Kansler radioed another correction, however, I

looked up to see the bird beginning its firing run and aiming directly toward me, apparently preparing to unload a salvo right into my half of the platoon. I clutched at the radio handset and snapped, *"Checkfire! Checkfire!* This is One-Five, I want a checkfire *now!"* I watched, stupefied, and suddenly the gunship's nose rose sharply and the pilot veered away, the rockets still in their pods.

We all compared compass azimuths, made sure the pilots knew there were two groups of us throwing out smokes, and finally told them to go ahead. The Cobras tore the bamboo apart, blasting mats of vegetation and pieces of trees into the air. When the ammo was expended we got ourselves together and moved forward to see what had been accomplished and bring out Peterson's body.

There wasn't much to see at first—the expected froth of wrecked, whipped bamboo, a bunker with the roof blown off, a gray, dusty litter of leaves and shredded bark. Then someone spoke or made a noise of some sort and I looked to my left to see what he had found. There was a jungle boot that stood by itself, and around it was draped the faded, rolled-up green cuff—only the cuff—of a set of fatigue pants. Out of the top of the boot extended a leg, very pale, there wasn't much blood, and halfway to the knee the leg stopped. For a few moments that was all of Peterson we could come up with. Then another portion of leg was found, and then part of the torso. That was it—that was Peterson. That was what would be sent home to his parents. And shit, what was there to say or feel or do? I stared at the boot, unable to comprehend it fully, feeling sucked empty and thinking absurdly, "So that's what happens when you get hit by a rocket."

We acted as if the platoon collectively had been hit over the head with a plank, barely able to speak, moping back and forth, stunned. When the enemy fired another rocket, which burst well before it reached us, we hardly took any notice, didn't jump or hit the dirt or even mutter "incoming."

What was left of Peterson was wrapped in a poncho and then Meager called to say that battalion wanted us to break off the action and return to the perimeter. On any other day I would have been astonished. Break off a fight and walk away, with Captain Meager at the helm? It just wasn't done. We fought them, or we moved back and called in artillery or rockets or whatever, but we didn't just walk away. But this time Meager said, "Fuck these gooks, over," and I just nodded, it seemed like a good idea, time to get out of there.

As we walked grimly into the perimeter, a helicopter descended above us carrying Lieutenant Frank, spiffy in clean, starched fatigues but looking tense. We must have looked like a scraggly bunch of whacked-out shell-shock victims. Certainly, we had just come from somewhere far into the war. Some of us gingerly lifted the poncho onto the floor of the Huey cabin and for a second I thought Frank was going to reel back from it. He must have known he was on his way out to pick up a body, but when he saw how pitifully small the bundle was, a brief flurry of disgust and disbelief blurred across his face. The two of us stared at one another for a moment, not even trying to shout above the roar of the chopper. I just shook my head. There weren't any words and I was close to weeping.

Battalion told us to link up with Bravo Company about two thousand yards to the northeast for the night. After covering barely three hundred yards we ran into more North Vietnamese. The clatter of shots from up ahead sent us to ground. I knelt against the inside of a crater and waited. We were weary and wasted by the morning's anxieties and horror. We had had three separate contacts with the enemy within twenty-four hours, and now, stepping out in a new direction, we were again brought to a halt. Was there any way out of here? Did the gooks lie in every direction? Were they setting a trap? Were we trapped already but didn't yet realize it?

No one wanted to fight. No one seemed to give a damn about anything that was happening outside his immediate field of view. I felt detached from the skirmishes up ahead and the voices on the radio were distant and unreal. When a wounded man was helped back past my spot, I barely looked up. Then the gunships came in and under the cover of their firepower 3rd Platoon drew back and sought a better route toward Bravo Company.

Now the battalion commander's bird appeared overhead and began guiding us, shepherding our long file along the axis of an old B-52 strike, where the vegetation was less thick and afforded the enemy fewer places to hide. Nevertheless, the point man sprayed magazine after magazine of bullets ahead of him, shooting up every tree, every clump of bamboo, every clot of vines and brush, every spot that might conceivably hide an enemy. Word came back that we were too close to Bravo's perimeter to keep that up, and then 3rd Platoon passed a Bravo outpost and radioed that it was in our sister company's position.

There was a weird sort of hysteria loose that evening. We were told battalion had concluded that the enemy unit we had been tangling with was part of a North Vietnamese medical brigade. I pictured little men in white coats, pushing their stethoscopes aside as they launched their rockets. Howie burst into a harangue, imagining the headline in *Stars & Stripes:* "NVA Medics Beat Shit out of Hard-Core Cavalrymen!" but our laughter had a saw-toothed edge. Somewhere in back of our desperate hilarity, laughter and weeping merged, you really couldn't tell them apart any more.

Suddenly, in the midst of our operations, the higher-ups spun us out of the field, through LZ Jamie and into the massive Tay Ninh West base camp, miles away on the other side of the dark, stumpy pyramid of Nui Ba Den. Tay Ninh West, home for elements of both the 1st Air Cav and the 25th Infantry Division, meant "stand-down," the so-called VIP Center. A rest. Two days of no guard duty, no bunker-building, no patrols, no details, no listening posts or ambushes, just showers and shaves, new socks and boots and fatigues, and quantities of booze, sleep, hot chow and dope. After rummaging through the jungles of War Zone C, VIP Center was a spike of super-speed.

That first night in Tay Ninh found me standing on a picnic table, harmonizing at the top of my lungs on some country and western song, "Pour me another cup of coffee...," one arm draped over Lt. Frank's shoulder, the other waving a fifth of bourbon. Three in the morning, body and mind flooded with liquor and Cambodian red. Kneeling by the front steps of my barracks and heaving it all, I already looked forward to more of the same the next evening. That night in the barracks I found Mike and Howie and Johnny Velez with a guy from another platoon who freaked when they addressed me as "Sarge." One of the guys calmed him down, saying it was okay, I was cool.

A South Korean rock band showed up for that second night's debauch, and a guy I had met in Sydney on R&R somehow found me and by the time the band was warmed up we were both down in flames. The young woman singer, during a long, crackling version of "Light My Fire," sent us howling into the midnight sky when she reached down into the front of her panties (which, with a T-shirt, was all she wore) and withdrew a few pubic hairs to give to the guys in the first row of our mob. And despite what might appear to be contradictions, the rock music and the determined, monotonous thudding of the base's artillery, a slender, half-naked young woman and the sputtering, swaying flares in the night sky, the scene holds together in memory and makes perfect sense.

―――――

Of course, the break wasn't enough to do us any good. Two days out of Zone C didn't give us any chance to re-wire shredded nerves and repair short circuits. We knew that only a few hours, in either direction, separated us from the forest and the fear and the blood. Our tensions, instead of flowing out and dissipating, merely drew us to any available stimulus. Drunk and stoned as we were, a sober streak ran through us like the mother lode.

The second afternoon I left the VIP Center and walked out to the base perimeter. There was an empty bunker there and I sat inside for a while, gazing across a field of dusty grass and barbed wire and hidden mines toward a village and a busy dirt road. At that moment the Vietnamese I could see—boys and girls walking and playing, farmers with carts drawn by water buffalo, travelers aboard a blue-painted, fantastically ramshackle bus—appeared to be the most peaceable, content people on earth. I was ready to chuck it all and join them, live on a diet of rice and fish and become an Indochinese Gauguin, minus the artistic skill but more than appreciative of the female form. The scene filled me with a weird sense of warm, comfortable melancholy.

That was the last time I saw a Vietnamese village. By noon the following day, the dark lump of Nui Ba Den was back in its accustomed place, scowling over the western horizon, and the Company was lifting out of LZ Jamie on air assault, back to the Mustang Trail.

Several miles to the south of our operations sector, through the maze of trees and bamboo hells and narrow paths and craters, a North Vietnamese heavy machinegun was in position. Doubtless the crew occupied a cramped, circular trench of the sort we occasionally chanced across in our wanderings. Once every day or so, one of our choppers, a resupply bird or the battalion commander's ship, would stray into the airspace overhead and attract the enemy gun crew's attention. We would hear the fading drone-clatter of the chopper, then the slow, flat-sounding fusillade of shots from the gun. Once or twice a doorgunner on the targeted bird thought he had the enemy position pegged and fired back and we would hear the banging of his M-60. No chopper, as far as we heard, was ever hit; it was more as if the gun crew was using bullets to thumb its nose at us than to actually do some damage. Likewise, no one aboard one of the choppers ever claimed to have hit the gun position below. It was just there, part of the peculiar scheme of things in War Zone C. One became used to it and we could count on hearing it whenever we saw a Huey flying toward that part of the landscape.

One day a Huey pilot got fed up and called for jets to silence the gun once and for all. I remember thinking, as the high explosives and napalm went in, that if they happened to find their mark, I would miss the sound of the gun, and in the oddest way the forest would seem all the more lonely. But the jets missed, of course—probably never came close—and a couple of days later the enemy gun crew was happily potting away at a resupply bird.

In retrospect, the enemy gun was not only a theme but a message. Pity that no one ever found the key to unlock it. By its simple continued existence the gun told us most of what we needed to know about War Zone C, or for that matter about the war in general. Its staccato cough told us how vast War Zone C was, and how impenetrable. It seemed to chide us for being so few and so impotent. The North Vietnamese were going to be there for a long time, it said, as long as they pleased. If we really wanted to trudge around the woods and pick fights with them, that was fine, but in the end we would leave. The North Vietnamese would wait. There was more than enough space there to absorb the blood from both sides, and someday we would all be back across the Pacific, and Zone C, despite its shattered trees and broken ground, would be about the same as when we found it.

———

Third Platoon's point man led the company into a small clearing nowhere in particular when, much to his surprise, a lone North Vietnamese jumped up and ran into the woods. Neither the point man nor the grenadier behind him had time to shoot. Twice already that day, Third's men had spotted enemy troops and on both previous occasions there had also been no firing. Now, the third time around, Meager called it quits for the day and told us to form a perimeter encompassing the clearing and start digging in for the night. I chose a spot directly behind and against a huge, thick termite mound; I figured its packed, rock-hard earth would cushion the blow from anything that might come booming in at it. Meanwhile, Kansler told Roy Stern to pick two men and go out front on a security patrol.

Less than thirty yards out, Roy was knocked to a halt. Something at the base of a large tree, visible from our position on the fledgling perimeter, erupted in his face with a mighty crash. Then a machinegun cracked down and it looked to me like a replay of my rocketed patrol several weeks before. When I heard the blast and the subsequent crackle of bullets, I thought, There go those guys. And then all three of them, came tumbling back toward us, running in the jerky, desperate gait peculiar to combat, where the most frantic efforts seem betrayed by lack of progress, little over-burdened marionettes in calf-deep mud.

Meager, of course, ordered us to get ready to fight and here we were again, in the shit, resignedly throwing on our bandoliers and field dressings and grenades, slinging the belts of gun ammo over our shoulders, adjusting our helmets—time to do it again. But this time, without our realizing it, we were reaching a sort of finale, the point to which the grim weeks had been pushing us all along, where nothing would go quite right and what wasn't supposed to happen did, all at once. And just out to the front, in among the trees and the vines, the ugly dreams would begin, even if they didn't show up for a few more months.

As we formed up to advance from our perimeter, all the bafflements and stresses seemed to roll to the surface at once, as if all the undercurrents that had been churning about finally broke to the surface. When Kansler directed 2nd Squad to take point, half the platoon simply refused to follow his directions, at least until some changes were made to his plan. Some of the guys were just not going to walk upright toward an automatic-weapons position, not again, not after Barrientes and Peterson and all the others who had been hurt or killed. That was that, and if Kansler wanted to make an issue of it, well, okay, but the guys were not moving.

I watched this happening, realizing with a kind of naive bewilderment that I was witnessing a mutiny—the refusal to carry out orders in combat—and that the platoon was on the verge of imploding. Nobody spoke loudly, or even impolitely— or at least no less politely than usual—but Kansler was told in no uncertain terms that about half the platoon was standing pat. Period.

I refused to interfere. As platoon sergeant, it was my job to stand by Kansler, back him up and advise the men to do as they were ordered or face court martial. But I could not do it. I had not lived with 1st Platoon for six weeks just to treat them like so many dogies and try to herd them forward against the bunkers, certainly not for someone they clearly did not trust. Perhaps I was splitting hairs, but it seemed to me that the platoon was not refusing to fight, it simply felt there was a better way to manage things just then and that rather than commit suicide by following Kansler's orders, we ought to think this one out.

Whether the guys were right or wrong, they had a total of many months of combat behind them and it seemed to me their collective wisdom ought to be considered. Perhaps Kansler caught on and realized, the hard way, that in the end, an infantry platoon in combat is a democracy: a lieutenant can push his men, coax them and order them and threaten them only so far, and when all that fails it is time to abide by the majority decision or bog down utterly. Whatever happened in Kansler's mind, he changed his plan, the platoon quieted down almost as quickly as it had bridled, and the specter of mutiny faded away. We began creeping forward, knowing perfectly well that the enemy was out there, waiting for us.

Stepping away from the perimeter, listening as the last mortar round plummeted and blew up, I tried to calculate the chances, all the awful angles, the standard vain computations, trying just to avoid freezing up and jamming like a fouled rifle under the ferocious emotional chill. As Ropp, who was leading the way, reached the base of the big tree without drawing fire, the fears careened in from ever-more frightening directions: they've moved, now we don't know where to look for them, we've no idea where they are, we're just blundering around out here. What do we do now? What the hell is happening? Where are they? When? How? Questions running into each other, overlapping, plunging like lead into the pit of the stomach, whirling up and around the scalp, feeling heavy as a stone and lightheaded all at once, pretty soon it was hard to follow my own thoughts. Difficult to imagine feeling any worse, weak and hollow and taut, brittle with tension and rubbery with resignation.

Kansler had us pivot to the left until the platoon was more or less on line and facing into the deeper forest. We went to earth, hugging the forest floor, amazed that no shooting had begun, hunting whatever bits of cover were available. I found myself wedged behind a small hump of earth with my radioman, Johnny Velez, hoping that we were protected by the slight fold in the terrain. One of the new gunners, Larry Hohman, was a few yards in front of me, also prone, peering into the trees over the sights of his M-60. Much to Larry's surprise, two North Vietnamese appeared, walking into view on the far side of an old, shallow, grassy bomb crater, seemingly unaware of our presence. Larry flipped his gun's safety to rock and roll, pulled trigger, the two enemy soldiers dove headlong into a bunker, and within five seconds the forest was suffused with a crescendo of pops and bangs, bullets were humming and cracking, and we had a full-tilt firefight on our hands.

With gunsmoke beginning to settle around us, fogging the scene, I noticed Lt. Kendall, on his belly like the rest of us, about a man's length away from me, between my position and Meager's. We stared dumbly at one another for a second before our attention was distracted by the eerie dance of sticks and leaves between us, jumping and twitching about as they were plucked by the bullets passing among them. I remember thinking idiotically, The enemy is firing so low that if I have to stand, they'll only hit me in the legs. The duff on the forest floor continued to jerk and dance.

The company had been through it all before, and I found myself, despite the adrenalin tide and the noise, sinking into a sort of mechanical boredom. I knew that, without heavy artillery and bombs, or at least extremely accurate rocket fire from gunships, we might as well spend the afternoon banging our heads against tree trunks as firing a lot of bullets. Second Platoon had been ordered far out to the right flank, to try to envelope the enemy position, but it appeared to have wandered out of the fight entirely. Of course, Kendall had long since alerted the artillery on LZ Jamie, the gunships based at Tay Ninh and the liaison with our jets—they were all on call, ready to come to our support whenever we gave the word—but Meager held off, he wanted to think about beating the North Vietnamese right then and there.

Instead of telling us to withdraw, Meager yelled across at Hohman: "Gimme some fire on that bunker!" When I saw him stripping off his pistol belt, I realized with a sort of morbid fascination that he was really going to try it, this was for real, he was going to *charge the bunker!* Hohman was blazing away from in front of my shelter, hot pink tracers streaking off into the trees, and I felt paralyzed, sure that I was about to watch Meager get himself killed and who was going to run the company? For Chrissakes, Captain….

Meager unpinned a frag grenade and dashed into the open, sprinting forward and out of sight from where I lay. He yelled something and Hohman shifted his aim slightly. There was another yell, then the punching, metallic crash of the grenade, and Meager shouted in fury and triumph, "You didn't get me, you son of a bitch!"

And it made no difference at all.

The grenade had failed to actually enter the bunker, the enemy gun was still spitting at us, and now Meager was hugging the far side of the crater, under the enemy's sights and out of the stream of fire but cut off from the rest of us.

The fight clattered on in stalemate while Charlie Hamilton crawled back to the company perimeter to round up some more light anti-armor weapons (LAWs). A team of gunships was orbiting in the vicinity, and the mortar crew was lobbing shells into the woods behind the enemy line. During an odd lull in the shooting, Hohman and some of his crew ran forward to join Meager and they, too, managed to avoid being shot. At Kendall's urging—he was ready to tell the gunships to begin firing at any moment—some of us were tossing smoke grenades around to outline our position. The woods turned into something straight out of a bad acid trip. Everything was shadowy and silhouetted among the wild swirls of colored smoke, red, violet, yellow all mixed together, and in the lurid gloom the forest resounded with the snarls of the gunships overhead, the muted discharge of the mortar answered by the quick, slamming detonation of its shells, and the continuing, spasmodic crackle of small-arms fire.

Charlie made it back with a few LAWs and took them forward to the crater, not that they made any difference now. It was past time for them and Meager had already called back for Kendall to turn the gunships loose. John Routt scuttled over to join Velez and me in our jammed little spot, and suddenly the air was suffused with the hideous guttural roars of the air-to-ground rockets being released by the Hueycobra pilots, the forest thundered in a long roll, the bamboo around us quivered from the concussion, and we could hear the little *clip... clip...clip* sounds of the steel splinters as they spun by. It took all the nerve I could summon to keep from jumping up and running for the perimeter. I don't know how long it went on. The gunships seemed to make one long, devastating firing run, and there was barely time to look around and peer through the smoke after one barrage before the appalling noise broke over us again.

Finally, the inevitable happened—a round ripped through Charlie's helmet and into his skull. For a moment I was aware only that a checkfire to the aerial barrage had been called and the horrible crashes had halted, and then the word was passed along and we could only stare at each other and think bitterly, Well, what the fuck did they think was gonna happen? Meager came creeping out of the murk like a bespectacled Faust, I didn't recognize him in the untimely twilight until he spoke to me: "We ain't doing any good. Get your people and bring 'em out."

The North Vietnamese were quiet for the moment, probably still huddling in their bunkers from the rockets, so Hohman and his crew were able to drag Charlie back to us. When I was able to see their spectral group, I crept from behind my shelter to lend a hand, praying the enemy would hold fire while I was upright and lugging one more casualty out of the way. As soon as we were out of the worst of the tangle, we stood erect and jogged the rest of the way to the perimeter. We put Charlie down at the edge of a shell crater next to my bunker.

He was dying. There was not a lot anyone could do for him, although Mike tried to facilitate his breathing and covered the wound in his head with a large bandage. I told the rest of the guys to go to their holes and build bunkers for the night. I hacked at a sapling with a machete, and after a little while Mike walked over and said, very quietly and without preamble, "Charlie didn't make it."

A long time before, during a different war before the Tet Offensive, when many of us thought that maybe the war had a point, maybe there really was a light up ahead and not just the gleam of some general's stars beckoning us forward, I was on a truck rolling north along Route One out of Hue City, heading for Quang Tri and the legendary DMZ—the big war. The whole battalion was on the road, trucks and jeeps to front and rear as far as we could see, comforting gunships circling overhead, and all around the lovely green villages and paddies glowing in the afternoon sunlight. We laughed and yelled at each other and everyone we saw, waving up toward the gunship crews when they circled close overhead, making obscene gestures to any Marines we saw headed in the other direction. When there was a halt we bought beer and Coke from roadside vendors. We were violently young and we thought we had the world by the tail. We were heading north to face the North Vietnamese in case they came over the border *en masse,* ready for them, in the best of spirits, sure of ourselves, immortal. A gunner named Van Weeks and I tried to harmonize on a Beatles tune, "I'm a lo-o-o-o-oser, and I'm not what I appear to be...."

But we didn't know what it meant. Not then.

The forward air controller sent two Super Sabre jets winging in with high explosives and napalm, the usual mix. The first two passes were too far out to the front to strike the enemy, but shortly the blasts were throwing out shrapnel toward us. I had had just about enough metal tossed at me for one day and I walked away toward Meager's CP, behind a tall, thick tree trunk. When the bombing was over, I would return to my hole.

Two things went wrong at once. One of the jet pilots performed an inexplicable ninety-degree change in his angle of approach, which meant he was now flying directly toward us instead of across our front. Then he delayed a split second or two in releasing his ordnance. He dropped napalm.

A massive wall of flame roared up in the woods in front of the platoon's sector and seemed to rush at us like a fiery tsunami. I glimpsed a few of the guys running from it, and noticed a huge glob of thick fire sailing past me to the right, across the thin line of brush between me and the platoon. The forest had burst into a wild red-orange hue, and for a moment I went berserk, convinced my guys were being immolated in front of me. Calloway sat a few feet away at Meager's CP, holding the handset of his radio, and I rounded on my old 3rd Platoon buddy, yelling wildly. "That's my platoon! That's my platoon!" Calloway looked scared and disbelieving. I sobbed with rage and frustration and it was not until the other jet made a pass without dropping anything that I knew someone had gotten through with a demand that the pilots hold off.

With the brush still smoking and burning to my front I raced back to the line and found to my astonishment that people there were alive and only one man had been hurt. Bub Stites stood with his head down, while Mike treated a four-inch-long football-shaped blister that had risen on the back of his neck. The full force of the napalm had been expended in turning everything right up to the bunkers into ash and cinders, and only isolated hunks of the flaming jelly had crossed into the company's perimeter. Howie walked over, still pale and shaky. We stared at the smoldering forest. He muttered something about our having a real field of fire to the front, no need to clear one with the machetes.

Toward dusk the bombing resumed. Afterwards, 2nd Platoon left for a night ambush and Kendall called in artillery fire from Jamie. By this time I was so tired and overloaded that the heavy booming made little impression. I felt as if nothing could penetrate the layers of weariness that enveloped me and when, as might have been expected, something went wrong and a close shell wounded a man in 2nd Platoon, the mishap seemed an afterthought.

The next morning, Kansler took us forward on patrol, and almost before we had started, one of our grenadiers put out a shell, reconning by fire, and a fragment flew back and cut the medic, Mike Bodnar. I told him to go back to the perimeter to be medevacked out, but he said he couldn't do that—if he left, who the hell would take care of us?

I never went on a more bizarre excursion. We advanced no farther than we had the day before. As we approached the near edge of the crater where Charlie had been hit, we all lay down as if a silent and invisible signal had been given—all but Hohman. He propped his machine-gun atop a thin tree stump in front of me and leaned against it, standing rigidly with his legs braced slightly apart, ready to fire, as if he were daring someone to fire at him first.

No one spoke. Breathing, the occasional shifting of a leg or arm, the turning of a man's head as he tried, discreetly, to make himself more comfortable, were the only motions and sounds, and the forest became haunted to an unearthly degree, even for the fucking war.

I stared at the dead leaves and the bits of bamboo in front of my eyes, at the weapons and gear on the men to my right. It appeared that the platoon had achieved petrifaction. It went on for the better part of an hour, or maybe several hours, time simply dissolved and we were all under a spell. When I looked up at Hohman, I wanted to snatch his legs out from under him, make him lie down like the rest of us. No one else was on his feet, or even kneeling, and Hohman seemed a beautiful, unavoidable target, I waited for the bullet to snap out of the forest and crumple him. I wanted to order him to get his ass down with the rest of us, but in the silence I found it impossible to speak.

The forest around us seemed tense to some fantastic degree, as if the slightest disturbance would cause it to explode. I felt as if the earth itself were about to burst, and I was struck by the idea that the atmosphere itself had forced me to the forest floor. I looked at the man next to me, but I neither spoke nor was I spoken to, and I have no recollection of who he was. When Kansler decided we had been out long enough and it was time to return to the perimeter, we rose silently and skulked away.

I sat at my bunker's entrance, three in the morning, with the earplug of someone's transistor radio stuck in my ear, listening to a jazzy instrumental version of Simon and Garfunkle's "Mrs. Robinson." It was a stupid thing to do, something one would expect of a shithead recruit. The music in one ear fouled my sensitivity to any other sounds around me in the night and left me uncertain about the direction of anything I did manage to hear. When I thought I detected some faint rustlings, I imagined they were from Howie's hole a few yards to my right—perhaps the guard was being changed—or even from Roy Stern's listening post out in the woods to the left front. The music continued to play. John Routt was asleep on the ground right behind me. A yard or two away, Donnie Farley and Mike were lying rolled up in their liners in our poncho hooch. In front of me, on the roof of the bunker, our two Claymore mine detonators lay handy, their wires running around each side of the termite mound and off into the charred brush. A clutch of hand grenades and three rifles were all within arm's reach. The peculiar noises persisted.

    Something, some sudden, untranslatable knowledge that things weren't right, finally warned me. I was already sliding down into the bunker when the first rocket smashed against the other side of the termite mound, outlining the earthen hump with a blinding yellow flash in my face. I grabbed for Routt, screaming for him to get inside. Before he could react, even as I was calling, "Incoming! Incoming!" a large burst of smoke appeared at the far end of the hooch. I heard no detonation, but something had exploded, rocket or grenade, and I figured Mike and Donnie had had it. No time to worry just then, bullets were starting to gust by in sheets, and Routt was plowing past me to the safety of the bunker. Before I could poke my head outside once more, here came Mike and Donnie, diving in headfirst, and for a second I thought I heard enemy mortar fire. The four of us sat in the underground blackness. My back was pressed against the forward wall across from and to one side of the entrance. The desire to hide from the onslaught left us incapable of taking any effective action, like setting off the claymores, grabbing our rifles to return the fire, or tossing grenades.

A rocket slammed into the roof directly over my head, blowing aside most of the sandbags and leaving only a few slim logs between me and the uproar aboveground. A deep, penetrating *whumph* filled the bunker and something concussive thudded hard down the length of my back. For a moment I remained calm, or perhaps stunned, but then I groped around with one hand to feel for any damage. When I touched the back of my shirt an awful wetness seemed to press against my palm, and in my mind's eye I saw my own death, back torn open, ribs, spine and organs laid bare, all splintered and bleeding. The complete absence of any pain interfered with my imagination not at all.

I panicked. Everything rational—thought, logic, training and the months of experience—simply fled. I scrambled my way toward the bunker entrance and began to claw my way up. Anything was better than bleeding to death underground and then being dragged out in the morning from what was beginning to seem more like a tomb than a protective fortification. I had to get out of there.

Mike yelled, "Get back here, Mark!" He grabbed at me

and tried to haul me back down and at that instant, as quickly as it had enveloped me, the panic passed, replaced with the absolute knowledge that I was not hurt.

Slumping against the back wall where I could crane my neck at the entrance and peek outside, I tried to think of something to do. Automatic fire and explosions continued along the platoon sector, and flares lit up the night. When someone popped a star cluster overhead, I could at least see from my cramped position that the North Vietnamese were not swarming all over the perimeter. And then, quite rapidly, in only a minute or two, the firing slackened to a few scattered bursts of shots and then died away altogether. Several more minutes elapsed before any of us felt like creeping outside. None of us in my bunker had fired a shot.

My lower back began to stiffen up and when I twisted to one side to rub it, I felt something small and hard—a minuscule bit of metal. There was no blood, it had barely broken the epidermis. I put the splinter into one of my shirt pockets, forgot to button it closed and lost it almost immediately. It was the only piece of enemy shrapnel to hit me during a total of twenty months in the war.

Daylight arrived with no one having gone back to sleep and as soon as the sun was above the trees 2nd Platoon took off on patrol, then came back a few hours later with that great rarity, a living North Vietnamese solder. He had been discovered lying against the base of a tree, not in the best shape, abandoned by the raiding party during its withdrawal. Our medics went to work on his wounds while the rest of us stood around and goggled at him. A couple of us offered him a cigarette, a sip of water, some C-rations.

We stared at him with a respect that went far beyond the event's novelty. It was an odd fact that most of the brutality I witnessed during the war—and there was much of it—was directed against civilians and so-called Viet Cong suspects, which meant anyone whose allegiance was questionable. Things were different where the armed North Vietnamese and Viet Cong were concerned. We appreciated what they were going through and how profoundly they must have believed in what they were trying to achieve. If we felt down and out and bitched about the rain and the mud and the heat, we knew they had it a lot worse, facing the napalm, the artillery barrages, and the B-52 strikes, firepower the likes of which had never been seen. They had no bases like Quan Loi and Tay Ninh West, or even LZ Jamie, where they could walk about in the open, enjoy the sunlight, and feel a breeze. They lived in dank, remote corners of the jungle, their hospitals were squared-off holes in the ground, they never received a week's respite in Taipei or Penang or Sydney, and they did not go home at the end of a year. Despite a lot of tough-guy talk, we seldom abused them when they fell into our hands.

What surprised me was the knowledge that the North Vietnamese were human. I was unprepared to see emotions play across their faces or to hear their voices. What this particular gentleman had to say gave me the heebie-jeebies. This guy's crew, an element from a heavy weapons company, had marched for three hours to get at us. That shook me up. These guys had been actively hunting us and, minus the wounded man, were still out there.

The prisoner's information produced no noticeable change in our operations. Meager decided we had been in one place one night too many, and in the afternoon we marched a couple of hundred yards east, to where a sluggish, cruddy little stream stagnated alongside a narrow north-south pathway. In the evening, Kansler took half the platoon off in one direction on ambush, while I took the other half north for fifty or so yards. A narrow, shallow ravine, choked with thorned brush, led from the trail to the creek, and that looked to me like a natural defensive position, offering cover against possible enemy fire from the front as well as from any shots from the company to the rear. I was haunted by the possibility that the enemy raiders of the night before might already be moving toward us for a second raid and after having had a rocket blow up only a couple of feet from the top of my head, my nerves were none too steady. I knew perfectly well the position I chose was much too close to the company perimeter—in effect, I turned half the platoon into a glorified listening post, barely outside the line of trip flares—but I was emotionally incapable of moving any further away into the darkening forest.

In the morning the company packed up and we led the way north along the path, but the trail platoon had hardly cleared the perimeter when battalion called and told us to turn around, aim for the nearest clearing and be prepared to lift out to LZ Jamie for a turn as security force there. For a moment it failed to register, but then I felt an incredible rush. We were going in. After four weeks that, cumulatively, were rougher than any four weeks I had experienced in nearly a year and a half of combat operations, the order made me goofy. I felt the awful strain recede, the tension begin to flow out of me, and I could see it in the others. No one had to give directions. We knew the route to the clearing from which we had evacuated the wounded the day before, and we pushed off with such vigor that Meager had to caution us against hiking too hastily through the woods. Just because the recall had been sounded didn't mean the North Vietnamese were absent.

But our luck held. We marched to the well-worn perimeter and immediately broke the platoons down into individual aircraft loads. Meager assigned my platoon to the first lift. I wasted no time in getting my gang together and having one man at the ready to guide in the first of the Hueys. As soon as the pilot spotted our smoke and identified the landing zone, my man was out there with his rifle above his head, ignoring the streams of violet smoke and the hurricane of dust and grit thrown up by the helicopter's propwash as the pilot jockeyed his way toward the tiny opening in the woods. The guide leaned one way, then the other, motioning for the pilot to jog ahead a bit, now slightly to the left…, to the left some more…, now right…, forward a hair…, now, down!

Six of us hurled ourselves aboard, sprawling across the small cabin, leaning against each other's packs. I rested my back against the co-pilot's armored chair and then we were lifting away from the woods, up from the scarred dirt and burnt brush and the shorn-off trees. Within five minutes we had settled onto the pad at LZ Jamie and stepped gratefully to terra firma. My legs were rubbery but I was high as a kite, almost giggling as I watched the crewmen inspecting the bird for holes. I walked unsteadily toward the gate into the perimeter. It was Independence Day 1969 and I was still alive.

The company never went back to the Mustang Trail, although other units did. From time to time, whenever we were on LZ Jamie, the monotonic beat of artillery and the muted booms and thuds of air strikes would resound to the northwest, and we would know that someone was out there, not liking it very much. We didn't talk much about our operations there.

Through July and August the company marched and patrolled and ambushed along the Saigon River corridor, which now seemed an innocent place. Once we passed near the spot where Mac had died, and even found the lonely, unmarked grave of an enemy soldier, but in the weeks since late May, the vegetation had already taken over and I was unable to make out the location of our fight.

At the end of my first tour, the bad times had not seemed all that bad. The deaths and injuries, horrible as they were, had washed by without eroding too deeply. The moments of fear and depression were isolated against a backdrop of largely innocuous patrolling and choppering about. Three months might pass without a death in the family—a pretty good bargain, by war standards. The experience had still offered a sense of directed adventure, a feeling that what was happening all around us would lead to … well, to something tangible and worthwhile. That was in 1967.

War Zone C had been a shock. Enemy troops were everywhere and they almost always had the advantage. Averaged out, elements of the company exchanged shots with the enemy once every three days for a month and sometimes twice a day. Save for the hallucinatory visit to VIP Center, there had been no real relief the entire time. It just went on and on like a crazy drama where every scene ended the same way, the North Vietnamese mysteriously gone and a few of us left bleeding in the spotlight. When one troupe was wrung out, another was sucked in and smashed. There never was an audience, really, just clean, concise little synopses in the newspapers and on TV that never told anyone anything at all.

Anyway, the definitions everyone else used meant nothing to us. Infantrymen have tunnel vision. This is not a matter of choice. When you're lying in a paddy under machine-gun fire, or walking toward a patch of bamboo that looks ugly, you're not concerned with strategic progress, how Hanoi is going to react to this escalation or that peace feeler, or how the Marines are doing up at Dong Ha. You're wondering whether the damned gun crew is in position, whether your M16 is going to fire or jam. You hope there will be time to put up a hooch before it rains, and that 2nd Platoon's new lieutenant knows what he's doing out on the flank. It is a view that twists and limits words like "victory" and "defeat," even "good" and "bad." You make up the definitions as you go along, according to what occurs in front of your eyes at a given time.

Back in '67, when we managed to pitch the enemy out of a

village, there was the sensation of winning. In Zone C, we couldn't even pick out the places we'd been a few weeks before. After all we had given to the Mustang Trail, the North Vietnamese were still out there, still ready to take on all comers, and it was as if we had never gone in. Against the actual record of our operations, the high-spirited stories in the service newspapers appeared unutterably grotesque. A story might appear in *Cavalair*, the division newspaper, to the effect that this or that unit had trained some South Vietnamese rangers or sprung an ambush over by Song Be and the only reasonable response was to ball it up and throw it into a sump. "Man, this fuckin' crap ...."

At odd moments the war might retain its glow, as when I watched Roy Stern's men charging through a sunny field of high grass the week before Mac died, or when Meager yelled, "You didn't get me, you son of a bitch!" But those moments faded quickly or turned out to be pointless and vain. Somehow, it came to appear, our bravery and willingness to sacrifice were being taken advantage of and betrayed.

———

Nine o'clock one evening near the end of August, on ambush by the river, someone called from the Company CP. I recognized Collins' voice when I took the handset: "You're supposed to be in Bien Hoa tonight, to catch your flight home." Eighteen hours later, Howie guided a chopper in to a patch of elephant grass as I ran around shaking hands and slapping shoulders. Then I hustled out and threw myself aboard. Catching a glimpse of familiar faces as the pilot took off, I managed to gesture with a V-for-peace, and we were dodging rain showers under the low-hanging scud, and the platoon and the company were gone.

War Zone C looked especially funereal that afternoon,

morose and depressed under the leaden sky. Despite my joy at leaving the field alive, my mood was in keeping with the grim landscape below. And I suppose that, as I do now while writing this, I took one long, deep breath, shuddered, and let it go.

There it is.

WAR AND MEMORY
SUSAN R. DIXON

42

What's War Got to Do With It?

The seat had a slight bucket shape, not like the chairs in my living room. An overhead light illuminated the pages of my journal, a ring binder that I had not yet learned was too bulky to bring on a trip. The noise of the propeller engines was so loud I felt like my seat and the little cabin around me, were inside them. It was my first time on a plane and it did not feel at all safe. But then the stewardess brought a folder about KLM with a puzzle in it, and a book in French, and then dinner. I was completely reassured. I reasoned that they would not be serving this adorable food-in-a-kit if the plane were in imminent danger of crashing. It was 1961. I was 13 and on my way, with my family, to Europe for the first of four extended trips that would constitute the greater part of my education, socialization, and adolescence.

We landed in Amsterdam and picked up our new car, a red and white, first-generation Volkswagen camper bus, fitted out with Formica cupboards, a small fridge, and adjustable seats. Five of us were to travel for three months in this car, camping so as to afford it. Problems with the bus's interior design delayed us, so we were installed in a hotel while a variety of imaginative Dutch mechanics and carpenters devised a solution. The hotel had stairs that were steeper than any I had ever seen and a dining room in which I counted 65 plates hung on the wall. I smelled the air, noted the width of patterned runners on the staircases, and marveled over door handles, faucets, and light switches. When the car was ready for us, we packed our belongings—my father's camera equipment under the back seat, our matching dresses (in case one of us got lost) into the latched cupboards—and set out. In the hotel, I had experienced the physical details of a way of living very different from my own. Now I observed that life through the windows of a tightly organized vehicle. It was a paradox: my world expanded in all directions—physical, intellectual, spiritual—from within the boundaries of a VW bus. By day, everything was new. At night I retreated to the narrow space between the cupboards, pulled the top of the sleeping bag over my head, and tried to keep up with the onslaught of experiences by recording their details.

My journals continued for nine years, detailed while traveling and intermittent when at home, in a charmingly awkward mashup of chatty travelogue and 'Dear Diary' angst. I was a Southern girl being brought up in a strict household and marking time between trips to Europe and the Middle East. In my journals, I desperately wanted to make my own way in the world, putting a lot of emphasis on "personality." I wanted action, and meaning, and something to believe in and fight for. I wanted a man, but not just whoever came along. I had standards and every conversation with an unsuspecting classmate was measured against them. I was tired of sitting on the sidelines. I wanted to be the author of my own story and I wrung my hands dramatically over how to make that happen. I played both sides of familial and cultural expectations, wanting my freedom, but in some acceptable way. My imagination grew beyond my ability to focus it so every new thing I saw had the potential to be my new life. Over these years I swore I would go to Israel to defend it, or Greece to lead a kind of Kazantzakis life, or Paraguay after I fell in love with a visiting student. It was all emotion and confusion and intensity and sincerity. I wrote a note to my future self at the beginning of one of the volumes intoning a warning that while whatever was written there might sound naïve, it was meant sincerely. I spent a lot of my time being depressed and exhausted.

The trips to Europe fueled my imagination but gave me either no tools with which to navigate the physicality of adolescence, or too many. I cobbled together a confused sexuality from fiction, culture, and family expectations of appropriate behavior, the contradictory messages leaving me paralyzed. Long hours spent in the museums of Europe exposed me to explicit renderings of the female body in masculine oils or marble but when I hesitantly inquired, I was informed that such depictions—male hands forever arresting the soft flesh of fleeing nubile women, for instance—were meant solely to depict "form" and "beauty." Fair was fair, though. I had plenty of opportunity to gather information about male anatomy in spite of these high-minded instructions. It made listening to the throbbing rhythms of the rock music I was coming to adore bewildering, the lyrics meant, evidently, only as metaphor.

―――

There were other lessons that the adults seemed to think they didn't have to explain—the remnants of war.

We visited the beaches of Normandy, read plaques commemorating reprisals for a resistance actions, and toured churches in Cologne built from their own rubble, but it was all as though war were simply the past condition through which these things existed in the present, something regrettable but only occasionally worth comment. We visited relatives by marriage in Germany who treated us with the most elaborate hospitality. My mother wondered where they had been in the Second World War, but I was too dazzled by the needlework kits and bottles of N° 4711 cologne they gave us to think much about it. Even in Nuremburg, where we bought a deli chicken that we ate with buttery crackers and white radishes and camped in Hitler's stadium, it all seemed long ago, an evocative and vicariously thrilling past, but the past, nonetheless. That changed, forever, in one place.

We set out that morning on what felt like an unscheduled trip. My parents were almost silent, wrapped in themselves; I watched to see what would happen. The place we were going had something to do with the war. Maybe they told us this, or maybe I saw it from the signs. I began to have a sense of foreboding.

We must have walked a good distance, perhaps seen barracks first, or a gatehouse. I look at a map of the place today, trying to recall how I arrived at the only memory I have, but I look away again for fear of creating a narrative that does not exist. I walked into the passageway of a dark building. Ahead of me was a metal door with an arched top and heavy hinges and latches set in a brick wall. I read the plaque. My mind both fled and remained planted before a revelation that I felt changing me, building new pathways in my brain to accommodate knowledge I did not know existed in the world. I was in the crematorium at Dachau and this was an oven in which human beings were burned.

Later, in the camperbus, I tried to piece together a moral structure in which such objects could exist. In order for that oven to be there, people had to have taken a journey into an evil I did not know was possible. I revolted against it, and yet I did not push it away. I wanted to close my mind, but I did not. Nothing but time separated me from what had happened there and though my mind, in self-preservation, assumed that such a thing would never happen again, on that day I knew better. Watching trees, grass, and fields move past me, nothing deformed or blasted, nothing in nature that rebelled against this history, I knew what I had seen was not "war," but something darker and no longer beyond belief. I had nowhere to put this knowledge and no way to come to terms with it. It compelled me in the way forbidden knowledge does. It was irrational, immoral, sadistic—everything my sheltered upbringing had sheltered me *from*. It was too late now. I knew —*I knew*—that what I had seen done *to* human beings was done *by* human beings. I had learned not about a war in the past, but about human nature. I had learned not what happened within the boundaries of one war, but what any war could unleash. I knew. It had happened there and then. It could happen again and anywhere.

From then on, I lived with a kind of existential dread that, in a 13-year-old, felt only like an underlying doubt, like a low-grade fever. I did not think much of it, not consciously, but I watched World War II movies and read what books I could find. I was trying to understand. I was looking for something deeper than what I had seen at Dachau, some firm ground on which to stand that could take the place of the ground that had been destroyed there.

All of this meant that by the fall of 1965, when Mark had set his sights on the Army, I was just trying to make it through another year of high school and I was seriously out of step with my classmates. I wanted to be a part of high school life. I wanted to be outgoing, go to football games and pep rallies, experiment and push my limits. Or at least I wanted to want to.

But I had learned something I could not talk about.

When CBS announced, in July of 1965, when Mark and I were both juniors, that the action in Vietnam was now "an American war," it stood to reason that I heard it. We ate every dinner as a family, at a table set with place mats and napkins, the heart-warming, Norman Rockwell-ness of this practice disrupted every evening by the intrusion of the Evening News. We would eat in silence while Chet Huntley or David Brinkley, or Walter Cronkite, informed us of the state of the world. When the commercials came on, my father would lean over to the television that sat on a cart by his chair, turn down the volume, and then turn it up again when the news resumed. We would take advantage of the intervals to refill water glasses or ask for seconds. So in all likelihood I heard about the escalation of the conflict in Vietnam, but it had no particular impact on me. It was too far away and too far out of my world.

Closer to home was civil rights movement. The marches from Selma to Montgomery had happened in March. I had watched film (in black and white) of hoses being turned on peaceful marchers and listened in awe to the cadences of Martin Luther King Jr.'s speech. Alabama also seemed a long way away, but then somewhere out on the edges of Chapel Hill, a woman urinated on a protester, an impropriety I found so shocking it invalidated, in and of itself, any argument in favor of segregation. I had only recently come from a segregated junior high in Florida, so the African-American students at the high school seemed exotic to me, but the justice of the cause was, to my mind, beyond question. In such a charged environment, Vietnam was, as yet, more than I could handle.

The music was confusing, too. The hits in 1965 included Herman's Hermits's "Mrs. Brown You've Got a Lovely Daughter," and Tom Jones's "It's Not Unusual." I was a big The New Christy Minstrels fan and loved—it must be said —"Green, Green" in which Barry McGuire sang lead to a chorus of exuberant guitars. The bouncy syncopation made me happy, certainly in a way that the sinister "Up With People" show that visited my high school did not, and I wanted to be happy. A darkness was coming. I knew it just as I knew my body was changing. I resisted both with the rollicking and often defiant Irish rhythms of The Clancy Brothers and Tommy Makem. I could count on them to sing the old tunes, the ones that wouldn't change, the desperate, tragic songs about life under British rule, but also drinking songs about corpses reviving. It was all of life, and it helped. I loved The Beatles, and I hung with them as they changed, too, moving from youthful exuberance to haunting evocations like "Norwegian Wood," which matched my mood. And then the same gravelly-voiced Barry McGuire of The New Christy Minstrels released "Eve of Destruction." It scared me, what he was singing. It was an early warning—there are always early warnings—not just of raging injustices, but of the forces that perpetuate them. I didn't want to know those things about the world, forgetting entirely that I already knew them. And while the song did not explicitly address the gathering storm in Vietnam it was all connecting for me—fire hoses on unarmed marchers and fighter planes over a country I could not yet find on the map.

―――

Storms were gathering in another part of the world, though, and a trip was being planned right into it. In the spring of 1967, while Mark walked endless patrols in Binh Dinh Province, I prepared for a university-sponsored trip to the Middle East. We were to go to Egypt, Lebanon, and Jordan, and then cross into Israel in Jerusalem through the checkpoint at the Mandelbaum Gate in Jerusalem. Once our passports had been stamped in Israel—this felt very dramatic to me—we would not be able to go back to an Arab country. There was an orderly plan, in other words, for navigating an excitingly volatile situation.

I read Leon Uris's *Exodus* and James Michener's *The Source*, and imagined myself into a thrilling story more ancient than anything I had ever known. At first, the rattling sabers made it seem like all that history had come alive but then I began to fret. In my journals, I wrestled with the question of war and my role in it. "I would rather die *asserting my personality*," I wrote, from the sanctuary of my room, "than sit aside being safe." I decided that maybe I shouldn't reject war out of hand, and that people who fight for what they believe in should be admired for their courage. I did not yet have room in my worldview for people who fight with courage in a war they do *not* believe in. When Egypt blockaded the Gulf of Aqaba and the stalemate became the Six Day War as we were leaving the United States, I felt like I was going to where something real was happening, something I could see and not just read about. I felt a visceral anticipation, an almost electric thrill of excitement, driven by the haunting, *"Yerushalaim Shel Zahav"* ("Jerusalem of Gold") that had begun to play on the radio like a soundtrack to my story.

News of events in Israel came by way of the *International Herald Tribune* and frequent calls my father made to the American consulate and organizers of the study tour. Plans shifted day by day. All travel in the Arab countries was impossible on American passports, which meant no pyramids, no Petra, and no Mandelbaum Gate, but we would be allowed to go to Israel. This meant a longer stay in Greece and a bonus trip to Turkey. I soaked up the Greek sun with no anticipation of danger. I imagined myself vaulting a Cretan bull, pretended I was a goddess brandishing snakes, and developed a secret crush on the magnificent marble Zeus, in Warrior Pose, hurling a thunderbolt. At Delphi, I watched a storm come in from the Gulf of Corinth until it got close enough to agitate a goat tied below my balcony. I walked out in the early morning into a deserted monastery complex at Mistra, along a walk lined with pungent thyme whose smell clung to me in memory for years. In Istanbul, a young man fell in love with me, invited me (and my family) for a dinner of fish in his mother's apartment overlooking the Bosporus, and serenaded me with "Strangers in the Night." On the way to Israel we stopped in Cyprus, landing in the now-deserted Nicosia airport, and visited a convent with rosemary hedges that were taller than me. "Rosemary for remembrance," the guide said.

In Israel we traveled by bus with students and faculty members, headed, by an educational route, for an archaeological site the Negev Desert. On the day we visited Ashdod and Ashkelon, we drove south along the ancient Way of the Sea, the road that at one time led to Egypt. Suddenly, the program leader announced that we were going to the entrance of the Gaza Strip and were going to ask permission to go in. Several faculty members stood in the aisles to fill us in on the history. When they told us we would be the first outside group other than journalists to go in since 1948, a buzz of excitement ran through the bus. When we arrived at the check point and received permission to enter we felt triumphant, as though it were a personal achievement.

We entered Gaza City at a careful speed, passed the United Nations headquarters and a damaged and deserted Egyptian military post. White flags hung from the windows of dusty houses. Damaged or destroyed tanks angled onto piles of rubble in front of collapsed buildings and walls pocked by bullets. Children shouted and waved to attract our attention to whatever they had found to sell.

Our excuse for going into Gaza was to see an Early Christian church that had been discovered a few days before on the beach. We admired the only thing left of the structure, a damaged mosaic floor, and then some of us walked along the sand looking for seashells. The afternoon sun shone through the clouds in long rays onto the water. An Israeli soldier with a rifle attracted attention. Some of the girls clowned with the rifle and had their pictures taken with the soldier, who then walked to the water's edge and shot it out over the sea.

We had had a glimpse of the destruction of war, the poignancy of white flags, and the desperation of children, but those memories melted before the seduction of the handsome soldier and the vicarious thrill of the weapon. At the time, I felt judgmental, but at the same time I understood. I myself had felt it before I had left the United States—the adrenaline rush, the *frisson* of war.

By the spring of 1968, I was trying to play both sides of the fence. The dorms at Carolina were not yet co-educational because the University of North Carolina was, at that time, still thought to play the role of *in loco parentis* (in the place of a parent). I wasn't living in a dorm, though. I was living at home where I had literal *parentis in loco*, with rules that were far more restrictive for being largely unspoken. It was simply assumed I would hold the same moralistic, judgmental values I had been raised with and Lord knows I tried. I had not yet realized that attempting to be a Southern lady and wanting to throw myself into the excitement I saw all around me was inherently contradictory and could lead only to what in a college sophomore was assumed to be "normal stress." The sensible course of action would have been to rebel, which would have meant letting go of one or another of the expectations, but I didn't. I tried to do it all. I tried to feel passion for my classes, because that was what I was supposed to do. I didn't understand what the "youth movement" was, but I knew it was important because so many people scorned it. I got no help on any of my questions from my family, so I ended up thinking my questions must not have been that important. At the same time, I took my cues from the music I heard on the radio and movies that appealed to my romantic imagination. Inspired by *Doctor Zhivago*, I sewed myself a dress with a red paisley print and deep cuffs on which I attached wide gold braid. I was costuming, but there would be no tie-dye for me. In the midst of all my angst I wrote in my long-suffering journal: "name of the psychedelic group—The Iron Butterfly. Reminds me of The Doors—"before I sink into the big sleep I want to hear the scream of the butterfly."

43

The Monster in the Labyrinth

A TIMELINE OF THE VIETNAM WAR GETS STUCK IN 1968—THE Battle of Khe Sanh, the Tet Offensive, the Battle of Lang Vei, the battle of Ben Tre (during which an unnamed US major was quoted as saying that it became necessary to destroy the town in order to save it), and the record for the highest number of casualties in one week. And that was only through February. But so many other critical events were happening, too—the assassinations of Martin Luther King, Jr. and Robert Kennedy, Lyndon Johnson's decision not to seek re-election, the Black Power salutes at the Mexico City Summer Olympics, the police violence at the Democratic Convention in Chicago—that I began to feel only a generalized sense of dread. If I had given any thought to the soldiers returning from Vietnam (for the most part I thought of them only as actors in a gruesome production being beamed from the other side of the world) I would have thought, good luck getting any attention just now. There was a song on the radio with a refrain that went, "Love is kind of crazy with a spooky little girl like you," and that worked for me, the world I was trying to learn to love seeming very crazy just then. It wasn't until many years later that I learned that one of the most vicious weapons the Americans were using in Vietnam, a modified gunship that could rain bullets down on an area the size of a football field in a matter of seconds, was nicknamed 'Spooky.'

Classes just could not compete with all this; they went on the back burner. Living at home provided a predictable rhythm, but I needed excitement and inspiration. I found both in the Campus Y (then the YM-YWCA), an organization with a long history of involvement in social justice issues. It had a reputation that often made it a thorn in the side of administration but it was an incubator of ideas and action. The little building that housed the Y occupied a central point of the campus, its plaza, called Y Court, a crossroads of activity. If one wanted to get a petition signed, recruit volunteers for committees, or galvanize interest in any cause, the table would be set up in Y Court or the building's lobby.

I chaired the Y's major fundraising event, the International Handicrafts Bazaar in the fall, which meant I spent a lot of time hanging out in the offices. I sat on the communal sofa reading *The New York Times* and listening to conversation and debate. I saw the interwoven forces that linked racism and war and yet the vibrant life of the Y, where new perspectives could and did walk through the door at any moment, gave me the idea that things might change. If we just got the strategy right, chose the right words, held the right energy together, bad as things looked, we could make them better. Our outrage always seemed paired with an optimism that came from not ever having experienced defeat or even much of a need to compromise. Someone always came up with a wild strategy—paint a peace sign on the outside wall, fill the quad with crosses to represent the casualties in Vietnam—and if these weren't always effective, they always led to something else. We were working together and loving it. I craved the excitement of sharing a cause we knew was right. It began to dawn on me—

and the idea did not seem unreasonable there in the Y—that we could stop a war.

———

I didn't know very much about this war I wanted to stop and I did not view it in any larger geopolitical context. The winning of previous wars, even the rightness of previous wars created no moral manifest destiny in my mind. Indeed, I felt something sinister beneath the pious ideals of my elders, whether elected or familial, precisely *because* there had been the precursor of a war so self-evidently just that it created its own logical argument: because it was right to fight in that war, it was not only right but also *required* to fight in the next one. I felt it when I watched Lyndon Johnson—a father-knows-best paternalism that hid, but not so well I could not see it, a deep cynicism about the lives he was willing to sacrifice to preserve it. Those lives were the young men around me, who were having to face, in a manner far more immediate than my own, the harrowing collision of patriotism, family expectations, fear, and the growing communal sense that the elders were, in fact, wrong.

Actually talking to these young men about such things still filled me with adolescent terror but I could see what was happening to them and there were moments when it filled me with rage. No manufactured fears—and that's what I saw them to be—justified the manipulation of events, language, values, and lives that I saw happening around me. How could these elders who had fought so valiantly against a tangible threat now be so cringingly fearful of an ideology? In any case, I did not trust Lyndon Johnson and I had not trusted him since he had started beating war drums about something that had happened in 1964 in the Gulf of Tonkin. When I heard about this incident my first thought had been, seriously? One incident with something called "torpedo boats" and we are going to war? Are we supposed to be channeling Pearl Harbor or something, getting all called to arms over some kind of flouting of our dignity when our destroyer was… well, what was our destroyer doing there anyway? I decided, based on no knowledge whatsoever, that the incident had been manufactured and once trust is destroyed, it is very hard to get it back.

In the spring of 1969 the war had become all too real for Mark. For me it was still a cause, made more distant by the fact that I was again in Europe, this time in Florence, Italy, where I attended language school in the mornings and practiced my Italian in the afternoons in museums, churches, and cafés. In a cloister, while I slowly studied the paintings of Fra Angelico, an artist sketched my portrait. I was so accustomed to being harassed on the street that I rebuffed him, kicking myself as I stalked away. I saw my first beehive hairstyles in Italy and yearned to imitate my Italian teacher's dramatic, winged eye makeup. An attack of appendicitis put me to bed with Italian "sick peoples" food of pasta and stewed zucchini. When that did not cure me, I had surgery in a small hospital where no one spoke English. On my last day there, the nurses taught me how to eat an artichoke. Letters from home told me about tensions boiling over on campus when food service workers in the dining halls went on strike over employment issues and the right to organize. The Y was the hub of activity and my friends were in the middle of it. Meanwhile I sat at a table in a Florentine kitchen reading the news and listening to The Beatles singing "Ob-La-Di, Ob-La-Da." I was close to fluent in Italian but I couldn't wait to get back home.

My plans for a polite honors thesis on Florentine Annunciations went out the window as soon as I returned to the Y and found that, even though it was summer, not only was everyone there, they all seemed to have just come from a meeting. I was taking summer school courses to make up for my absence in the spring, but classes in general were becoming an excuse to hang out at the Y. Finding my place again was a challenge. I had a boyfriend, but no idea what I wanted to be when I grew up. I signed up to tutor in an elementary school, but the required education courses bored me.

Meanwhile the war was becoming more insistent. Every night I ate dinner while watching reporters duck against a backdrop of bamboo, their microphones held up to strained faces. Every night I heard the soundtrack of helicopters and turned my eyes away from the graphic that tallied the body count. I felt pulled apart, trying to plan for the life that was expected of me while the war created a cataclysm that fascinated and engulfed me. Although, much later, I learned that young women not much older than I had simply walked away from their expected lives to go to Vietnam to write about the war, that possibility never once occurred to me. It was not a choice that I rejected. It was a choice that was simply not there.

I had learned at Dachau what human beings, of any nationality, are capable of doing to one another. When faced with the issue of the war in Vietnam, therefore, I thought beyond "my country, right or wrong." I saw "my country, wrong" and I wanted to make it right. I felt a sense of urgency because by the time I was paying any attention, the war had changed. No longer was there any real hope that something good would come of what we were doing and I knew what forces could be unleashed in conditions of frustration and desperation. Every night, on the evening news, I saw only fear, pain, and destruction. When I heard the reports I had begun to focus on what was out of camera range—in the burning villages, the edges of the rice paddies, or on stretchers—and to wonder what had come before and what would happen next. At the same time politicians and military leaders announced without emotion that the numbers showed we were winning and that what we were doing was right. I could only imagine that either they did not choose to see what I was seeing, or they saw it and were lying about it, or they saw it and didn't care.

I thought Americans cared. I thought Americans saw something going wrong and tried to fix it. In Vietnam things were going wrong, we were making it worse, and I wanted it stopped. The only way available to me was to ally myself with the anti-war movement. If I had thought it out I would have known that I was not necessarily anti-war; I was anti-*that* war. I had no sympathy for the North Vietnamese or any desire for the South Vietnamese to achieve anything at all. My travels abroad had given me an enticing view of other cultures, but returning through JFK International Airport always restored my sense of home and country. I was an American. Even taking the side of an enemy I did not think should be the enemy was not an option.

We were making things up as we went along, though. I experimented with intellectual argument but was more comfortable distributing postcards with a quote from Kenneth Patchen's *Hallelujah Anyway*. I fretted and tormented over everything. As anti-war activists we were being accused of malingering. What if that were true, I thought. How would I be able to tell? We were accused of aiding and abetting the enemy. That one worried me because I could see their point but my moral compass told me what was happening in Vietnam was wrong, no matter who did it and for what reason. We were accused of not loving our country. I was on firm ground here. I knew I loved my country. I just wanted my country to do the right thing. For a time I could recite much of Langston Hughes's "Let America Be America Again."

Night after night I took the dinner my father had served onto my plate. I ate meatloaf and boiled potatoes, or tuna mixed with mushroom soup and wrapped in a biscuit roll, or a kind of stir fry with strips of beef and cabbage marinated in soy sauce, with the war playing on the television in the background. Night after night, I swallowed the war, choked down helplessness and grief, empathy and galvanizing fury. I knew my father opposed the war but he also believed in the transcending authority of the university and saw anti-war activism as violating its sacrosanct boundaries. One evening after dinner, I stood in the kitchen, my back against a counter, and listened to him complain about the students. "They are so *undisciplined,*" he said. "They have no *organization*, no *plan.*" I'd had it. "If you think we are doing such a bad job," I said, "do it better. Stop criticizing people who are actually out there saying what they believe. Take some leadership." I don't think I had ever spoken like that to him before, but it worked. Our household soon became such a hub of activity that we began to suspect our phone was tapped. We took it valiantly in stride, though, my sister even having the courtesy to greet the wiretap whenever she called home.

———

In November 1969 I marched in Washington. Many of us carried small American flags as a way of reclaiming the symbol from those who, challenging our patriotism, had used it against us. At the White House, which was ringed with school buses, I had a momentary vision: the buses became soldiers with guns turned on the demonstrators, and then they were buses again. I pushed the vision away. A few months later, at Kent State, it happened.

In May, 1970, President Nixon expanded the war while saying he wasn't. I didn't know what made me more angry, the lies or the assumption that I would believe them. When four unarmed protesters were shot at Kent State, business-as-usual stopped. Grief and fury threatened to overwhelm strategy as campus leaders cast about for a focus. As an officer of the Y, I helped plan a candlelight vigil. We decided there should be a procession and there should be coffins. It was easy to get enough candles but the coffins were a challenge. Somehow they were found and that evening I stood in a circle of little lights, close to the Old Well, holding papers and a small book. We were poised to begin when someone told us there were students running through the dorms and coming toward us. We waited in silence. The group arrived at the far side of the gathering, their grief and anger surging up against our calm. They were given candles and drawn into the group, which grew quiet again. When my part came, I let the air settle and then read a prayer for the dead.

So many students, faculty members, and townspeople attended the vigil that when the first people following the coffins had left the quad, circled the arboretum, turned back on Franklin Street and returned to the Old Well, the last of the procession had not yet left. The energy shifted, not just in the frantic students, or even just in those who walked in procession; the energy shifted on the whole campus. Later there would be explanations for why the UNC campus did not grow violent, as it could have and others did. Many explanations were reasonable, including the one that credited the fundamental "gentility" of the South. But the energy had shifted in that circle; I felt it happen.

Through the combined efforts of the Y and Student Government, we formed a plan: we would go to Washington to meet with our congressmen and senators. One a few days later, seven buses and an uncounted number of cars converged on Washington where we fanned out through the offices meeting with our own representatives, or with anyone who would let us in. The group was so large the North Carolina Congressional Delegation met with us in a hearing room. Senator Sam Ervin, the venerable "Senator Sam," annoyed me with his strict interpretation of the Constitution that he used to defend the president's incursion into Cambodia and then excused himself on account of the many important things he had to do. When the junior senator, B. Everett Jordan, said he would give attention to the next bill about the war that came to his desk, the room erupted in applause. When he repeated his statement more forcefully, we gave him a standing ovation. He was our new hero and he was as good as his word: when the Cooper-Church Amendment limiting the president's war powers came before the Senate, he provided a swing vote in favor and credited the delegation from the University of North Carolina for playing a role in his decision.

Our experience in Washington was a rare triumph for activists and should have given me a sense of power and commitment, but I was already withdrawing. I graduated a few weeks later, and a few weeks after that got married. The Y community dispersed to new jobs and new lives. I moved with my new husband to Ithaca, New York, where he immersed himself in graduate school, and I took a job in a bookstore and set up housekeeping as a married woman. Our tiny apartment did not have a television, so the war in Vietnam became distant and abstract. Only a matter of weeks earlier, my soundtrack had been Buffalo Springfield's "For What It's Worth," and The Doors' "The End" but I needed a community to sustain that kind of energy. Without it my way forward was cloudy and it suddenly telescoped down to a pinpoint of anxiety.

My new husband's draft number was 138, low enough that

the situation was no longer abstract, no longer a cause. He began the process of applying for conscientious objector status and his father, a lawyer, brought legal and financial resources in support. I was not involved in this campaign, which so far as I could tell had become less a matter of war resistance than of individual conscience, and so I was left in a state of terror. I had just achieved my new life away from my family and outside of the South and it might at any moment be snatched away. I had nowhere to turn. My husband had draft counsellors and support centers. I had no groups, no mentors, no friends. I was trying to learn what being married meant and what it would mean in the event that any of the many possibilities my husband was not talking about came to pass. I admired Joan Baez, whose husband had gone to prison for refusing induction, and tried to identify with the songs she wrote about him, but was not entirely successful. I wanted something more satisfying than waiting. I wanted to have the opportunity to feel heroic and instead, my husband, whose situation might confer this status on me, had buried himself in graduate school.

Meanwhile, the anti-war movement, with which, for want of anything else, I had identified, had taken on a dark, violent tone that was too close to what I had learned, so many years before, could be unleashed. I had known only the world of opposition, the dangerously-disembodied, spectator world of newscasts and ideas. I wanted to know not how to oppose, but how to heal. Embarking on a completely unfocused spiritual search, right in line with the mood of the early 70s, my personal soundtrack became Cat Stevens's "Morning Has Broken," George Harrison's "My Sweet Lord," and "Jesus Christ Superstar." My husband faced his draft board twice, going to New Jersey by bus and staying with his parents, and both times they rejected his application on the grounds that he "was not sincere." His status became 1A and stayed that way. Month after month nothing happened. Finally he received a letter saying that because he had been 1A for a year and had not been called up, his status dropped to 4F. It was over. There was a gathering in our little apartment for which I no doubt made sangria with Rioja I could get for one dollar a bottle, but it was all a little desultory. I felt relieved, but also cheated, as though a chance for heroism had been snatched away, even if my role would have been only that of Stoic Wife.

Soon after that we moved to Washington, D.C. where I attended graduate school in art history (it seemed the logical thing to do). Two children arrived, one of whom needed several surgeries. Saigon fell and I must have seen the images but they made less of an impression on me than the murder of the Olympic athletes during the Munich Olympics and then the Watergate hearings, happening only a few miles away from our house in Alexandria. I thought less and less about the war in Vietnam until I did not think about it at all. I buried it; I did not realize it was lying in wait.

———

After returning from his second tour, Mark attended classes at The University of North Carolina for two years, hanging out on the same lounge furniture in the Y building that I had only recently vacated and coordinating protests as a part of Vietnam Veterans Against the War. He came back to a world utterly different from the one he had left three years earlier. He had enlisted in the optimistic post-Kennedy world of black-and-white, superior technology, and (male, military) arrogance. He came back to disarray, disunity, and disillusionment, within a cultural free-for-all. He took two years of classes in history and threw himself into '60s hedonism. He moved to Boston and then to Juneau, Alaska, and later to Las Vegas, Nevada—glaciers and desert, both landscapes utterly different from

Vietnam but both, as I later put it, bigger than he was. These were landscapes capable of absorbing what he could not speak.

He wrote. He wrote about his first tour, typing on whatever paper was available. He wrote in vignettes, with dates and place names and characters moving in and out just as they had in his experience. Some years later he began writing about his second tour in a letter that turned into a complete narrative. Then he put it all away. He began a career as a newspaper journalist and photographer and though he had supportive friends, his writing about the war had no audience.

―――

Meanwhile, I earned a Masters Degree at George Washington University, completed an internship at the Smithsonian Institution, moved back to Ithaca, and earned a Ph.D. in the history of art at Cornell. I worked as an editor at Cornell's American Indian Program and started my own business as a web designer, editor, and writer.

In all that time I kept my distance from politics, considering that a kind of non-cooperation strategy. I kept my distance from activism as well. In the conflicts that followed the war in Vietnam I could find no lessons learned and without the Campus Y, I had no community to challenge and inspire me. Simply being a part of a "peace movement" did not attract me, but I did not know what would. It was as if I had briefly crossed paths with war and then thought of it only as something distant and tragic.

I did not know and I did not choose to know what the young men were facing who had come back from the conflict I had hated. I had no experience talking to them and had no reason to think they would be interested in talking to me. Veterans were, for me, like members of the International Brotherhood of Electrical Workers: people who by virtue of specialized training and experience hung out together because they understood each other. I was not qualified. I was not part of the military and I knew nothing about it. I would have felt confused and shy, unsure what to say, as one does with someone recently bereaved. To me the war was in the past, its unresolved trauma playing out in movies and books. I assumed that those who participated thought of it much as I did my trip to Israel—exciting, life-changing, and *over*. It was a benign disregard, but disregard, I later came to believe, is a form of disrespect. I was a living example of the enormous gulf that separates veterans from civilians.

It took decades for that to change. Caught up in raising children, pursuing and leaving an academic career, and enduring various personal crises, I gave little thought to Vietnam or to the war that had happened there. I read none of the books, watched none of the movies, and visited The Vietnam Veterans Memorial in Washington largely because of the beauty of its conception. Having been raised in one, I thought I needed the church and devoted energy and time to teenagers, committees, the choir, and liturgical seasons. I was searching for something I had not yet defined and I thought I would find it there. In fact, I thought it ought to be there already and I annoyed many people by advocating for it— passion, trust, cooperation, and deeply-held values expressed creatively. It took many years for me to realize: I was looking for the Y. I missed my youthful idealism, the shared belief that things that had gone wrong should and could be changed. I missed the energy. I missed my friends. I missed being *involved*.

I did not, of course, miss the cause. In spite of seeing that its lessons had not been learned, I thought the war in Vietnam was behind me and that it was past time to move on, or at least to move forward. I held the war's betrayals deep inside and shut them away. The effort was like trying to cage the minotaur: the monster may be hidden deep in the labyrinth, but it is *there*, pawing and snorting. It was about to claw its way to the surface.

———

In 2011, John Peters-Campbell, a friend from graduate school, told me that he had accepted a job at an American School in Hanoi. My mind did the thing a mind does when confronted with information it cannot process—it chose a plausible explanation. Without thinking further, I decided he was going to Saigon (I certainly did not think of it as Ho Chi Minh City). That he was going to Vietnam was difficult enough: "John is going to Vietnam" still meant, "John is going to war." Similarly, "Hanoi" meant a conceptual, almost existential place where one was taken or dropped into. It was like the bottom of the sea, reachable only by the very brave, the very foolish, or the very unlucky. Hanoi "wanted" things and "refused" things and "declared" things and attacked and defended and kept coming, relentlessly. "Hanoi" was Tolkein's Mordor or The Borg from *Star Trek*. That John was going there was in a literal sense absurd, in that it was utterly and obviously senseless, and without any place in what I thought was normal life.

Several months later, he invited me to visit. I accepted before I could talk myself out of it.

44

Finding My Way Back To a Place I Had Never Been

Giving up all my beliefs about Hanoi did not come easily. However outmoded and ludicrous those beliefs were, they were mine, and they were deeply embedded in my psyche. Agreeing to go there called all of them into question. If they were true, it made no sense to go and if I was going, what I believed would have to change. I tried to think it through rationally, but my brain froze and my body took over every time. I fought nausea. I shook uncontrollably. I read a guidebook and shuddered. I watched a travel show and couldn't breathe. In the night, when I woke, I sobbed. All those many years earlier, I had learned that "Vietnam" meant cynicism and despair. I had learned that my leaders would use the power of words to make people see what is not there or not to see what is. I had buried that knowledge and, left unexamined for forty years, it had changed shape, and was now bursting from within me in a cascade of sorrow.

Forty years earlier I had walked away from trauma that I had, however distantly, endured. Now I chose to walk toward it. The war in Vietnam was at the core of my coming of age, the glue that bound me to my generation. I had watched a beautiful country being torn apart by American explosives, huge fighter planes, gunships, and fleets of helicopters raining terror from the sky. I had seen men being carried screaming to helicopters and women and children shielding one another in rice paddies. I had listened to politicians betray no emotion in the face of cascading disaster. I had felt the anguish of a divided nation. I had lost something of myself then. I had to go to Vietnam to get it back.

On my first night in Hanoi we walked to one of John's favorite spots for dinner and then a few blocks further to a traffic circle where we stopped and just watched. It was impossible to tell how many lanes, as we would measure them, made up the intersection. No one was observing lanes and it occurred to me that it might have been suicidal to try to do so. This traffic, if that is what it was called, flowed according to a rhythm of its own, like starlings that swoop and turn according to an inner knowledge known from birth. When watching hundreds of motorbikes navigating under the streetlights and surrounded by neon signs threatened to overwhelm my senses, I watched one, following it as it danced among the others, moved into the quieter inner circle, and then threaded out among the other dancers to find a side street. The sound became the roar of the ocean. The only thing that kept me from falling into a trance was seeing again and again the improbability of the motor bikes' passengers and cargo. What did not stand to reason to me was second nature to them.

Dinner had already challenged my assumptions. I had not one single reassurance, by my expectations, that this would be a safe and sanitary experience. We had sat on child-sized plastic stools at a plastic table right on the sidewalk with traffic swooping past us, kicking up dirt and exhaust and *germs*. There was litter on the ground, sticky condiment bottles in front of us, and chopsticks loose in a jar, but I had surveyed the lively scene and decided that, well, this was what was happening. Besides, the smells were intoxicating, so I let go of maladaptive anxiety and was rewarded with food that was heady with spices and herbs, rich with grilled meat and deep broth, like nothing I had ever tasted in a "proper" restaurant.

―――

The Hanoi experience came, as I had wanted it to, in homely ways. People were constantly sweeping up, and with good reason for the city was a construction zone. As most building was being done in concrete and each construction project began with the destruction of something else, a fine limestone dust shrouded everything. With no apparent zoning or city planning, sudden concrete skyscrapers filled with scaffolding rose up next to two-story shops and houses, separated only by rubble. In some of these incomplete buildings, workers lived and hung out their laundry. Small shops crowded the street level, their signs jostling one another and climbing up the sides of French colonial buildings that had a melancholic air of patience or chagrin.

―――

To the dismay of my host, who had preserved more of an identity as an art historian than I had, I showed no interest in the temple complexes of Angor Wat in Cambodia or Borobudur in Indonesia. He wanted me to take full advantage of the resources I had expended in getting to that part of the world, but I had only just arrived and besides, I was after bigger game: errands.

    I went with John to order a new jug of water for the cooler

in the apartment because one must drink bottled water in Hanoi. We found a cord for his computer, and specialty coffee, and, of course, groceries. Errands got me out with a purpose and into the little shops, each one of them on the ground floor of the building where the proprietors lived, and each one exuding urban entrepreneurial energy. The shops sold colorful textiles or gifts or gadgets or pirated movies. In the computer shops the items in the dusty cases were refurbished or repackaged and nothing was the latest version. Because of the veil of limestone dust, everything felt drab, metallic, and gray. But in every shop—every single makeshift shop—there was a little shrine, usually on the floor near the entrance, red and gold, with lights, incense, and offerings. The shops were all part of a black and white world, but each had a beating heart in technicolor.

Everything was made in one of these little shops—windows, tiles, doors, clothing, food of course, lots of wedding dresses, signs for Vietnam Airlines. This meant there was an organic quality to everything and a lack of uniformity. In some ways, the city was a contraption but that also meant, as John pointed out, it was handmade. I stumbled on the steps leading up to the apartment the first night because one step had been repaired and, as the city lacked uniform building codes, that step was taller than the others. Many of the shops were organized by street—kitchen wares on one street, ceramics on another, children's clothes somewhere else. I thought it would have made more sense to sort by neighborhood so that everyone had easy access to everything and I wondered how customers chose among the many shops that seemed to duplicate one another. But that was how it was done.

John's apartment building had shops and offices on the main

floor and several floors of apartments surrounding a central court. Inside the main doorway hung the bright red flag of Vietnam and a bust of Ho Chi Minh. The apartment had much of the loveliness I had looked for—high ceilings, gracious proportions, a small balcony, and heavy, hard, carved dark wood furniture, not at all suited to curling up with a book. Over the door hung a loudspeaker which came to life from time to time with urgent and incomprehensible announcements. The loudspeaker, together with the presence of two attendants sitting at a small table in the lobby, led us to believe that the building was owned by the Party. The attendants watched me come and go and never smiled.

The screenless windows were left open during the day for ventilation and closed at nightfall, when the lights came on. Failing to do this resulted in an invasion of insects. Every day my host left early for his teaching job at the American school housed in the university. I ate breakfast on my own, usually a cup of complex, chocolate-y coffee, a bowl of slightly sweetened yogurt with a handful each of cashews and tiny dried baby lemons. A morning broadcast in the street over a public address system began with music I found surprisingly pleasant, followed by a woman's voice speaking at a rapid but not urgent pace. When she had finished I listened to the normal morning sounds of a city, sounds from other apartments in the building, and a bird, possibly caged, that I never found.

On many of the mornings during my three-week visit I took a cab to wherever I was going, usually the Hanoi Cooking Centre where I took as many classes as I could. Taking a cab gave me the opportunity to observe, much as I had done from the window of our VW bus. I came quickly to like the white noise soundtrack of the motorbikes, but never adjusted to the horns. They were sudden and sharp and there was a language to them. At first, when I was walking, I took them personally. I thought any horn anywhere near me was directed at me. I responded with a startle reflex, which was not good. Horns could mean any number of things but they never, ever, mean to freeze, jump, or make any sudden movements. Drivers counted on all other occupants of the road to hang loose, move rhythmically, and, insofar as possible, behave predictably. Horns could mean, "Be careful, I'm here," or "I see we are on a collision course and I am coming through," or "Don't cut in, I'm right behind you," or "I'm a taxi on Important Business." The cab drivers were all young and as driving seemed to approximate playing a video game, their youth was an advantage.

I never got over my terror of crossing the street. While there were the occasional traffic lights with little signals for pedestrians, the principal and accepted way for pedestrians to get from one place to another was to step off the curb and enter the dance, which, so far as I was concerned, involved making out my will. Although I came to sense the rhythm, I never mastered it. It all seemed to happen on the basis of a social contract much less rule-based than ours, a contract that relied on awareness and predictability and cultural knowledge. My reflexes had been calibrated to a different standard that I did not know how to change.

―――

In other areas, I made compromises. Before I left home I decided I would not eat anything that was endangered or anything that had knowingly been made to suffer. I would not eat dog or cat or that very foreign Asian delicacy, fetal duck egg.

Things looked different when the situation arose in context, though. In my first class at the Hanoi Cooking Centre we toured the nearby market and our guide and chef walked us back, carrying a string bag with eggs in it. "Fetal duck eggs!" he announced, and he was going to teach us to eat them. The eggs cooked in a little pot during class. I eyed them warily. When he shelled one it looked like a mottled hard-boiled egg, the embryonic duck revealed as he pulled it apart. He spooned it up, added a little lime and chili salt and held it out to me. The room grew silent. I had a moment to remember my misgivings and then yielded them for the sake of learning, which is what I had come to Vietnam to do. It tasted like a cross between a hardboiled egg and very tender duck, which made me wonder why I would object to the intermediate stage. With the lime and chili salt, it was delicious.

The stunningly beautiful vegetables and fruits in the markets looked like they do in the travel posters. Laid out on counters or carried in woven baskets, vegetables are part of the visual and emotional appeal of Vietnam. But Vietnamese do not live on vegetables alone. They eat meat, lots of it, and much of it in forms we would shun. I had helped butcher chickens at my grandmother's house and my grandmother loved to gnaw on the feet. I don't remember any unlaid eggs within the chickens, but here they were laid out on the concrete counter in neat piles, separated from the feet and the innards, each its own specialty. Whole birds were piled on top of one another, wings and legs folded in, and on top of each pile there was one plucked bird sitting up, its beak open in a macabre scream that horrified me. Later I learned those birds were intended for an altar offering, the open beak meant for holding a coin, but at first I thought this chicken would show up in my dreams.

There were two areas in the market for aquatic creatures, one for the coasts and one for the rivers and rice paddies. Frogs fit in the second area. At the stalls with large net bags of black frogs, the women sat behind their wares waiting for customers and chatting together. From farther along the aisle came a rhythmic sound—*whap!* ... *whap!* ... *whap!*

We turned the corner and our guide, without changing his tone, talked about the fish in plastic tubs or styrofoam coolers to the left. To the right, though, one of the vendors was picking up the frogs by the legs, one by one, and slamming them down against the side of the tiled wall. One frog—*whap!* another —*whap!* When one of them slipped out of her hand and jumped into the next little walled stall, she went after it, brought it back and killed it—*whap!* When she had a good supply she sat on her stool and skinned them, expertly, almost in one pull. Meanwhile a snakehead fish from the stall opposite escaped its tub and flopped on the pavement until it was retrieved.

In cooking and travel shows, stories like this are used to demonstrate "extreme eating," or the utter foreignness of a culture, strategies that erect barriers or hold Vietnam at arm's length, finding ways to see it as Very Different From Us. I recoiled from the frog stall but at the same time remembered my distance from the sacrifice that gives me my dinner. Nothing is hidden in a Vietnamese market. They eat *anything*. Although the Buddhist monks, of which there are many, are vegetarian and much of the Vietnamese daily menu—rice, rice noodles, tofu, and produce of all kinds—is vegetarian or vegan, the culture is permeated with meat-eating. The recent memory of famine has created a food culture in which there is little room for refusing an entire category of nutrition. The idea that an ordinary person (not a monk) would choose (have the luxury of choosing) some things and not others is not an easy concept. Frogs breed in abundance in the paddies and are an important source of protein. If the killing and skinning is done in the market, the frogs are fresh and the customers know it. So when the man in front of me said, "There has to be a better way," I thought, "This *is* the better way." It was an honesty I was not quite ready for, though. I fled, meaning I continued to walk, pretending to a cultural openness I did not feel.

We stopped at the herbs and the lotus root, and admired the deep baskets of fresh noodles. Behind me, *whap! whap!* and the silent scream of the chicken.

———

"The old people say that if the dragonflies are flying low, there will be rain."

Cheung, my guide, spoke softly, his voice barely disturbing the heavy air. He occasionally explained things or pointed things out, but mostly I heard the dip of the oars and the water slipping along the side of the boat. The smell was rich, dark, and fertile. Dragonflies in all shapes and colors flitted along in front of us, flew over our heads, and perched on every stalk sticking out of the water.

We had driven several hours from Hanoi through tiny villages and past walled fields that held water buffalo and the tombs of the family's dead. We were making a pilgrimage to the Perfume Pagoda, a complex of Buddhist shrines in the mountains south of Hanoi. I wished it wasn't just me making this trip. I felt curious, alert, devout even, but self-conscious.

We had arrived in a larger village that was a gathering place and point-of-transfer to long rowboats for an hour's trip on the Yen River. Our boat was metal and had been sitting in the sun so Cheung put down a piece of cardboard for me to sit on. He sat beside me and the young man who rowed stood in the back.

All along the embankments in this town were stairs down to the river where, at festival time, rowboats would be lined up five or six deep. Today it was quiet. We were the only ones to set out and we encountered only fishermen and people, mostly women, checking on the rice paddies we could glimpse through the grass along the river's edge. I took an occasional picture, trailed my fingers through the water, and lost myself to the heat.

Making the journey to a pilgrimage site is part of the healing process, as is seeing the holy relic or image housed there, touching something, bathing in water, smelling the air, listening. There is always a journey and always the earth. At the major sites—and this was one—there are also souvenirs.

We arrived at a ramshackle dock with corrugated metal buildings lining the waterfront. As recently as three weeks ago, this site would have been crowded with the faithful and the vendors who besieged them by aggressively hawking fans, temple supplies, plastic tchotchkes, water, and soft drinks. Today, only about one in ten stalls was even open. The rest were shrouded in tattered tarps or being dismantled or repaired. The vendors who were open tried to get me to buy, but the season was winding down and their hearts were not in it. There were a few stalls with baskets of fruit or boiled potatoes and all along the way were displays of traditional medicines.

We stopped at a few of these stalls and Cheung pointed out dried herbs to strengthen bones, to ease sleep, to soothe stomach aches. I saw snake wine ("good for the man"—and any time something was described as either good or bad "for the man," the speaker illustrates the point with a meaningful crooking of the index finger) and bee's nest wine (honeycomb). There were roots and powders, leaves and funguses. The dried medicines were laid out in baskets. The tonics were in large glass jars, perhaps gallon-size, and most contained the thing that was imparting its strength: plants, a snake, even a bird.

By the time I reached the cave, I was in an appropriately altered state of consciousness. I had slid along a river in the sun, climbed hundreds of steps, flown over the trees in a creaking gondola, and climbed more steps. At the entrance to the cave I looked over a wall to an open oven where the peoples' offerings were being burned. The air was dense and steamy. I walked through an arched gateway, down a long flight of stone stairs, and into the cave.

The floor was barely leveled with stones and in places slick with water. Saffron-robed monks lived in tents up on a ledge. Stalactites formed a curtain above an enormous stupa-like formation. It was raw stone, a gaping, numinous mouth of the earth open to the thousands of people who come here to pray.

Everything in balance, Cheung had kept saying when he explained *feng shui* and tattoos. A dragon or lion tattoo, he had said, has to be balanced with something small. Yin and yang, male and female, heaven and earth—all must be in balance. Inside the cave, though, it seemed to me that earth had the upper hand. There were the usual offerings of flowers and water and Choco-Pies, red and gold, metal and paper, but over it all loomed the great mouth of the cave, all stone and dripping water.

On the trip back along the river insects hummed and a monkey called from the forest. The dragonflies, no longer over our heads, had left their stalks and were flying low against the water's surface. Heavy clouds gathered ahead of us and the wind picked up. By the time we reached the highway, lightening was cutting across the sky, torrential rain had reduced visibility to only a few feet, and the radio said there was flooding in Hanoi.

In Hoa Lo Prison—all that remained of the infamous "Hanoi Hilton,"—I looked for the story I knew had happened there, my certainty in no way marred by the partial nature of my knowledge. This was where captured American pilots were kept and tortured, for years at a time. That was the only story I knew and I expected it, entirely failing to remember who, now, was telling it. The prison had been built by the French to hold rebellious Vietnamese, those who had dared to resist their colonizers. Room after room memorialized these prisoners, the displays highlighting their suffering and heroism. Plaster mannequins were shackled on long stone ledges in heartrending poses of dignity and compassion for one another. A recording of moans and screams made me shiver in a dank hall of solitary cells, the walls built of heavy blocks of cut stone, blackened by years of dark energy. A real guillotine, I learned, is much narrower than the ones I knew from movies.

In a shallow alcove of the last hall hung a photomontage of anti-war demonstrations in the United States. The black-and-white images showing marches and banners proclaiming opposition to the war was labelled "Demonstrations in Solidarity with the Vietnamese People." In the last two rooms, painted in soft colors and well lit, was a plexiglass case holding John McCain's uniform, photographs of American prisoners playing volleyball and having Christmas dinner. There was also a photograph of McCain's plane in the lake after it had been shot down. McCain was surrounded by swimmers who are variously described on plaques, or maps, or guidebooks as having attacked him or having saved his life. Both are probably true. They pulled him out of the water but they were none too pleased with him, as he had been bombing their city.

I had demonstrated against the war, but not "in solidarity with the Vietnamese people." The American prisoners had played volleyball but they did not nickname this place the Hanoi Hilton out of affection, as a label suggested. Prisoners, American and Vietnamese, are long gone from this place but their stories are still being contended to the point that they are forever linked in a fog of ambiguity.

I came to suspect that Vietnamese knew more about us than we ever knew, or know now, about them. They were *interested* in Americans.

In the gardens of the Ho Chi Minh Mausoleum, I found a bench in front of two shrines holding offerings and burning incense. The sun dappled through the leaves and birds flew high among the trees, too quickly for me to see. A group of Vietnamese people, mostly women in conical hats, arrived, passed in front of me, sat cross-legged on the ground farther on the path, and got out a picnic. One of their group, a man wearing a pith helmet, approached me with a platter of cut pieces of watermelon. He bowed and made the offering gesture, extending the platter with both hands. Behind him the women beamed. I took a piece, thanking him softly. The sweet fruit was sticky on my mouth and hands. When the group left, each one nodded to me and smiled. I felt welcomed. I felt *noticed*.

I was a woman of an identifiable era in a country that respects elders. I had wondered (and been a little hurt) that no one asked my age, something the guidebooks assured me would happen. Vietnamese need to know one's age so as to know which term to use, which is always relative to the speaker. Evidently, I comfortably occupied the *ba* category, an older woman.

Accordingly, the drivers of the cabs I took seemed to think that I, as an American *ba*, merited, if not protection, at least *management*. Somewhere in the city, for instance, I knew there was an American B-52 bomber sticking out of a small lake in the middle of a residential district. It had been shot down in 1968 or 1972 and left there. On my Vietnamese map of Hanoi it was called the Monument to B-52 Victory. I wrote down the address on a card, marked the place on my map and hailed a cab by pointing to the ground. As usual, the driver was a young man. Although at no time during my visit to Hanoi had I felt threatened, or even ill at ease, I was stupidly aware, as I showed my card to the driver, that I was an American woman asking a North Vietnamese man (in my mind he was no longer just "Vietnamese" but *"North* Vietnamese") to take me to an obscure site associated with the war. He did not seem to recognize the place, so I showed him the map where it was marked and labeled. He pointed to the place on the map and asked if that is right. "Yes," I said and pointed, too, for good measure.

Soon, the one North Vietnamese man became several North Vietnamese men, because my driver consulted others along the way. There was much discussion and looking to me. We made our way to the general neighborhood and my driver asked directions again a few times and was directed back and then across and down another street. Finally, he made a satisfied sound and turned into the gates of … the Botanical Gardens. He waved toward the gardens, which surround a lake and looked at me for approval. "Are you sure?" I said, in English, but clearly doubtful. He gestured again. This was where I wanted to be, or he wanted me to be, or someone somewhere along the line had decided I should be. I paid him and got out.

I walked along brick paths under towering trees. I visited several monkeys and two peacocks in cages. I sat on a bench beside the lake. It began to rain so I opened my umbrella and continued to sit. I watched a fisherman with a line and any number of drenched brides having their pictures taken. The rain stopped and I walked some more, passing pairs of lovebirds snatching some privacy. I climbed stone steps up the side of a mound to a little abandoned café that had been taken over by playful rats. The sun came out, the air got steamy, and I began to be bitten by mosquitoes. I walked back to the entrance, hailed another cab, and went back to the apartment.

John, upon learning my story, told me that the mound I

had climbed was almost certainly the gun emplacement from which the B-52 had been shot down.

———

It was evening on Halong Bay after a day of surpassing beauty. Most of the tourist boats took a popular, cluttered route, while our junks—three that could hold fourteen and the lovely couples' boat that I had inadvertently hired and had to myself—explored quiet caves and environmental projects designed to bring balance among the fishing villages, the press of tourists, and the health of the bay.

We pulled into a cove to anchor for the night and found we shared our seclusion with four Vietnamese Navy ships, the engine of one chugging at a low, steady pulse. My guide, on behalf of the captain, apologized: they had not expected anyone to be here. They were sorry for the noise.

I sat on a deck chair and took surreptitious pictures of the boats. Evening fell. Dinner was served. One of the men turned on a light on the side of our boat, shining it into the water to attract squid. My guide called me over and showed me how to distinguish schools of little fish from the more fast-moving squid. I had to retrain my eyes, which expected to see something much larger, like what I get when I order calamari. Once I learned to see what was in front of me rather than what I expected, I noticed the greenish light reflecting on luminescent bodies that darted among tiny fish.

The Navy boat's engine chugged, its armaments shrouded and its towers and antennas askew. I made out what looked like fishing nets hung from lanyards and tarps slung along the side. Like most else in Vietnam the boats looked like contraptions. If I had been on an American battleship forty years ago and boats like these had crossed my path—all cobbled together out of whatever was to hand and made to work—I, too, might have been looking for something more substantial.

On my last day in Hanoi, John and I had lunch with friends at a food stall in an alley just off the university campus—rice with dried shredded pork and shallots, and sticky rice cake in banana leaf with cucumber salad. On the walk back, John bought mango slices dusted with chili salt, which we ate out of a plastic bag with wooden skewers. We came to a pagoda he said he had never seen open and went in. On one side of the courtyard men were building something from a stack of bricks. A circle of women prepared lunch on the veranda. Other women counted money on the ground beside two old women, old enough to have lived through the war, their weathered faces lit with animated conversation.

I removed my shoes and stepped over the wooden track that held the now-opened carved doors. The usual host of statues crowded the central hall: birds, urns, flowers, warriors, scholars, and guardian figures, each taller than I. Red and gold and light and incense held the room together. I moved slowly, as through a quiet forest. Far in the back, against the wall, I saw a figure dressed in gold, smaller than all the others and yet compelling, a mother goddess or a Black Madonna. Older than all the wars Vietnam had been in, she anchored the hall like a holy mountain. She presided over the prayers and the offerings, the lunch and the conversations. Wordlessly, I sought the thing I had come to find. I had no offering or joss stick, only my seeking. I felt her eyes on me long after I had gone home. There was work for me to do.

45

Survivors

Now Vietnam was never far from my mind. It was not just Vietnam-the-country or even Vietnam-the-war. It was Vietnam-the-situation, the-state-of-mind, the-unfinished-business. Each person I talked to carried it still, in different ways, and with different reactions. I began to feel intuitively how much had been left undone, how little the failure, betrayal, and anger had been brought out into the open. The energy that had been generated during the Vietnam years had not disappeared but had burrowed beneath ordinary life, hidden within rueful memories, and triggered by shared language or snatches of music. These were the echoes of shared trauma that had been left untended, like the wounded soldiers one is never supposed to leave behind.

Ever the idealist, I wanted to help. I thought the answer would be to encourage others to start where I had started, by going to Vietnam, to the country whose name was, for most of us, synonymous with whatever our experience had been. I began with my anti-war companions, hoping we might journey together, reconvene the impromptu meetings, the passion, the creativity. I talked to people I had stayed in contact with and people I had not spoken with in decades. Apart from two who agreed immediately, they would not come. Admittedly, there was much I had not taken into account. That various family, professional, financial, or health considerations made such a trip impractical or impossible did not surprise me, but something less tangible played a role. They looked away, not meeting my eyes, with expressions of anguish and grief. Experienced travelers who had never been to Vietnam said they didn't want to go "back there." Others worried about security and danger. I had the occasional beginnings of conversations—a partial narrative of memories, a halting story of a father killed in the war—and the conversation would break off. Eyes blurred as though seeing something from a great distance. "Not now," they said. "Some day … maybe …"

I began to see more than was there, to hear more than had been spoken. I tried to begin a conversation about the aftermath of the war and how it might have affected all of us, but I could not find the words. I could not find a way in. Some people resented me, as though I were speaking out of turn. We had all agreed, after all—had we not?—not to talk about it.

"I've moved on," some said. Others reminded me that we had done what we could forty years ago and that was an end to it. No need to revisit it.

So I set out on my own, not sure what the mission was, where it would take me, or indeed if there was a mission at all.

―――

Without his name in the lower part of the frame—Mark Smith—I might not have known him. His brows were drawn together slightly and the muscles under his eyes made shadows along his nose, remnants of repeated expressions of intensity and alarm. He spoke quietly, softly, the goofy kid I had known in high school subdued. He spoke of the beauty of Vietnam, the intensity of its colors, "especially the greens."

I had been watching a documentary about the war, a documentary I had chanced upon because it reminded me of the war the way I had experienced it: on television. Several veterans were being interviewed and, against all odds, Mark was one of them. He described the boredom contrasting with the sudden, intense excitement when his unit made contact with the enemy. "You couldn't go through combat," he said, "and remain detached. It was the idea of someone shooting at you, someone was trying to kill you, you were trying to kill someone, you were using that finger [here he crooked the finger of his right hand] to try to take someone's life, and that sends a real charge through you."

His words shocked me, but I hardly heard them. I was taking in that it was him and studying his face for what it showed me.

He appeared one more time, this time talking about his disillusionment with how he and his fellow soldiers had been treated within whatever plan there had been for conducting the war. "After a while," he said, "I began to feel that someone was taking advantage of our bravery and our courage to no good end. So we were being used, really, for God knows what purpose, at least in terms that we could understand and appreciate on a gut level, which is the level on which you operated in Vietnam. Words like 'peace with honor' and 'negotiations,' they didn't pay the bills in Vietnam, not when you were out in the field."

That connection with how the soldiers on the ground felt, quite apart from the moral and political issues, attracted me. He had a story to tell. I wanted to hear it.

He wasn't easy to find. He had, it turned out, gone to

ground in the northwestern corner of North Carolina and had not left much of an online trace. After a year of looking off and on, a short trail led me to his Facebook page where I learned he'd had a stroke the year before, almost exactly when I had started looking for him.

From his page, I formed a picture of a lively, opinionated man who had been working for a newspaper and was angry that someone had abandoned a puppy on the Blue Ridge Parkway. He had posted photographs of Juneau, Alaska, and friends, various local items for the newspapers he had worked for, and the natural world, along with paragraphs of commentary. And then, suddenly, it had stopped and the only information I could find were requests for prayers. Dismayed, I knew that just as the face I had seen in the documentary was no longer who he had been in high school, now I knew he would no longer be that face.

When I saw that he had returned to Facebook, albeit in a limited way, I contacted him and asked, by way of opening a conversation, was that really him in the documentary? He responded immediately that it was him. "Two tours," he said. "Twenty months. I miss it still."

―――

When I asked Mark about the war I discovered a man who was not only living with his memories, he was living *in* them. My appearance in his life after so many years opened a vein that lay close to the surface. I wrestled with the wisdom of this, knowing my desire to care and to learn might be at odds with my complete and utter naiveté. I was acutely aware that I was inviting myself into his life, with consequences I could not foresee. Having been a part of the culture that had not known how to bring the Vietnam veterans home at the time, I wondered what made me think I would do a better job now. I harbored these doubts as though the only question was how this conversation might affect him. I had not yet wondered what it might do to me.

Once begun, though, I could not back out. Remembering that he had been a journalist and photographer in high school, I asked Mark if he had written about his experiences. He sent me the rough manuscript of his second tour and then I had to read it. Perhaps he did not realize how little I knew about the context of his story. Perhaps he didn't care. My intellectual mind wanted a coherent narrative, a story with a protagonist, an antagonist, a quest, a climax, and a resolution. Instead I was dropped into a violent, on-going conflict without anything to ground me. The story was disorienting. It breached any defenses I had put up, any secure perimeter I had built for myself over the years. The conflict between whatever I expected and what it relentlessly gave me destroyed any distance I might have clung to between myself and that war. I could not stop reading. Immersed in a world without redemption, in a war that was coming apart, I read into the night. When I put the manuscript down and turned off the light, I thought I heard helicopters and realized it was my own blood pounding in my ears.

―――

"Helpful Suggestion for Supporting Veterans," from the website of a psychiatric social worker: Find a veteran and offer to listen to whatever he or she needs to say. That did not seem like a good idea to me at all. I thought that should at least come with a warning—you must be prepared in case the veteran decides you are the right person to hear it. In any case, buttonholing a veteran out of the blue and expecting their confidence and trust seemed grossly disrespectful.

And yet that was exactly what I had done.

Recklessly, I asked Mark if he would go back to Vietnam. He said he would in a minute if it were possible. As my desire to focus on anti-war activists was not making progress, I shifted toward any trip that would get Mark back. I needed help, though. Three weeks in Hanoi had reconciled me to the city and given me a glimpse of the lively and very entrepreneurial tourist industry, but that did not qualify me to make decisions for a group traveling throughout the country.

I contacted an organization that had been making healing journeys for veterans for many years. I told my story and made an impassioned appeal. John Fisher, a veteran with experience in such trips, responded immediately. In his emails and subsequent phone conversations, I learned that he had been drafted, served one year, mostly in the Central Highlands, had become a chiropractor after the war, and returned as often as he could to hold clinics for veterans, elderly, and Agent Orange victims.

John had a boundless faith in his joyful belief, often repeated, that "the Vietnamese have forgiven us." This idea took me by surprise. I was not looking for forgiveness and did not know how such a thing would be negotiated. I was looking for understanding. Something like accountability made sense to me, but I thought that if we were to go there, each of us would have to wrestle with memories we had carried for decades and learn something new about them in the company of a supportive community. John's cheerful promise sounded a little too easy to me, but he had begun calling me "sister" and I had begun to get caught up in his optimism.

John had an undeniable love for the country he had fought in and he prided himself on having made a minor specialty of its history. Trained as I was in academia I frequently swallowed objections to his sweeping generalizations as I could see they came from a place of open-heartedness and respect. He had found his way of working out the demons he had brought home with him and I admired that.

We ran into a quiet collision of worldviews, though, when we tried to recruit people for our trip at the University of North Carolina, where I still hoped for some kind of co-sponsorship. At a workshop in the Y and a private event at a local home, I was on my territory. This was my town, my campus, my friends. I felt empowered, even imbued with some of John's optimism: we could do this, we could make it work. John's lack of academic grounding, though, caused some of our audience to pull away. Academics have a healthy skepticism of generalities. They want analysis, research, and citations. It is their comfort zone and respecting that is the way to gain their trust. John's language was foreign to them and that foreignness was, for them, too open-ended. They shut down, doubt or outright disagreement written on their faces. Sadly, but perhaps inevitably, John interpreted this as hostility. "They are the kind that would have spit on me when I came home," he claimed. That was not true. They would not have spit on him, but the world of academic standards had collided with the world of happy endings. I belonged to both worlds now so I yearned for a path through the confusion, a mapable road that would bring resolution and release. If a happy ending were to be had, though, I wanted it, even—perhaps especially—for those whose long history of hurt, regret, and disappointment had turned them into skeptics.

I put my misgivings on hold. John's can-do energy was the most immediate way to get Mark, me, and whatever group might be assembled to Vietnam, and I wanted to go.

———

With this talk taking place, Mark began sprinkling photographs from the war among his frequent social media posts. Many were of himself, taken by his buddies. There were also more recent images of himself, usually alone and unsmiling, and often taken with the timer on his SLR—old-school selfies. The images from the war were in some ways like graffiti—"I was here"—but they also recorded the process of being changed by the war. The ones from the first tour seemed to say, "Here I am, in this war." In the second tour they had lost their optimism—"The war is getting worse but here I am." The post-war images seemed more melancholy statements of fact —"Here I am. I am alive" and "I am getting older but I am alive." That impression was reinforced by the inclusion of images of men who were identified by name and then their status: WIA (wounded-in-action) or KIA (killed-in-action). The photographs documented a survivor, and one who was living uneasily with that fact.

———

One day Mark posted a picture, black and white, the image printed with rounded corners on a white background. At the top, in strong black ink, he had written: "Me June 28, '67 An Hoa Village." He was sitting on what looked like a sandy bank, scrubby brush in the background. He was holding a cigarette in his left hand, his right bent back at the wrist against his hip. His shirt was rolled up above the elbows and his hair, way too long for regulation, was pushed up in a wind-blown pompadour. He glowered at the camera, eyebrows drawn and mouth tightened.

    I would look at the picture later and wonder why I reacted as I did that night. It was as if I saw *into* it. Mark insisted later that according to both the inscribed date and his own memory, what I saw had not yet occurred.

"What happened on that day, June 28, 1967?" I asked in a quick email. He gave me a military answer. I said he looked fierce. He said he looked tired. I let it go.

That night he sent me an electronic file and told me to try to open it. The text came up with lines of symbols at the top and fragmented in places but what he wanted me to read was intact. He had given me the story of the death of the villages of An Hoa and An Quang. It was there, he told me, in those villages, that he had begun to have doubts about the war. "This is the moment that turned the tide," he said. "The village was a charnel house."

He had signed and dated the account—"Mark M. Smith, 8 October, 1968, West Berlin, Germany"—which gave it added weight. It was less an account of an experience and more the formal statement of a witness. "These are the facts," he seemed to say. "This is what happened." I recognized the boy I had known in high school, who would have been furious that the American medic would not help the villagers. At the same time, I saw the boy the war had begun to transform get frustrated when he couldn't get "action" and who participated in shooting an unarmed man. Both were true. In my world they were contradictory but both were true. In spite of his best intention—to go to war as a witness—he had been drawn in. The change in him was not a sudden break. It took place gradually, the blurring of the line between who he had been and who the war wanted him to be.

———

Often, in conversations with civilians, I encountered the mostly unspoken assumption that Vietnam veterans would have or *should* have a sense of remorse, regret, and contrition. There did not seem to be any malice in this, just what I came to see as a kind of entitled righteousness, an unspoken "I told you so."

The speaker was *right* about that war, had been right all along, and still was right. The subtle implication was that anyone who had been involved in the war was wrong, and surely, by this time, they knew it.

If Mark had opinions about this, he did not show them. Such expectations seemed almost to have nothing to do with him. "It was war," he said. That was his answer even to my concerns that at times, it seemed to me, a line had been crossed. The idea of a line at all was not much on his mind. He had gone there to do a job and he did it. He had documented himself as honestly as he could. He owed no one more than that, not to make *them* feel better.

———

Mark took an interest in my great-grandfather, John Thomas Dixon, who had fought for the Confederacy and had survived Pickett's Charge at Gettysburg after being wounded. After learning the military specifics—Company I, 56th VA Infantry, Garnett's Brigade, Pickett's Division, Longstreet's Corps—he sent me maps, marked with the route my great-grandfather would have taken, with speculation about where he had been wounded. I read the book he recommended and learned terms like "flanking maneuver." When I mentioned that I would be giving a talk at Wilson College in Chambersburg, Pennsylvania, I told Mark that I would run over to Gettysburg to see the place. He offered to drive from Sparta, North Carolina, where he lived—six-hours away—and meet me there. It would be the first time I had seen him since high school.

Gettysburg is a strange place to me. In the fifth and sixth grades I had lived in Carlisle, so I had come here on class trips and have blurry black and white snapshots of classmates climbing on cannons, taken with my now-impossibly antique Anscoflex II. My great-grandfather had fought here. My uncle, a professor of American history at a nearby college, had led family tours of the grounds. I felt a deep connection to the countryside, the rolling fields with their stone walls, but almost none to the great battle that had happened there. I had wanted to see the ghosts I had read about and felt a little cheated that I never had. It was very different for Mark. He described Gettysburg as a lodestone. It was a place of emptiness he peopled with what had happened there.

He was standing by his red Ford Focus at our agreed meeting place, wearing ill-fitting pants and a denim jacket that obscured a beer belly. Impulsively, I gave him a light hug. He patted my arm and murmured, "Thank you."

We left my car and drove in his through the lanes, occasionally getting out to visit a monument. We went into the gift shop where I bought a novel. We had a picnic on the grass next to a rail fence. I told him if I had not recognized him in any other way—and I might not have—I would have known him by his walk, the slow, careful walk of a tracker in the forest that had later become the slow, careful walk of an infantryman. He took my picture on the wall the charge had been trying to reach. I wanted at least to experience an unexpected breeze or a shiver, some presence that would approve or disapprove what I had undertaken, but I felt nothing. If there were ghosts, they seemed to be waiting for me to make the first move.

―――――

Mark's maps of the battles at Gettysburg involved long parallel lines, straight or curved, continuous, with arrow points on the ends and converging at The Angle. All hell broke loose in the process, but the soldiers wore uniforms, were coordinated and organized, and opposed one another in planned and to some degree, predictable ways.

Mark's maps of the war in Vietnam, hand-drawn in letters and notebooks, or, later, as annotations on topographical maps, showed the movements only of his own unit, patrolling, day after day. The lines appeared aimless, meandering, with large or small starbursts to mark encounters with enemy forces. From time to time the line was broken and in the gap was a mark that looked like a flattened figure eight, a literal and metaphorical infinity symbol. These were the places where the unit had been picked up, flown across the intervening terrain in choppers and deposited in a new location to begin new meanders and new encounters. These markings, I came to see, were almost diagrams of his thought process.

―――――

Mark wrote to me almost every night telling me the places he wanted to see on the trip that, by then, was taking shape. There was not a whole lot of negotiation. If I asked *why* he wanted to go to a particular place, he would say it was "important." He wanted to go to so many places, I began to wonder if he were trying to retrace his steps, on some level to relive his entire experience.

He breezily dismissed my concerns about access to the jungle. "It's all right there," he said. I finally realized how deeply he was living in memory. He had not yet come to terms with a country that would be at peace, and a mode of transportation that no longer involved choppers.

―――――

They called it the 'snapshot war,' he said, everyone taking pictures of everyone else. I had seen several of him, including one from early in his first tour, where he and some buddies lounged against the parapet of a bridge, scruffy, shirtless, no doubt the worse for days without bathing. He had adopted a pose designed for an effect of maximum coolness, but he wasn't even the most obnoxious. That was the guy who looked out at the camera insolently and had his thumbs hooked in his low-slung pants. "Frat boys," I began calling them, all of them, not just this little gang, especially after one particularly lively email discussion.

Mark had shown me a photograph that I did not properly appreciate. I was supposed to comment on the tracers coming from the choppers. Tracers are, he instructed me, rare in photographs, so these were notable. Instead, I asked what they were shooting at, as all I could see was a densely-wooded hillside. "Occasionally we got return fire," he said. "Occasionally?! You bombarded a hillside just because you occasionally got return fire? You were blowing things up just to blow things up!" He acknowledged that that was true. "You were acting like frat boys over there!" "Frat boys" became a shorthand for "careless, entitled, unable to have empathy for the suffering of others." That was my definition. He said that was him.

———

He posted a picture of himself, shirtless, holding a pistol with both hands and looking up with a strange, manic smile at something beyond the camera. I asked. He said he had taken the pistol from a wounded NVA in a place they called Ralph's Valley.

The conversation veered into the history of the pistol. Mark thought the wounded man might have taken it from someone else and then Mark took it from him and then two more people at least had it and it was stolen some time in the 70s in Oakland.

"So why were you so interested in this pistol," I asked when, a few weeks later, he posted the photo again. He was regaining his verbal ability, the result of weekly speech therapy at the VA, but he was still communicating through photographs, assuming that the meaning he knew was there would be clear to his viewers.

"LOL, it was mine!"

I wasn't buying that explanation. Something did not fit. I waited.

"Artillery lieutenant, mortally wounded," he said. "Sad to say."

Still I said nothing.

"We looked into each other eyes," he said. "There aren't the words for it. He held his arms up. I held fire. Thank god."

And then, "I never knew his name."

I don't know if they were Hueys, such as Mark described coming into the assault on An Hoa: "twenty-odd Hueys delicately maneuvering their way onto the sand was beautiful—the epitome of the airmobile concept." I only saw a fleet of choppers coming out of the clouds and in from the sea. For a moment I saw it as beautiful, too, and then the beating rotor blades became menacing and I jumped out of the vantage point the director had created for me and into the village, running from the terror approaching from the sky, a terror that, I had no doubt, was part of what some saw as the beauty.

I was making up for lost time, taking remedial courses in "The Vietnam War" so I could share in the common language and I was always going to be playing catch-up unless I watched *Apocalypse Now*.

I could not keep my distance, no matter how many times I reminded myself it was only a movie. I would try little tricks, noticing how much Robert Duvall looked like Robert Duvall and goodness, Marlon Brando, he's still with us? It didn't work. There were the women running from the choppers, the man screaming in the night beyond the perimeter, and the sampan scene—I wanted to throw myself into the screen, shield the family with my body *stopitstopitstopitstopit!* I knew it was not a documentary, but I also knew that it spoke truth.

———

When taking domestic flights in Vietnam, checked luggage must not weigh over forty-four pounds and carry-on luggage no more than fourteen. Plan accordingly, we were warned. Consequently, I became preoccupied with my wardrobe. Mark, however, had other concerns. It turned out he was deathly afraid of flying. He had hung onto the edges of choppers, or had been held on so as not to slip off, but fixed-wing aircraft terrified him. I asked him why, then, he agreed to fly to Vietnam. "It's the only way to get there," he said.

———

We were an assorted group that included three veterans and five civilians. John F. had told me he might not offer his usual chiropractic clinics on our trip because I had asked for something different in my inquiry, but then clinics were what was happening. I did a poor job of defending whatever vision I had had, mostly because I only dimly understood it myself. It soon became clear that we were going on a trip that had been made many times before and had a comfortable and familiar format both for the Americans and our Vietnamese hosts.

John had what I called the gift of "upbeatness," an optimism and excitement that was infectious. His wife joined us for this trip, bringing her gifts as an energy healer and a generous supply of essential oils. One of their friends, a veteran who had become a massage therapist, came as well. They shared a common language of breathy spirituality that meant nothing at all to Mark and in spite of—or perhaps because of—my familiarity with it, quietly annoyed me. There was also my husband, Joe, and Dan, one of his close friends from high school and college, an earnest United Church of Christ minister who had picked up on my invitation immediately and spent much of the trip trying to figure out what to do with it. The three of us had been active in the Y together and had kept up for several years afterwards, and then had, until recently, lost touch. Dan had recruited another friend, for whom he felt some responsibility and with whom he spent most of his time. I was overly watchful of Mark, who managed just fine except in just that moment when he didn't.

For the required group discussions, John brought a stick he had picked up on his land, which we were to hold when it was our turn to speak. Although I was familiar with the "talking stick" practice from Native culture and retreats, I thought it out of place in our context, especially when we were encouraged, over the course of the trip, to decorate it with feathers and rice and such.

The trip followed an itinerary adjusted to the needs of the veterans who were able, on their own "day," to visit sites of importance to them. Mark was the only veteran to be returning for the first time and I watched him closely. In a real sense, his "day" began the moment he stepped off the plane, as sensations and long-buried memories cascaded over him. He barely noticed that his experience was supposed to be scheduled; *everything* had enormous meaning for him.

―――

In addition to visiting sites connected to the war, we brought gifts—cows for "poor farmers," washing machines for orphanages, monetary donations for organizations—and stood for commemorative photos. I had told John that I would prefer to just leave the items on the back porch and go away quietly, but that was not an option. There was always a ceremony of exchange: they got a cow and we got a photograph. The local economy seemed to rely on these gifts, but I was never quite sure what happened to them after we left. What I had wanted —or imagined I could have as a well-meaning American— collided with the mysteries of these encounters, leaving me perpetually uncertain if I had received what I sought, or something else entirely, or even if I had understood the exchange at all.

———

Our heaviest baggage was the stories we came with that both determined what we saw and shaded it. For the most part, we saw what we expected to see, what we were told to see, or what we were guided to see. For the veterans, the visits to war sites, the small ceremonies conducted there, the repeated narrative of forgiveness and the evident welcome of the Vietnamese seemed, in fact, to bring about something, and perhaps it was peace.

The story for the civilians was more ambiguous because, after all, why were we there? We were not veterans, family of veterans, therapists, social workers, or journalists, so why had we come? Because I had not adequately anticipated the need to show a more united front, it was awkwardly determined that we were there to witness the stories of the veterans, the tacit assumption being that the war belonged to those who had fought in it.

———

Mark and I walked along Dong Khoi, which the French had called *rue Catinat* after a warship they had used when taking control of Vietnam. The street name had been a reminder, a place holder—"*rue Catinat,*" it seemed to say, "and we can sail back whenever we choose." In the end the *Catinat* did sail away, along with the French, leaving the street, renamed Tu Do, to become a hotspot of exotic pleasure. The open doors of shops and sit-down restaurants advertising steaks in English breathed memories of the mostly-vanished bars and brothels that had catered to men not old enough to know their desire except to feel it.

A little stand selling trinkets to tourists caught our attention, the owner encouraging us with a knowing smirk. Mark looked for a "hard-core hat," paying no attention to the Zippo lighters, which swam in front of my eyes, conjuring images of Mark's endless cigarettes, heat tabs for his cocoa—double sugar, double cream—and the thatch of the last home in An Hoa. These were fakes, decorated as cheap souvenirs. I dismissed them with a flick of my fingers. I might have bought a real one but then, caught in a web of irony, would not have wanted to keep it. Instead, I wanted a drink at the Caravelle Hotel, just to be able to say that I had had one. I nodded to the owner, who grinned back. He might have lost me, but he was playing the odds.

No longer the black-and-white bastion of journalists who watched the war from the rooftop and beat out their stories on portable typewriters in the rooms below, the Caravelle had morphed into a high-end hotel, with a curved driveway leading to enormous glass doors, uniformed doorkeepers, and hostesses wearing graceful *ao dàis*. Smoothly intersecting spaces flowed from lobby to conversation groupings to bars. It wasn't the atmosphere I had imagined. I appreciated it, but all the sparkle didn't make up for a suppressed disappointment I was hesitant to acknowledge. I wanted a glimpse, just a glimpse, of the world I had only read about. I felt some guilt at this—how could I wish for the violent decadence of wartime Saigon?—but I could not avoid a sense of loss that it had all disappeared while I had been doing other things.

A hostess led us to a round marble table with two upholstered chairs. Mark faced the square with a view out toward the Opera House and the Hotel Continental. I faced the elevators.

A lacquered box of crackers and dried fruit appeared. Mark ordered a Scotch. I veered away from the "B-52," which, under the circumstances, I considered tasteless, and chose a Gimlet, which was hard-boiled enough for the moment.

"God-amighty," Mark said, several times, shaking his head. "Whew!" He kept looking out at the Continental as if he thought it had come to life out of *The Quiet American.*

"You were never in Saigon, were you?" I asked.

"Bien Hoa the first time and Quan Loi the second," he answered. "Never any reason to go to Saigon."

I fingered the stem of my glass. I had read stories about how veterans react when they return to Vietnam the first time, but Mark appeared to be nothing like them.

"Where did you go," I asked, "when we went to the market?" I had looked for him, thinking he might need support, but he had been nowhere to be seen. So we had plunged into the indoor labyrinth, gotten lost among claustrophobic stalls selling fabric or cooking supplies or baskets. I had bought a bag of candied young coconut that the stall owner insisted was just what I wanted and over the next days, on the bus, I would find she was right.

"I walked around. Taking pictures," he said. "I went to the Reunification Palace."

"But you'd never been here before," I exclaimed. "How could you just take off like that?" I expected, I don't know, awe or *gravitas,* but he was unperturbed.

"I'm home," he said and sipped his Scotch.

Meanwhile, just beyond our table, young Vietnamese women dressed in short, tight clothes went into the elevators or emerged from them, most in the company of older and much larger Western men who held their hands or draped an arm over a shoulder. One heavy-set lug, wearing a loose shirt with a tropical print, carried a bouquet of shopping bags and looked down shyly at the tiny young woman by his side.

Evening fell. The lights of the Caravelle sparkled. We walked back to our hotel through a night market, which was alive with people strolling among the open shops. We ate shrimp cooked on smoky, aromatic grills and watched vendors throwing pinwheel lights into the air.

———

None of us questioned the decision to begin our journey at the War Remnants Museum. We might have wished it were otherwise, but the war was why we had come. Difficult as it was to see, what the museum contained was the truth.

We walked through a plaza filled with abandoned American military equipment where I was able, for the first time to get an idea of the size of the various choppers I had read so much about. In a corner of the main-floor lobby some young people were making flower arrangements and figurines out of beads. They greeted us with radiant smiles, hugging John and eyeing the rest of us curiously. With only a brief hesitation, we moved among them, admiring their work, and thanking them for their welcome.

One young man was making a beaded cat. I told him how lovely it was. In a panicked undertone he called for help from his friend seated nearby. The friend knew English and translated while I showed off my miniscule Vietnamese by pronouncing the cat *con meo*.

We were told the group had prepared some songs for us so we gathered around while a young man with a keyboard found the beat he wanted and got them started. Another young man in the front swayed to the music, closed his eyes, and relished the rhythm. The songs were spirited and the young people sang with energy. They behaved like all young people: shy, proud, gracious.

The young man with the keyboard was planning his wedding. He had no eyes, just smooth, unbroken skin where the eyes should have been. The one making the beaded cat tucked the spool under his armpit and pulled the thread through with his teeth. The one swaying to the rhythm had a stunted torso and shortened limbs. He was stationed at the outside of the group greeting people. The crowd had to part so he could join his friends for the singing. He was a bit of a flirt, the way he grinned soulfully at whoever smiled at him.

These were the children of Agent Orange, the defoliant the United States had sprayed on the forests and jungles of Vietnam by the thousands of tons. The chemical was harmless to people and animals—so they said—but it was contaminated with dioxin, one of the most poisonous substances on earth. Contaminated accidentally. So they said.

They also said there was no way to prove a connection between drenching the land and the water with dioxin and the many illnesses of Vietnamese and American soldiers and of their children. The birth defects of the children of American soldiers are bad enough. The birth defects in Vietnam, where the women lived—and still live—on the contaminated land, were—and still are—horrific. The young people we met in the lobby of the museum were functional, charming, and full of life. We had not seen, and would not see, the children whose defects were beyond imagination.

I was uncomfortable with the way we had met them. I did not like them being on display in the lobby of the museum, but this place held what was left of the war. When the United States pulled out we left much ordinance, equipment, and supplies behind. We also left a poison which in the soil has a half-life of more than 100 years. No one treated the young people like circus freaks, however, and they were, certainly, the remnants of war.

In four cities, we arrived at an orphanage or rehabilitation center, were invited into meeting rooms, each place set with a water bottle, and were ceremonially greeted. Then we set up four massage tables and arranged folding chairs in rows. I greeted those who were coming for treatment, many who were still feeling the effects of the "American War." I guided old men to tables or helped move young people crippled by Agent Orange. I put drops of lavender oil onto hands for calming. I knelt, held dusty, calloused feet, and anointed them with oil. The Biblical allusion did not escape me. I touched with the intention to soothe, something I had never thought to be able to do as an American for Vietnamese. The clients, cheerful or wary, eager or fearful, invariably trusted us. Many of them were familiar with John from previous clinics and greeted him warmly. He wore a headband around his brow—it was hot work—and adjusted shoulders and backs. Mark hung on the edges of the rooms, sometimes walking out to a garden or lotus pool, always taking pictures. He longed for Binh Dinh Province, the base of his first tour and a place so familiar he called it "the neighborhood." It was two cities and two clinics before he got his wish.

If Mark had felt at home simply by arriving in Vietnam, on the drive north on Route One he played host, astounding our guide with his detailed knowledge of sites and place names. At LZ English we turned off the highway and stopped at a crossroads. Mark produced a black-and-white photo of himself, a cigarette dangling from his mouth, standing next to his friend Rolf on a dike between rice paddies and there, in front of us, were the very dike and paddies, in full color. We recreated the photo while young people rode by on motorbikes and greeted us. Mark looked at them, almost bewildered, as though he did not understand what they were doing there, happily waving to us. He was seeing double: his memory and the reality in front of him.

A woman in a café at the crossroads had seen us arrive. I had noticed her, wearing the print pajama-like cotton pants and shirt many Vietnamese women wear for daily work. When we walked back toward the bus and she invited us in for refreshments, she had changed into something more formal, let her hair down, and put on earrings. She brought us bottled drinks and we sat and talked about what she remembered and about the ways in which the American government supported the Amerasian kids, the children of American soldiers.

Suddenly Mark got up and walked out. I followed. He could not stay in the present, so he went to look for the past: the ammo dump that had blown up when he was not there. We walked through a little garden of pepper plants climbing conical brick supports and he saw it. With no hesitation, he went up to the house to ask permission to explore. It was just a hill now, behind the house but he knew the hill was made of rubble. On the bus he kept shaking his head in disbelief. The remains of his memories were still there. "It really happened," he said.

Throughout the afternoon he identified the Cay Giep Mountains and recognized Duster Hill, where he had seen the chopper crash, in spite of its growth of vegetation. We climbed a bank to the rebuilt Bong Son Bridge where his bunker named Desolation Row had stood. A conductor came out of his little booth to speak to us and then went back in to retrieve his hat for pictures. Many years before, Mark had observed the landscape so intently that he could now measure distance, spot landmarks, and know where to turn. He loved this country where he had come to fight. He came back to see if it was still there.

Mark deeply wanted to return to An Hoa and An Quang, the site of devastation and horror where doubts had first been sown in him. In this wish he had the support of Anh, our guide, who nevertheless thought the only road, which ran along the east side of the lake, was used by the military and so was closed to civilians. Mark yearned so much to get close that we decided to drive to the west side to be at least within sight. The road got narrower as it approached the shore until we had to stop. Mark took off down a little lane and out onto a dike between rice paddies. It was as close as we could get. Across the lake we saw only quiet houses and trees, making it difficult for the rest of us to imagine Mark's memories. I made a short explanation and we gathered in a circle with joss sticks lit. Mark carried his out to the water as far as he could go and lifted it toward the villages.

He and I walked back slowly, looking at flowers along the way, the others spread out ahead of us, until we heard voices calling us to come. Two former Viet Cong had come out of one of the houses along the path to greet us. The five veterans stood for photos, arms around one another's shoulders. The VC typically fought in their own districts, defending their homes and villages, so it was more than likely that they and Mark would have fought each other. This surprise meeting moved Mark profoundly. He felt a kinship with these men, a bond unlike any other, and rather than harboring hatred or resentment, they seemed to feel the same. To shared laughter Anh translated what they said, "We are glad we weren't better shots."

This meeting marked a shift in Mark. While the other two veterans traveling with us clung to the idea that "the Vietnamese have forgiven us," forgiveness was not a concept that Mark entertained. The way he saw it, he did the job he had come to do, so many years before, and meetings like these with the Vietnamese veterans allowed him to see that the VC and the NVA had done the same. So long ago they had been generic enemy identified only with a slur. Now he felt a kinship with them and admired them. "They were *patriots,*" he began to say.

Mark and I both found the scheduled group sharing times to be forced and, for the most part, not to suit our personalities. In different ways we sensed the ghosts and spirits, the interweavings of an other world understood and shaped differently from our own. During a visit to a noisy orphanage, for instance, we participated in the unsettling ritual of charitable donations. We were given a tour of the building and reached the nursery where half a dozen babies were sleeping or playing in cribs. We were invited, encouraged even, to pick the babies up, which most in our group did. The babies were cooed at, dandled, and admired. Pictures were taken: Americans holding cute Vietnamese babies. Then the babies were put down and we left. I joined the group listening to the chant sung as a thank you for our American generosity—a washing machine and a high-protein meal. Mark, unable to manage even that, went for a walk alone. When he returned he had a beer and photographs of a lonely royal tomb complex he had found down a lane—overgrown terraces and stone sculptures of elephants and guardian warriors, evocative remnants of a long-ago people. I was jealous of the stolen moments away from the ceremony, time alone in which he could sense the ghosts.

We sat on a veranda on the shore of the South China Sea, which the Vietnamese call the East Sea, the waves making a soothing, rhythmic pulse in front of us, going through Mark's photographs on my laptop. One photograph at a time we let the war reappear. We reached a picture I found particularly disturbing: a young Mark faced the camera, a cigarette in one hand and, in the other, a stick with a skull on top. The photograph had been taken after Mark had exhumed the grave and been given the nickname North Carolina Vulture. I had seen this photograph many times before and each time my visceral response was revulsion.

"Tell me about this," I said.

Mark chuckled. I bridled. I did not know what his chuckle meant and sometimes I just did not know what to say or think. I had long since accepted that war was a different country, a place where what I found unacceptable was, if not approved, at least tolerated. In that peaceful place, though, listening to the waves of the sea, I could not accept an image like that on any grounds.

"Why are you laughing?" I asked. I couldn't be angry. I wanted to be, but I wanted the answer first.

He shrugged it off. "It is the truth," he said.

That could have meant anything: that the photo was an accurate depiction of what happened that day, or an all-too-common incident in war, or a glimpse of the mood or attitude of the soldiers. But it was not so much the skull on the stick that bothered me. It was the expression on Mark's face, which was not the face of the boy I had known in high school. That Mark had been funny, goofy, curious, intelligent. The Mark in the photograph smirked, insolent, brandishing a trophy. I did not understand it and I refused to accept it yet, at the same time, I knew it would not help anything to be horrified.

I circled his face on the monitor with my finger. "Tell me about *that*," I said.

I waited for his answer. He waited, too, until the right words came.

"We all live in the thin veneer of civilization," he said. "Soldiers—on both sides—know what it is to slip beneath."

―――

A brightly-painted shrine, called a spirit house, hung on a wall, what I saw as charm and whimsy seemingly at odds with its purpose to honor and appease the dead of that place. A very different spirit house had hung in a side yard somewhere in the Central Highlands. I had seen that one when we had threaded our way behind some kind of machine shop to find a barely-enclosed toilet, meaning what we had called in Europe a "hole in the ground." That spirit house had been surrounded by litter and rusted metal and had been worn and battered. At first I had thought it had been discarded but then I had seen flowers inside and two ceramic candle holders in front. Each house told a different story about Vietnam. There was the bright story of energy and optimism but there was also the story of poverty and struggle within the detritus of industrialization. Neither represented the "real" Vietnam, the one Americans, weary of the confusion and alienation we associate with "Vietnam" want it to come down to. We want an end to the story, one that we can enjoy in our lifetimes. I could not enjoy the folkart quality of the second spirit house, without holding it together with the poignancy of the first.

On so many occasions there were what seemed to be contradictory messages, all of which had to be held in mind. The pleasing proportions, the tended gardens, the color and light of the Celestial Lady Pagoda in Hue conveyed the harmony of human-made creation within the natural environment, and the tranquility of a life spent in meditation. In an open shelter beside the walkway through the gardens, however, sat a robin's egg blue Austin, the very car in which the Buddhist monk Thich Quang Duc had traveled from the An Quang Pagoda in Saigon to a busy intersection where, in 1963, in protest against the government's treatment of Buddhists, he had set himself on fire. Someone had driven that car from Saigon to Hue, a distance of over 900 kilometers, where it had been set in the shelter—like a holy image in a niche—with a sign in front written in both Vietnamese and English. Malcom Browne's famous photograph of the monk engulfed in flames hung on the back wall. The sight of the car jarred loose the memory of the event, the horror of the act, and the discipline required to endure it. It was all of a piece somehow, fully coherent and yet mysterious to me. Understanding eluded me.

At My Lai I asked.

The village was the site of a horrifying massacre of civilians by American soldiers who had, for reasons they could not later explain, dropped beneath the thin veneer of civilization into a state of utmost depravity. The destroyed village had been consolidated as a memorial, its pathways paved in concrete imprinted with chaotic footprints, both barefoot and booted. Mark and I walked in silence. He stopped at mannequins of dead farm animals, smashed cooking pots, and thatched roofs. I remembered what he had seen at An Hoa and An Quang and thought he must be remembering also. Shaken and filled with grief, we joined the group to walk to a neighboring house where we were to meet with a survivor of the massacre. Shot through the hip, this lady had lain hidden under the bodies of her family members and friends. When she regained consciousness she had crawled out and was found. She continued to live close by in a small house where, with her son and two daughters, she received visitors from all over the world. It is said she thought she survived to help heal soldiers, especially American soldiers. I asked my question.

"I want to know," I said to our interpreter, "how does she do it? How does she stay serene and welcoming? What does she do with her memories?"

The question was presumptuous but it was the only thought I could entertain, the only speech I could tolerate. There was a pause. John, perhaps unable to endure the silence, spoke for her and the moment was gone. Everyone smiled. Many pictures were taken. Perhaps she would not have answered and I would have accepted that. She had answered the question for herself, in her own life; I would have to answer it for mine.

Back on the bus Mark stared out the window, watching the village slip away behind us. Suddenly he turned to me and said fiercely, "Do you wonder why I am always tired?"

———

On the old Route One outside of Quang Tri City Mark found the place where he had been dropped into the Tet Offensive, where there had been explosions from one horizon to the other. At La Vang, the Christian pilgrimage site where he had been stationed over the next two weeks and where his unit was later overrun, we walked in the relentless sun. The avenue of sculptures he had seen from above depicted the life of Christ, but their harsh, anguished forms bore witness to the years of war that had surged around them. I took Mark's picture at the grove of trees that had been the CP. I wanted to walk in the direction his unit had taken that day, thinking we would somehow know where to go, as though the remains of that firefight still clung to the soil, but a fence blocked the way. We lit a joss stick in their memory and stuck it into the sand of a massive urn that stood on the steps of the outdoor altar.

Wilted by heat that Mark hardly seemed to notice, I took shelter on a bench in a bit of shade. A nun in a pale blue habit and headscarf came and sat beside me. She had a gentle face and looked to be about my age. Nodding to Mark she asked who we were. "He fought here," I said, "long ago." She persisted, her eyes soft with compassion. "We have been friends a long time," I said, hoping to fend off any confusion. She said, "I think he is your brother."

We set up our tables and supplies in a sunny front room of Friendship Village in Hanoi, a rehabilitation center founded by an American veteran. Vietnamese veterans gathered along the wall awaiting their turn. They were gentle men, courteous, willing, even courtly. One by one I invited them to sit in a chair and bowed to them, a greeting they returned. I took their hands one at a time and rubbed lavender oil into each palm. I rubbed my own hands together and invited them to do the same. I held my palms in front of my face and breathed. They mimicked me, usually gasping a bit with the effort to please. I mimed breathing slowly and deeply. The lavender was meant to calm the nervous system and maybe it worked. What worked for both of us was my hands on their hands.

Sometimes they showed me where it hurt. Usually it was

their neck and shoulders, sometimes the lower back. I traced the line they showed me and reassured them that I would tell the *bác sĩ*, the doctor. Sometimes when I opened their palms for the oil they clutched my hand and squeezed it. I looked into their eyes.

Then I took a different oil blend and knelt in front of them. My knees protested. I was as old as they were and feeling it. But I knelt on one knee and took their feet. Usually they wore plastic scuffs, which they kicked off as soon as they understood what was happening. I traced a line of oil along the sole of the foot once, twice, three times. The foot was usually dusty, sometimes calloused. I wished I had warm water but what I had was oil and my own hands. I traced the lines and then I held the foot for a moment, saying a wordless prayer.

From my station they moved to the chiropractic table. I gestured for them to lie face down so that John could do what he could in a few minutes' time to realign vertebrae, unknot muscles, and ease aches. We all saw old bullet wounds or the tracks of shrapnel: their backs had been exposed before, when they were crawling through the jungle.

John always asked them, through our interpreter Anh, where they had served. There was excitement when it was discovered the first man had fought at Quang Tri.

"Mark!" John called. "Quang Tri!"

Mark came over. I gestured to him as I looked at the man and said, "Quang Tri!"

They understood. They looked at each other with wonder and delight. They wanted a picture taken, their arms around one another. Then that man moved to the table and when we asked the next one where he had served, it was again Quang Tri. Again Mark was summoned. Again the recognition, the arms around shoulders, the pictures. I returned to work bowing and anointing hands and feet. Around me I heard the questions. Again I heard, "Quang Tri." It became almost an incantation.

Mark was at Quang Tri only a short time before he left and his unit was overrun. Some of the men here today for treatment fought later, in 1972 or 1973, but for others the years had overlapped.

I spoke quietly to Mark. "It is hard," I said, "not to think about who might have been where on which day."

He waved it away with resignation and acceptance. There was no point in thinking that way. The dead were dead. The veterans had all suffered and on that day they were meeting in friendship. I held the next pair of feet in my hands, praying for the man's children, my children, the next generations.

There was a lightness to these men. They joked, they brought newspapers to show us, they greeted, they posed for pictures. It was all natural to them, as though they had been expecting us, as though this were the way you finish war, with arms around shoulders.

Was it really over for them, I wondered? Were they some different kind of creature? Did they all have a ceremony some time and decide just to let bygones be bygones? Did I understand or miss what was happening entirely?

―――

We left the bus in a dusty lot outside the gates of the village and walked along a path beside a stream that widened from time to time into pools reflecting the roofs and trees. The homes had their own distinct spaces and yet they interlocked in a tightly-woven pattern. As with so much in Vietnam, the partially-screened houses and balconies, the layered trees, and the curve of the paths simultaneously lured and concealed through a process of attraction and misdirection.

We had come as the guests of a young art student from

Hanoi. John knew her somehow and called her 'niece.' "Everyone is family in Vietnam," he said. The young woman's grandfather was a Viet Minh veteran who had served at Diên Biên Phú and had known General Giap. She said she could sit all day listening to her grandfather's stories, he held so much of their history. This would be a special experience, we were assured, an extraordinary opportunity. I quickened my pace to keep up with the young woman, who was anticipating her visit with her family. The lovely vistas of this village were tempting, though, and some of our group dawdled, taking pictures.

We met a man and stopped to chat. The occasional motorbike passed. We turned into a lane of one-story houses and then into a courtyard surrounded by small buildings and sheds. The family emerged to invite us inside. The veteran was a small man with a smile that lit up the room. Others of his family appeared. Extra chairs were brought and set alongside carved wooden furniture. Coffee and tea were offered.

John sat on the sofa and introduced everyone. I accepted some tea and, adopting an expectant expression, waited for the rhythm to shift to the storytelling. I knew only a little about that time period and wanted to listen to whatever the old veteran had to say. The ceremony took a different turn, however. There was the lengthy presentation of a gift to the veteran. It was the stick we had used in our required talking circles and each of its adornments was being explained. The speech became an end in itself and left no opening for questions. Plates of sliced fruit were passed. Neighbor children appeared and distracted some of the group with their friendliness and accessibility. My mind wandered.

I watched the women. The mother needed the daughter to help with something on her cell phone. Freed from the responsibility of being the center of attention, the two conferred in a way I understood, the mother happy to have her daughter home for a conversation of any kind. They stood in a doorway, the mother wearing a black skirt and a blouse with a high neck and a vining pattern in silver, the daughter in a colorful striped tunic. The grandmother, the veteran's wife sat in front of them, at ease, almost in command, one foot bent up on the chair she sat on, an arm resting on her knee. She gazed up toward the corner of the room, her eyes and mouth narrowed.

    I got up and went to a lovely piece of furniture with a case that held mementos, including an identity card with a picture of the veteran as a young man. I sensed a long, bitter, and proud history pulsing up from these objects that were kept in reverence in the center of the house. When I looked back, photographs were being taken, for some purpose I did not know. As usual, Americans put their arms around the shoulders of the Vietnamese and leaned into the camera, smiling.

    We drifted outside, said our goodbyes, and moved toward the lane. I glanced back at the grandmother, who had already turned away. We met no one on the path. At the village gate we gazed across a small pond toward a community center, like theater-goers admiring the architecture after the play is over. We were silent in the bus back to Hanoi.

    That night, a nightmare exploded my sleep. I was at the same time both inside and outside a village that had been caught in war and was the site not so much of violence as of madness. Someone with a sing-song voice was telling me to watch my step and not mind the mess. Things appeared before me that felt out of place or were missing parts. The more I looked, the more the voice told me, "It's all right now, everything is fine now, keep moving." I tried and tried to scream and finally did, sitting straight up before I was awake, my husband trying to soothe me.

    In the morning the dream shrouded me. I went down early to breakfast but the dining room was full of Laotian businessmen smoking, so I sat on a bench in the lobby. The first person down from our group was the gentle Anh who sat with me while I explained my dream.

"It's not enough, what we are doing, Anh," I said. "We come here carrying the burden of memory and wanting you and your people to take it from us." It wasn't Anh's job to make me feel better either, but he was the one that was there. "Either we are forever scarred by that damned war," I said, "or we need to learn from you how to heal. And I don't think we even understand what it means."

"Forgiveness is a simple thing," Anh said. "It happens because it is too hard to do anything else."

Images flew through my mind: Anh's infectious laugh, his love for his children who were with us much of the trip, the way he called his wife "my lady," his tireless devotion to solving every problem that arose, his defense of Mark's need to find a place in Anh's country where Mark had participated in senseless violence, the support he gave to those who had wrecked havoc on his land and to those who came here wanting Vietnamese to grant absolution. Somehow Anh had reached a place of peace, of vibrant life. He seemed to me, in that moment, to inhabit the world I strove for, a world that transcends war.

But I had seen the repeated acts of Lady Bountiful gift-giving and, notwithstanding the help I knew it provided, had increasingly found it almost insulting. No matter how needed the cow or the washing machine was, I could not help thinking what a paltry return this was for all the damage we had done and how false the display rang to me because of it. We had our pictures, arms draped in an overly-familiar manner on Vietnamese shoulders, and I could not escape the feeling that we were skipping the hard part, and jumping on through to a happy ending I did not feel.

Anh waited for my response.

"I can't, Anh," I said. "Not yet."

It was too soon. I had made this trip not knowing what I had wanted and now I did not know if I had gotten it. More than that, though, I was still clawing my way back from a nightmare that had taken me beneath the thin veneer in which all is forgiven and dropped me into a place where those whose memories I had not even begun to understand smiled for American cameras.

46

Looking for Answers

I HEARD A STORY ABOUT AN INFANTRYMAN WHO HAD THE USUAL infantryman's experience, was wounded, sent home, made a life for himself as best he could and then, suddenly, began going to reunions, writing long emails to other veterans, and posting to Facebook groups. When I asked one of his friends why he thought this had happened he shrugged and said, "Looking for answers."

So was Mark when he wrote and wrote in the 1970s, typing on whatever paper was available, wrote to say what he had seen, so that people would know. But the writing had no audience and life took him into the career in journalism he had always been suited for. He was still looking for answers when he came for a visit and walked through the door carrying an armload of yellowing files in battered manila folders and put them into my arms.

"What do you want me to do with these?" I asked, alarmed.

"I want you," he said, "to make some sense of them."

Because in life we can't see around the next bend in the path we are on, I took the files. I am an editor, I thought. I will edit them. It felt like the logical next step in a series of next steps I had already agreed to. It also felt like the ultimate sign of trust. I was honored. Mark had held onto those files for decades and now he had given them to me. To edit them would mean bringing our project to a logical conclusion and now, having walked at least part of the path with him, I felt qualified to accomplish it. Once again I did not realize where that path was taking me.

The folders held writing I hadn't known existed: short vignettes of his first tour, each written separately, like a newspaper column or feature article. There were no page numbers and only an accidental order to the sheets in the folders. I scanned the files, deleted the graphics the OCR program created and corrected all the little symbols it threw in when it could not make out the print. Coping with the physicality of the files gave me a way to begin, a way to acclimate. I liked the feel of the paper, the crinkle it made, the effects of age.

I began to put the files in chronological order, easy to do when there was a date on the page but there was still confusion and repetition. Mark had been constantly moving around from one place to another in helicopters and coming back to the same place but at a different time. I grew acquainted with the names and could notice if something appeared to be out of order. I needed lengthy explanations of things that seemed obvious to Mark. He had handed me his files; he was also trying to hand me his memories.

We had to sort out names. All the names in the original files were pseudonyms, including his own. His character was an alter-ego named Geoffrey Speck. "Geoffrey" because Mark liked the name and "Speck" …, well a speck, you know. Just a speck ….

I did not like Geoffrey at first. I wanted him out of the way, but then I grew fond of him. I could see his purpose. "Geoffrey" had given Mark the distance he had needed to tell the story. Nevertheless, in order to make his writing about the first tour more consistent with the second, which was already different enough, we decided to take him out. Then we decided to be true to the original writing and we put him back in. Then, finally, we took him out. Each time, I went through all the files, changing the names and the pronouns and making nouns and verbs agree. I fell into the familiar editor's role: cleaning up and organizing, deciding which vignettes to include and which to leave out, looking for segues, clarifying dates, and asking endless questions.

Those were the mechanics of the job. The real work was in taking it all in, letting it activate my all-too-vivid imagination. I did this not just as an editor but as a person, as an anti-war activist, and as a woman. The story engaged my humanity, so the going seemed slow. I could edit an academic paper quickly, scouring it for incorrect grammar, extra words, and organization, like a mechanical harvester. This work was different. Beyond the expected challenges of confronting the senseless violence, the twisting of values, and the relentless stress, I felt this story changing me. Gradually, I gained the autonomy I was going to need if I had any chance of making some sense of the story, as Mark had asked me to do, rather than simply telling it. From time to time I resisted the entire project, took a mental health break, or allowed myself to be distracted, but I always came back.

At first I idealistically believed that if people just knew the truth about war, war would stop. That was why I was playing a part in this project, after all: to make one small contribution to *stopping war!* The more I read, though, or asked Mark questions, or sat with him over a glass of wine, the more I had to accept war's attraction to young men and the bitterness that drives old men to exploit them. The problem of war began to seem intractable to me. The only thing that kept me going was my belief in the power of storytelling and my conviction that in spite of the thousands of memoirs, historical accounts, analyses, movies, and music, there was still more to say about the war in Vietnam.

———

I began to wonder about the purpose of war stories. Mark considered himself a witness, the man behind the camera. He was also the man behind the gun, but even then he had been a faithful witness to his own experience. As faithful as any of us can be, in any case. I had long considered any story to be worth telling, but I was deeply skeptical of war stories, wondering at what point readers of war stories—or viewers of war movies—become voyeurs, getting a vicarious thrill out of the violence, knowing it is temporary and will end when the lights come up. Or how often the authors of these stories, consciously or unconsciously, turn their experience into a soundbite: *horror! glory! sacrifice!* Or in what ways, conscious or unconscious, war stories conform to the stereotypes held by readers or viewers who were never in a war but think they know what makes a war story "realistic."

There was no agenda to Mark's writing, though. He did not spin the story in any way and he stubbornly refused to resolve his experience, not for me, not for anyone. I occasionally yearned for the kind of redemption that would reassure me that my time was being well spent. It was not there. There was only the truth, in all its ambiguity, complexity, and mystery.

———

The work affected our relationship. We bonded over the war—it is impossible to hear another person's story and not create a bond—but rifts appeared. They primarily concerned two stand-by and unhealed coping strategies in war: drinking and sex.

Years earlier, Mark's health problems had prompted him to give up smoking and Scotch. Over the course of our project, though, his wine consumption became noticeably heavier and he went back to Scotch. At first he just ordered a Scotch in a restaurant as a celebration, but then he started buying a whole bottle or bringing one with him to drink in his room. I began to blame myself, or blamed the memories I was stirring up, and tried to talk about it. He would not discuss it, and continued to consume more in an evening than my husband and me combined. When he drank he became maudlin. At first I didn't see the connection and thought he "needed to talk." Then I realized the talk never changed, so I drew a boundary. The boundary continually fluctuated but at least I knew it was there.

Mark's attitude toward women was more difficult to avoid and hit closer to home. Women did not play a large role in his story but when they appeared it was as far-away, idealized girl-friends or available, often desperate, prostitutes. As his sexual experience, learned in wartime conditions, increased, he began to confuse the two, fantasizing about the girlfriends based on the behavior of the prostitutes. War and sex, weapons and women, all intertwined and all mixed up in a brain not yet fully formed, the excitement of war confused with the excitement of sex, the one mimicking the other. It was a story as old as war itself and I hated it. He acknowledged my anger but he did not disavow his attitude.

From the beginning I had naively assumed the excitement he had told me he missed was the adrenalin rush of combat. That was what he had talked about in the documentary, but it turned out actual combat was only part of it. He also missed the almost limitless power that he spoke about in the section of his writing called "The Return." He missed that he could impress Marines by calling in helicopters at will. And he missed the easy access to women, an access he still had in the hedonism he had thrown himself into on his return. He never reconsidered it and the signs of it, when they appeared, made me uncomfortable. In many ways, the experience of war, at such a critical time, had frozen parts of his personality in adolescence and kept him blissfully unaware that the world had changed and that his overtures to young women were no longer appropriate, if they ever had been.

———

In spite of the challenges, we pressed on, trying to wrestle the past into some kind of détente with the present. I watched for recurring topics so as to learn where there might be controlling events that were outside the written text I had. All the while I was careful not to assume there was anything at all beyond what he told me. Once I asked him. "I am telling you the truth," he said, and I believed him.

Still, there was "The Month Everybody Got Shot," the account of a pivotal few weeks that had happened in the first part of his second tour. He had not included this month in the text that became "The War in the Jungle" so I had to piece it together as best I could from letters, diary entries, and transcriptions of his answers to my questions, knowing all the while that understanding that month involved more than the sequence of events. What had happened then could only be shared with those who had lived through it and especially one man, his platoon leader, Marvin Hasenak.

> I ran wild in February and early March 1969. We had a lot of contact, a lot of guys were wounded and killed, and I threw myself into it. My platoon leader [Hasenak] at that time, a draftee, no less, was as loony as I was, and we were

probably a dangerous pair to be around. Some of the things he would do (and I would do with him) would turn most GIs' hair white, but we were having a ball, dancing with Mr. D and taking our chances. He was wounded in the chin and lower arm late in February (he had the presence of mind to have one of the guys use his camera to snap a photo of him waiting for medevac—in Vietnam terms, he was a very cool dude!) and that was my guide to being a platoon leader.

I became friends with Marvin and his wife Sharon, who he called Red. They lived where Marvin had grown up, in West Texas, a landscape and culture utterly foreign to me. Marvin sent me stories about Texas rural life and recipes for traditional food. I consulted him on matters of tamales, chili, and chicken fried steak. I did not know his opinion of Mark's description of him and I did not ask. Watching him and Mark together I could believe that they had been quite the pair.

Marvin told me they had taken chances so the men would not have to. Mark, on the other hand, had reveled in it. At the same time, so many died or were wounded around him, apparently randomly and without touching him, that it began to affect with his mind. In many ways he was still a kid, playing a grim game of catch-me-if-you-can with Death, the almost embodied opponent he called "Mr. D." He had wanted to experience war, to know what it meant to be shot at. The logical conclusion of that game is the one he tempted. It was wild and exhilarating and in a way he never lost, he loved it.

Even for Mark, though, this month eluded description, which is why he had not written about it at the time. Both Marvin and Mark wanted me to *know* about that month and they both worked to ensure it was represented in the book, but there, if nowhere else, it was simply true that, as someone who had not been there with them, I would never understand.

From time to time there were lulls in our progress, sometimes long ones. I had other projects on my desk and this one had long since left the world in which I was just brushing up an existing manuscript and sending it out. Mark had given me thousands of words in different forms: rough manuscripts, diary entries, letters, and email answers to my endless questions. It demanded more of me than I had expected and much more than I had bargained for.

At the same time I felt myself searching for something I knew was there but could not identify, something just outside my field of vision. The feeling was not unlike what had happened when I was watching the film reports from the war, but this time I was looking for something less tangible, more mysterious, as old as war itself.

47

Ghosts

IN 2016 WE WENT BACK TO VIETNAM, WITH A GROUP I organized. By that time I had learned enough to feel confident, which is to say I knew people who knew people and everyone helped. John F. was more than generous, as was Anh, who put me in touch with Kien, a friend and fellow guide in Hanoi. I got past the stress of sending many thousands of dollars through the ether to someone in Vietnam I had never met and enjoyed the process of planning and introducing new people to the country I loved. Our group included Mike, a Marine who had served in two locations very close to where Mark had served but whose primary purpose in going to Vietnam now was to study the effects of climate change. There was also Chuck, who I had known for many years and with whom I had enjoyed rich conversations engaging the problem of forgiveness. He also had a professional interest in rising sea levels. The group I called Team Climate Change was rounded out by Edmund, a former graduate student at Cornell, now living and working in his home country of Malaysia. There was also Kip, a professional photographer whose keen eye helped us to see more intently; Debbie, a woman whose boundless curiosity stimulated our own; and Mark. We were a diverse group but we shared a sense of humor, a willingness to learn, and an openness to Vietnam.

In his welcome, Hai, the guide who traveled with us, repeated what I had so often heard, that the young people don't want to dwell on the war. "The war was bad," he said, "and both sides lost. Now was the time to be friends, for welcome and enjoyment." He looked at both of our veterans, touched his heart, and said what an honor it was for him to travel with them and help them find the places they had been. At the same time, we who traveled together were not the younger generation. We could not so easily jettison the baggage we carried.

Our bus stopped an hour out of Can Tho, somewhere along the old Route One in the Mekong Delta. Team Climate Change was in meetings at the university so Kip, Debbie and I were on a field trip. Mark had stayed behind at the hotel. Motor scooters appeared, summoned by a call from Hai's iPhone. We settled ourselves on the backs of the scooters, and were instructed how to do *xe om*—the "hug ride"—and then we were sailing along a path into a village completely hidden from the highway. Along the way I saw egrets in the stream, by ones and twos, but as we walked across an arched concrete bridge there were many more in the trees. And then I heard them—a chittering that came from everywhere. Like gossamer scarves they rose and settled above us in the treetops, fretting and fussing.

A tightly wound metal circular staircase led to an observation deck where we looked out on hundreds of egrets, as well as a sizeable cohort of night herons. The story was that they had started to come here when the people threw rice husks out for the few that were there and the others came for the safety to raise families, some of whom we saw being tended in the trees. The village took pride in the project and helped with the gift of land. We met the family who lived among all this activity, guardian angels of the trees and birds. They had invoked the help of the gods by building a shrine oriented in the *feng shui* direction to bring luck and protection to their creatures.

I sat in a thatched shelter among these birds and looked out of the dense trees to an expanse of rice paddies beyond, and then another stand of trees. Enveloped in teeming natural life, I understood, perhaps for the first time, what had been the personal geography of war, the sensory experience one person might have had in this space. My too-keen imagination imagined all too well what might have happened here, in another time.

We rode our scooters only part way back so as to walk through the village. Hai stopped at a house and asked permission for us to come in for a visit. We met the woman of the house, a beautiful lady of 77, and her sister, daughter-in-law and shy, eager grandson. They took us to their front room where their altar stood. While we chatted, the daughter-in-law brought in a joss stick, lit it, and put it in the urn on the altar.

The woman said she had retired now because her knee and her ankle were giving her trouble. I put my hand where she showed me, memories of the clinics I had been a part of on my last trip flooding back to me, with time only for the most fragmentary prayer for healing. She said we had to come back and visit her but we should come back soon because she did not think she could live for ten years.

While we were saying our goodbys she went to the side of the altar, produced a plate of boiled bananas, and offered them to each of us. We took them, sensing a sacrament, and bowed and smiled our way back across her little bridge.

On the path, Hai told us the bananas were an offering for

her dead husband. Giving them to us meant we had been blessed, we, our journey, and our families. Of course, I revelled in the blessing, honored by its gift, but I was thinking about the joss stick. They lit it because we had arrived, Americans, coming not across the rice paddies, but by *xe om*.

―――――

Mark and I were again at the Caravelle for a drink but this time we were on the roof. It was not hard to imagine what it might have been like, looking out toward the horizon and the war but I had little time for reverie. We had come to meet a friend, a Vietnamese woman we had met three years before, the daughter of a grizzled NVA veteran who had played songs for us in 2013 at the War Remnants Museum. He still had his guitar from those days and had sung the old songs that had kept up the spirits of the soldiers on the Ho Chi Minh Trail, songs about home and sweethearts. One of them had been funny. Then, as a special gift to us, this man and his daughter had sung "Where Have All the Flowers Gone?" There were tears in the room, just as there had been when he had seen a musician in a previous group play it and so had set out to learn it. The fact that he had no English had not stopped him. His accent was heavy and the rhythm was a little off, but no matter. The gift was profound. We wept for the time that had passed, the opportunities wasted, the soldiers—on both sides—gone to graveyards.

Since our last visit our friend had married an American veteran who had left his life in the States to live where he wanted, and how he wanted, and to make this woman his wife and Vietnam his home. They were building a house and they brought out the plans. She showed us the spaces, designated and yet flowing in the Vietnamese way. There would be a wing for her father and a conservatory for the butterflies the man raised.

I looked out across the cityscape below us, my mind carrying me west into the wilds beyond the Caravelle, beyond the city, beyond Saigon. A breeze softened the heat of the day; waiters brought our drinks.

"There were butterflies at LZ Illini," Mark said suddenly, "April 1967. Maybe one or two acres of them."

Someone should have taken notice of that, I thought, not waited until the war was over to mention it.

The man expressed surprise. No one he had asked since the war had seen butterflies, even those who had become entomologists. Or if they had seen them, they had taken no notice, not like the mosquitoes and scorpions and venomous snakes. Those they remembered.

Had butterflies been uncounted casualties of the war, I wondered? Or had they occupied some kind of space pocket, coexisting and untouched by the mayhem around them?

―――

Vietnam had created a thriving industry of leading groups of Americans looking for solace, or forgiveness, or closure. The industry employed not just guides, but all the standard support services—restaurants, hotels, bus companies, travel agencies, and so on. That was a lot of Vietnamese and, at least from what I saw, they did it without cynicism or bitterness. All the guides I knew were open-hearted, generous, constantly cheerful, and utterly devoted not just to the welfare of the group but to ensuring that we could get where we wanted to go. Very often those trips involved veterans finding places that aroused memories of trauma, so in addition to being a source of information about Vietnam's economy or politics or the finer points of rice-growing, the guides had to be prepared for whatever the sites aroused in their guests.

Hai was no exception to this. I had planned the trip over the phone with Kien, who we did not meet until we reached Hanoi, but Hai met us in Saigon to travel with us. He had sent me his picture before we left and told me that he was taller than most Vietnamese so I would be able to find him easily at the airport. This turned out to be true—I just looked over the heads of the crowd at Tân Sơn Nhất and there he was. He had the muscular frame and buzz cut of the West Point cadets who, he told us, he often led on trips to military sites. He had a strong voice that he frequently amplified on the bus with a microphone, forgetting that we were only seven people. He repeated directions, often multiple times, in case in the interim we had begun to come up with a different plan. In fairness, that sometimes happened. Once at a roadside restaurant half the group became intrigued with the house next door and went off to investigate. Alarmed, Hai headed after them like an overworked border collie to bring them back. Every morning on the bus he instructed us to make sure we had all our belongings until I grew impatient with being treated like a high school group on a field trip and then it was me that left my iPad in the hotel room and Hai had to make calls and the iPad was found and brought to our first stop by the next bus to leave the hotel.

Hai's job was to make sure our trip went as smoothly as possible. That meant that most of the opportunities for disaster that tend to happen during travel did not happen to us. We did not have to cope with lost reservations, or find safe places to eat, or put up with sub-standard hotels. It also meant our experience was choreographed, most of the darker side of Vietnamese life shielded from us. Our individual opportunities to get lost, or run afoul of something, or otherwise get into trouble were minimized but our chances for unscheduled adventure were minimized as well.

Hai made stops that I had not expected but also did not resist. The experience was not entirely under my control, nor did I want it to be. On Route One, in the bad stretch of road the French had called *La Rue Sans Joie,* "The Street Without Joy,"—and the Americans, with good reason, had kept the name—he had us stop by the roadside to light joss sticks that we left burning in the sandy ground to honor the dead. In Quang Tri City we climbed the steep steps of a monument with him to pay homage to those who had died defending The Citadel.

———

North of Quang Tri, close to the former DMZ, at Vinh Muoc, we visited one of many underground tunnel complexes scattered throughout the country. These tunnels, hiding only soldiers, or, as here, large enough for families, were critical to the war and in thinking about them here I gained an insight into the cultural encounter that our country had never learned to navigate.

The path through the park was a rough pavement of stones and cement, wide enough for two people to walk side-by-side, and easily visible between stretches of grass. We walked obediently, stopping occasionally to hear information and then continuing to walk. Our guide pointed out the bomb craters, which still remained and some of which were labeled, and the entrances to the tunnels that had provided shelter from the relentless bombardment from American ships off-shore.

These were no ordinary tunnels. Accessed through entrances hidden in little hills and protected by stone vaults, they were like a small town, with separate areas for living and cooking and storing supplies. There was a hospital, a maternity ward, and a nursery for the babies born there. There were multiple entrances and an elaborate ventilation system. The tunnels were brilliantly conceived and tunnels like these (although not all had facilities for families) existed all over Vietnam, including under American bases. It was all very Vietnamese and so not-American that it had baffled and foiled our military.

I hung back a little, watching. I began to observe that everyone stumbled, just slightly, from time to time. They wavered on an unexpectedly low surface or their shoes would catch on one that was unexpectedly high. It wasn't much, nothing dangerous, but on a subtle level it kept us a little insecure. The Vietnamese had constantly baffled American forces by appearing from nowhere, attacking, and disappearing, fading back into the landscape, which they knew far better than we did. Like this walkway, the strategy kept everything a little off balance. Our feet, accustomed to uniformity, had difficulty adjusting to the organic form of the pavement, which had been built with the materials at hand. What else did they have, after all, to combat American war ships?

―――――

From early on in my discussions about our itinerary, I had emphasized the importance of getting to the villages of An Hoa and An Quang. I was determined that it would work. Perhaps if we started early enough and asked formal permission we would be allowed to go there and pay tribute. I was willing to do my part to achieve this, although I was aware that the way things got done in Vietnam was your guide got on the phone. As a bonus, we had Hai who was like a dog on a bone when he set his mind on something, and that day he had set his mind on getting us to those villages. Beaming in triumph, he announced that there was a new road around the lake and that we could get there. It turned out that "getting there" meant following a narrow lane that ran around the southern end of the lake, called the Dam Tra-O, a name I found lilting and vaguely Irish but learned was of Cham heritage.

As usual, we were well into the trip before I began to wonder what I had gotten us into. We clung to the shoreline, took a wrong turn, had to back out, and stopped several times to confirm that we were headed in the right direction. At such times, I had learned to yield to the skills of the bus drivers, which were considerable, and trust that the little bus, which was still, after all, a bus and not meant for this road, was not going to tumble into the water.

Beyond being determined to get there, I did not know what to expect in the villages and I was apprehensive. As John F. had done on the last trip, I called this "Mark's day" because these were his sites, the places he had been and needed to go back to. As we got closer, though, I realized this was as much my day as his. The story of these villages had been profound for me. The horror of his story, coming so soon after I had begun talking to him, and disturbed me so much I had consulted John F. about it. He told me that by giving the story to me Mark only wanted to take one of the rocks out of the heavy pack he had been carrying all these years. Those villages represented a heavy emotional weight for both of us. The last I knew about them, at the end of Mark's account, they had been utterly destroyed, a scar on the landscape months later when he had flown over them. If I expected anything it was perhaps something like what I had seen in Gaza: pockmarked walls and broken masonry. On our last trip, when we had gotten only as far as a dike into the lake from the far shore, Mark had said he had seen them – "oh yes, they were there" – but I wasn't sure I believed him. How could they have been visible if they had been so utterly destroyed? There would, I hoped, have been rebuilding in the intervening years, but I expected the ghosts to be there, if only because they haunted me.

So I was stunned into disorienting wonder to find the

villages not only rebuilt, but thriving and vibrant with color. We drove in under lush trees, along little lanes with neat houses surrounded by walls covered in foliage and flowers. There were gates and courtyards and people out, answering Hai's questions. I would have gotten out and walked, just to rejoice in the ways life returns, in what *happens*, but as nowhere else in Vietnam I was overcome by awe, mixed with an awkward shyness and embarrassment. My countrymen had destroyed these villages, destroyed them utterly and killed their people. Whereas in all the other places we had been, where I had been able to relish the way things are now, to accept the welcome, and yield to the rebirth of life, here I was paralyzed, unable even to speak.

I glanced at Mark who seemed to be as stupefied as I was. He sat with no reaction, saying nothing, just looking. In other places we had been he had seen landmarks or landscape features he knew and then had to cope with the reality of the present. Here he saw nothing that was recognizable. I could see that he wanted to know he had come to the right place and that the only way to do that would be to get to the dunes, the place where the 20-odd helicopters had delicately maneuvered onto the sand in what he had called "the epitome of the airmobile concept." It was to find those dunes that Hai was asking questions.

We drove not far from town, the bus pulled over, and there before us was the expanse of sand the soldiers had crossed. Mark was off the bus and moving toward the dunes as soon as we stopped without waiting for any of us. We could not, in any case, keep up with him, so we took more circuitous routes, moving among clusters of tombs, which were poignant to me although most were not from the era Mark remembered. He had climbed to the top of the dunes and was looking out in wonder when we arrived, Hai not far behind, warning us to stay on the path because of the danger of unexploded ordnance.

I looked back and tried to imagine the past, while being suddenly sobered. There may have been survivors of the days Mark remembered living in the villages. If so, they now lived in a place of beauty, but also with the ever-present danger that the war would suddenly explode again if they strayed too far off tested paths.

Mark and I walked back together, slowly, commenting on the graves, the sand, the path he had taken so long ago. We had not found the exact spot where he had dug in for the night and posed for snapshots taken under fire, but we were close enough. It was all there, laid out in front of us but turned inside out, the villages bright with color instead of grimly gray and smoking, the only color that of fire. The shifting sands had absorbed the concussions, the beating of helicopter blades, the shouts and shots, leaving only the breeze from the sea.

———

We got back on the bus, teasing Mark for how quickly he had gotten across the sand to get to the dunes. We passed around bottles of water and pulled away. Not far along the road, Mark saw the place where one of his sergeants had been killed when he had stepped on a landmine and several more in the patrol had been wounded. In his description, the scene had been filled with confusion, fear, and decidedly non-regulation shouting because the radio had been knocked out in the explosion. Though he had not thought well of the man as a leader, Mark had been distraught at his death, as well as at the sobering realization of how many men could be taken out by the misstep of one. Without the urgency and screams in his account, the landscape seemed so much smaller than I had imagined, the hill low and innocent, an easy walk.

We drove west across the north end of the lake and back out onto Route One again where Hai began to look for a place for us to have lunch. There were many choices along the road, entrepreneurial, family-run kitchens with small indoor dining areas and little forests of hammocks outside available to anyone needing a nap for the price of a cup of coffee. He chose one on the basis of a standard of his own and stationed himself in the kitchen to oversee the preparation of our meal. We made ourselves comfortable under an open-air shelter which had tables and plastic stools scattered around a concrete floor. A glass china cabinet against a green wall held small dishes, mysterious bottles, and a vase of plastic flowers. On the glass front of the cabinet were large decals advertising the familiar dishes—*cơm* (rice), *bún* (noodle), and *phở* (soup). No further description was necessary. Everyone would know what to expect.

These three dishes were not the only ones the kitchen could offer, though. Five or six dishes emerged as they were readied and explained by Hai, who sent one back because the eggs weren't cooked enough to suit him. I felt gratitude to Hai not only for his mother-hen care but also for his willingness to stop at home-cooking places like this where the food was delicious, evocative, and a part of daily life.

With the food safely in hand, Hai struck up a conversation with the owner of the very nice car parked in front that had reassured him about the restaurant. We learned that he was a veteran who lived in Hanoi and was traveling with friends to visit places he had been in the war. Just like us. Hai said he was a well-known military writer. When he learned I was writing about the war, he got a copy of his book from his car, and inscribed it for me. The round stainless steel tables had been cleared of food and the three veterans gathered their red plastic stools, with Hai between them to interpret. They bent toward one another, at ease, elbows on knees. Behind them, our bus driver took a well-deserved nap in one of the hammocks slung from the walls. I stood apart from them, watching. Mark had fought here, as had the writer. Perhaps they had crossed paths at some point—if that is how one would put it—although uncovering that possibility would have taken the conversation in a direction it did not seem to be going. From what I could tell, the men were just sharing memories of places they knew and how bad it had been.

At My Lai we again visited Madam Qui and she recognized Mark and me. We sat with her and her son in a café, happy just to be with her again. Her beautiful weathered face had a few more lines and her warmth embraced us. We inquired about her health, her family. She had retired, she said, and I wondered what she meant, except that being there for visitors, a survivor, a reminder, might have in some way been her job. It was one of many questions I had in Vietnam that I had learned to let be questions. Some things were not my business, or would have taken a great deal of time to learn. I could have asked my presumptuous question of last time—how does she do it?—without fear of being interrupted, but the question now seemed to me to be out of synch with the rhythm of the place, too filled with talk and not enough listening. Also, since our last trip, I had read in other stories, by different storytellers, that this lady had not somehow miraculously transcended her memories. In other stories she bore the pain still, struggling with anger and depression. Knowing that she was human, a woman who loved and loves, and who mourned still, I was better able to honor her.

In the garden of a convent in Hue on the last trip, I had

encountered Quan Am, the Vietnamese Quan Yin, or female *bodhisattva* of compassion. Quan Am is honored everywhere in Vietnam and is usually depicted holding a vase of water, the water of compassion, which she pours out upon the world. The figure in the garden stood on a marble dragon above a rocky sacred mountain, and was surrounded by lush trees and flowering bushes. The size of the statue, carved of white marble, gave her a presence that stopped me, compelled me not only to give her reverence, but to carry away with me the heart of her action. She did not promise a happy ending. She poured her water continually, as though compassion is always available, but also always needed.

In the pilgrimage site at Quang Tri I felt I had encountered Quan Am, or one of her followers, in the nun who *saw* who I was, and who Mark was, who had spoken to me so kindly, and whose picture I kept on my writing desk. I felt I saw Quan Am again here, in a small café in My Lai. This woman had lost so much, suffered so much, and yet, it was said, felt she had been spared to help others. Chuck was seated next to her in the circle of stools we had formed. At one point she took his hand and from time to time she patted it.

We left a small gift of cash and a box of ChocoPies that Hai, knowing better than we did the requirements of hospitality on such occasions, had bought from a nearby shop. As a rule I found ChocoPies a little silly, a child's treat, cottony cakes sandwiched on marshmallow filling and dipped in waxy chocolate. I had had to somehow reconsider my judgment when I saw boxes of them on altars in pagodas as offerings. In that light, ChocoPies were a fitting gift for Madam Qui.

———

In Hue we did the things one does in Hue. We visited The Citadel, which was perpetually under construction to repair the massive damage it sustained during the Tet Offensive. On our last visit I had been deeply upset by the presence of tethered elephants who were kept to give rides to tourists, but they were no longer there. On the other hand, Celestial Lady Pagoda, where I had walked in the tranquil gardens and seen the blue Austin set in a niche as a relic, was inundated with visitors. I knew that crowds and tawdry souvenir shops had been a part of pilgrimage sites for as long as there had been pilgrimages, but after some discussion with Edmund of my idea that calling the blue Austin a "relic" was meant to link the physical vehicle to the spiritual path, I, too, was ready to leave.

Things got more confusing when it came to my request to visit the neglected statues that Mark had found when he took off on his own at the orphanage the last time we visited. I kept reminding Hai of that request and then began to wonder why I had to remind him so often. He was usually so meticulous and devoted to finding our every obscure site. Now, though, he kept "forgetting" or acting like he hoped I had forgotten. He was on the phone a lot, I guessed with Kien. Finally I told him to tell Kien it was my fault and I took responsibility but we needed to find those statues. And we did. The bus parked under a tree, we walked a short distance, and there they were: broken plazas guarded by weathered horses, elephants, and the occasional stone watchman at attention. Flights of stone stairs led to overgrown enclosures. We fanned out, explored different parts of the grounds, sat in thought, or wrote in quiet corners. It was all picturesque and evocative and we loved it.

Back on the bus an hour later Hai was elated. He hadn't wanted to take us there, which had become obvious, because in the past it had been littered with the detritus of drug dealers and prostitutes. Ever protective of us and of our opinion of his country, he had not wanted us to see that.

The ebbs and flows of fortune had affected La Vang, too. Mark and I wanted to go back because we thought this time we might be able to get over to the area his unit had gone on that day when they had been overrun. Although Mark thought there was no point in trying to find the exact place, the lonely stretch of ground beyond the fence still called to me. I thought if we could just walk that way, maybe there would be a sign of some kind, even just a shiver of recognition, or a bird calling.

From a distance, though, we could see that the site was undergoing a major transformation. No longer was the spire of the church Mark had seen from the air the only landmark. An enormous new church was being built on a hill I hadn't even realized was there and the surrounding area had been turned over to stoneworks, cranes, and the sound of hammers. The original church had lost its newer addition, now no longer needed, and it had been consolidated to the form it had been in 1972 when it had been destroyed. The enormity of the new structure, built in the style of an elaborate pagoda and accessible by flights of stairs, disoriented and dismayed me. I had seen the place only at a quiet time, the preparations for pilgrims evident but not obtrusive. Now great vats with rows of spigots held holy water, enough for devout visitors in numbers I could not begin to visualize.

Two centuries before, this forest, a part of which we saw on the hill, had been a place of refuge for Catholics escaping persecution. Here they had seen a vision of the Madonna, wearing an *ao dài*, and carrying an infant. She had taught them about the plants of the forest to help them survive and over the years the site had become a major focus of devotion. La Vang had been a different kind of pilgrimage place for me, a place of melancholy grief. I felt what Mark had been feeling faced with the peaceful rice paddies and cheerful people at LZ English two years before when he had seemed to want to sweep aside the present to reach what he held of the past. Now I walked about anxiously, looking for the scene I remembered. I found the later additions garish, a travesty upon the memory of men I had never known.

With no fence any longer blocking our way, we walked along a rutted path in the direction the men must have taken that day. Once again we were turned back, this time by a huge work shed holding enormous blocks of stone. Just inside the shelter stood the upper half of an enormous new statue of Our Lady, which seemed to rise up out of the earth like something from the last scene in *Planet of the Apes*. We stood together looking into the distance at the wooded hill where the combat would have happened, untouched by the construction. At Friendship Village in Hanoi, we had met some of the survivors of the years of war here, men who carried the memory of what had happened. No monument would mark the place on that hill where eight members of Mark's unit had lost their lives. It had been just one of many bursts of violence in the ten or more years of violence the avenue of statues behind us had witnessed, violence that had claimed many more lives than just the American eight. The earth remembered, though, as did the breeze that stirred the trees. In the midst of the hammering, I could hear their silence.

———

On the morning of Mark's day in Binh Dinh Province, his "neighborhood," I had put some photos on my iPad to show our fellow travelers. I included the picture we had re-enacted on our last trip with Mark and Rolf Beyer in front of the rice paddies at LZ English. I had the photo of Desolation Row at Bong Son Bridge, and one of the sands outside An Hoa and An Quang. Although it was not directly a part of the story of the day, I had included one more: the picture of Mark holding the skull on the stick, the one that was taken after he had volunteered to exhume the grave "to check for booby traps."

The iPad was passed around so that everyone could have a closer look while I tried to keep the story going from my perch in the front of the bus. I barely noticed when the iPad reached Hai, but then I saw him growing agitated. I was always self-conscious at times like this. Most of the Vietnamese we encountered may have come to some kind of terms with the war's reality, but I had not. Usually our guides participated with no personal reaction, but something had upset Hai and I saw that it was the photo with the skull on the stick. Distraught, he turned on Mark, too honestly emotional for his accusations to be hurtful. He must have seen so many pictures of the war we Americans had waged in his country, but this one crossed a line with him.

I wanted to protest that this was not the young man I had known in high school, but the thought died in my mind. To excuse the Mark of the photograph would have been to deny him the responsibility he now had to take, however awkwardly. In the past he had shrugged it off. He had seen worse, or would, and after all, it had just been a joke, the others thought so, too. ... But he had always known there was more to it than that.

Every time I had tried to talk to him about that photograph Mark had said, "It's the truth." As a storyteller, I agreed. Things that are hidden become monsters under the bed. But Hai was not asking that anything be hidden; after all, he was spending long hours with us finding our places of truth. It was not the reminder of war, however ugly, that troubled him. It was, it seemed to me, that war's brutality, its victimizing even of the dead, had been turned into a sordid joke. War is a serious matter, he seemed to be saying. Show respect.

They were at an impasse. Mark saw the incident as just what happens in war, and not something still alive in the present. In a way, he was at an impasse with himself, living with the pain of past actions and yet clinging, still, to the memory of the excitement. Even the comment he had made about the photo when we had sat by the shore of the South China Sea, that soldiers on both sides know what it is to dip beneath the thin veneer of civilization, held within it a smug note: he had learned something others who had not seen war would never know. He took bitter pride in that, in many ways feeling more of a bond with enemy soldiers than with allied civilians. But now, for the sake of moving forward, he was being asked to reconsider the way he had learned the lesson. This was especially difficult because the incident had been a rite of passage. He had done the gruesome thing that no one else wanted to do and had thereby gained both a reputation and a name – the North Carolina Vulture. He had *liked* that. He still did. To give it up, even to let it undergo a metamorphosis of sorts so as to exist in the present day, was to give up part of his identity. I could see he did not know what to do, what to say, or what to think. No one had ever called him out on this, except maybe me. Certainly no one in Vietnam.

Almost in desperation, Hai asked Mark what he had done with the skull. Mark answered that they had reburied it. Hai's demeanor changed completely. There was relief, which became approval and then deep gratitude. "You did well," he said. "Thank you. You did the right thing." And then, "That man's spirit—I believe this—that man's spirit is what is calling you back to Vietnam."

The bus approached LZ English from a different direction this trip, coming in past the landing strip, still visible in a wide area cleared of trees. At the far end farmers were spreading rice out on the hot surface to dry. I walked along the battered pavement, in some places covered with sand and in others eroded with vegetation. If this had been a movie there would be flashbacks now, film of C-130s screaming down the runway, mechanical noise tearing at the horizon, but on that day all was still, only the crunch of our footsteps and the low murmur of our voices.

I saw from both sides now. On the one hand, I rationalized that Mark had been young, it had been war, it had all happened a long time ago. But Hai was right. Some things went too far. Perhaps it had been the excess of the moment, adolescent bravado brought on by isolation, horror, and complete dependence upon one's companions in a strange land, but this apparently small incident had gone too far and no one had pulled it back. I could not defend Mark, even in my mind.

Much worse desecrations happened in that war, as well as all others, but that did not lessen what had taken place there on that hillside. Mark had resigned himself to carrying the memory, but in that moment, on that bus traveling the land of Vietnam, Hai had offered something different. He had offered a way *through*, back across the thin veneer. What he offered was distinctly Vietnamese and equally foreign to American thinking: that the shock of the body's disturbance had created a bond between the dead man and the soldier that had the power to bring Mark back to Vietnam.

This was not the first time I had heard this idea. In all the stories of the United States and Vietnam there has run a mysterious emotional and psychic connection that weaves through the increasingly frantic and desperate actions of the war, persists in the sad, unresolved aftermath, and shows up in the stories of individual people. The connection is most apparent in veterans. Many, many veterans, some immediately after the war and some to this day, have returned to Vietnam to open schools, clean up unexploded ordnance, and create clinics. Others just want to lay something to rest by going back to places of fear and violence and what they find there allows them to release painful memories. Many refer to Vietnam as "home." Even the anger, hatred, and desire for revenge that other veterans still feel speak to a powerful connection.

And it is not just veterans. There are the former anti-war activists I spoke to who got a strange look in their eyes at the thought of going to Vietnam. There were my own panic attacks at the idea of traveling to Hanoi. Others (I was one of these, too) are drawn to the journey, as though to complete, or enlarge, or understand something still alive within themselves. One man who had spent some time in Vietnam said, "Though I was never a soldier, I feel a bond with Vietnamese I have never felt anywhere else. I don't know why."

I looked out toward the farmers, their conical hats bending and moving over their work. A breeze stirred the trees of the nearby forest. I had not been an innocent bystander in this incident, after all. For some reason I did not now know, I had included that photograph, even though the incident had not taken place where we were going. Mark had always justified showing it because "it was the truth," and maybe I wanted us to face the truth together. But simply telling the truth no longer seemed enough. Or rather, it no longer seemed enough simply to tell *our* truth. Hai had offered us a truth that reached beyond the desecration of a grave, even beyond the desecration of a country. In that moment it was not important to justify the incident in any way, or even to apologize for it. What was important was to see the incident through Hai's eyes, to understand what crossed a line for *him*, and what *he* understood as the remedy.

Could we understand it, the idea of a dead man calling a living man back? Could we learn to see that not as terrifying, but as redemptive? And what if we were all here—not just Mark but all of us—because we had been called here by the dead?

48

The Old Veterans

I WANTED TO GET US TO FRIENDSHIP VILLAGE, THE rehabilitation center on the outskirts of Hanoi, founded by an American veteran and once again Hai had to be persistent and not give up on the mission. A festival in a village along our route kept us from taking a direct path, so we meandered along tree-hung lanes and through clusters of shops and houses, the tall buildings of the city off in the distance. Finally we turned into the complex and parked the bus in the circular driveway ringed with the flags of many supporting countries. We were welcomed in the reception room where we gave a donation and then were taken on a tour of the grounds. We saw Agent Orange-disabled children and young people learning vocational skills. We greeted a few veterans and then walked through the dining room. Everywhere the young people waved and flirted and called hello. The veterans smiled and held out their hands for me to shake as I wished them *xin chao*.

I was outside again when one of the men appeared and pulled up his shirt to display a heavily scarred abdomen. "The bullet went in here," he said, pointing to his upper rib cage. He had had surgery, and it appeared to have been a pretty rough field operation, to remove it. These are my scars, he seemed to be saying. My story. Another man, dressed in a full khaki uniform and cap, lifted his jacket to reveal a back puckered and rippled by exposure to chemicals.

There was much commotion when they found out Mark was a veteran, everyone trying to make a speech at once. One man pointed his forefingers toward each other, shaking them a little for emphasis, and then clasped his hands together. "We were shooting at each other," he said, "but now we are friends." The men lined up for a photograph. The man in uniform put his hand on Mark's shoulder. The man with the scarred abdomen stood especially proud. He was stunned by what was happening. Mark was the first American veteran he had ever seen.

We walked away and I saw that Mark was crying. It had been a difficult trip for him. He had not always been happy, the more annoying aspects of traveling in a group wearing on him. We had had some high moments but there was a distance between us now. The rhythm of travel had not bothered me. The more boring bits gave me an opportunity to take things in and reflect. Mark, though, would have been happy just finding the remains of yet another landing zone. Meeting Vietnamese veterans had taken him out of himself, the only thing that had. With them, if with no one else, he could be comfortable with who he was, more at home with those he had fought against than with those he had fought for.

Mark had done what he had set out to do: to experience war firsthand, and though he never regretted his decision, it had brought him no satisfaction. He was a walking memorial to the horrors of war, a silent witness, identified not by medals or maiming injuries but by a cap that read "Vietnam Veteran." The night custodian at the VA hospital in San Francisco told me that he knew of many veterans who had gone back to Vietnam. "'Crossing over,' they called it," he told me. Mark had crossed over the first time, when he went to fight his country's war without his country telling him how to cross back. No one had told him that it is okay to come back different. No one told him that is, in fact, how it should be, how could it be anything else? "Tell us about it when you can. If you can. Take your time." He had crossed a boundary, the thin veneer of civilization, and learned skills he could not unlearn. So now he made long road trips to visit the long-empty battlefields of the United States: Gettysburg, Antietam, Little Bighorn where his unit in his second tour, 7th Cavalry, had met its match. He drove, took his pictures, wore his cap.

He bore his grief as a duty, not caring any more to lay it down. I asked him once, "Would Mac want you to live like this? Mac and Woollard and Peterson and Danny Dodd and the others?" He just shrugged. He didn't know and didn't care. It was what he did and he had done it for too long to stop. He had worn his battered fatigues when he got back, he said, as a reminder to society of who they had sent to die. He wore the cap now for the same reason: to remind people, as he told me once, stabbing at his chest as he spoke, that there is a cost to war and the cost is *me*. I resented that he had not seen that coming when he chose to go to war. At the same time, I understood.

Mark knew he had been a part of a losing cause and he took no offense from it. He came of age in war and part of him never grew out of it. He came to think of Vietnam as home and to recognize Vietnamese veterans as brothers. In that he found what peace he would know in this life. His story had grown timeless: the old soldier, left to wander the earth, haunting empty battlefields, more comfortable with the dead than the living.

MEDITATION
SUSAN R. DIXON

49

Seeking Quan Am

NEITHER MARK NOR I FIT THE USUAL STEREOTYPES OF A Vietnam veteran or an anti-war activist. Mark was not a sniper, a LURP, or a member of a small unit abandoned in the jungle, like something out of *Rambo*. He was an infantryman, witnessing the war first-hand. I had marched in Washington once, carried petitions, and coordinated a candlelight vigil, but when said I was an anti-war activist my audience imagined drugs, sex, and riots in the streets. In a time of extremes, our stories were ordinary. Neither of us saw war or its opposition as an opportunity for heroics. In very different ways, both of us wanted to throw ourselves into the experience that was shaping us, to learn what we could from it, and to report back. That had not proved to be easy.

Writing in the 1970s, Mark said, "If one talks too much about the good times, people perceive a candidate for the VFW. The one that pours out all the horrors is seen as a basket case. Try to balance it out and tell the truth, people haven't time to listen." Fifty years later, I found that the situation was much the same. Conversations still began with enthusiasm and broke off for no apparent reason. People still got a faraway look in their eyes. It even seemed to me that the Vietnam generation—the younger ones, not the ones who had learned ruthlessness in the carpet bombing of Japan or the proposed use of tactical nuclear weapons at Khe Sanh—was still in shock. We famously changed societal rules and upended norms, but the rule-changing had already begun when young men like Mark, raised with the expectations of triumphal newsreels and *Victory at Sea*, were thrown into a system, a mindset, a morality that counted victory not in land gained or cities liberated, but in numbers of dead bodies. The twisting of the values we had been raised with produced hopelessness, cynicism, and withdrawal. I could hardly blame those whose unhealed grief kept them from engaging what could only reopen their heartache.

I still had no answers, but I wanted something to show for the passion and idealism of my twenties. I wanted something to come of my good intentions, however late in the day. I sought insight in the books that by that time lay in stacks on chairs and cabinets in my office. Surely, in all the time I had been otherwise occupied, someone had found some explanation. But all my books told me was that there are no answers, not to that war, not to everything that led up to it or came after. We could argue about facts or motivations or what *could* have happened, and probably would, but there are no answers and all my searching would not lead to any. Mark had asked me to "make some sense" of his files, by which I came to understand he meant "make some sense of what happened" and I could not.

By turns, I berated the gods and sat in numb paralysis, grief-stricken. All my activism, my indignation, my *rightness*, fell away and I was faced with what I did not want to know. I knew it to be true but I did not want to *know* it: my beautiful, extraordinary country, whose best I had believed in—and still did—was built on the moral, political, social, and psychological belief that some peoples' lives are worth less than others and that any action, no matter how violent, is justified if it defends that belief. I had wanted to dismiss this knowledge, set it aside in favor of the energy, the optimism, the good that my country does. I had wanted to dismiss it because I knew—I had learned the lesson as a teenager—where such a belief could lead. I had wanted to dismiss it and I could not. Bombs, napalm, Spooky (how many Americans know that such a thing as Spooky existed?) were not aberrations. They represented, in tangible, deadly form, the dark side, the shadow side, of my country.

The shadow side is the part of one's identity that is lied about or explained away or ignored. The shadow side haunts the present and it haunts the living. Lying about it does not make it disappear. It is still there, the monster under the bed, driving conscious actions through fear. The shadow side is what the soldiers came back knowing—not just what war was, what it means to drop below the thin veneer of civilization, but what *that* war was. They knew what the war-makers did not—and do not—want anyone else to know.

Not wanting to know was—and is—my own shadow side, the dark side of living a protected life cocooned in what commentators call "our freedoms." I say I did not know what to do when the soldiers came home, and that is true, but it does not change the fact that I did nothing. I do not know how many opportunities I missed simply to listen, how many times my silence, my looking away, steered the conversation into "safer" territory. That others did better at listening—and there were many—does not change the fact that I waited decades to learn what I wish I had known then.

To blame myself, though, would be to miss my own point. For whatever reason, I had needed that time, I had needed the journey I had been on, I needed my *age*, to arrive somewhere I could not have been at an earlier time. I arrived, not at any resolution that made sense within my cultural framework, but at the mystery of Vietnam.

No political explanation for the perverse path that led us to what the Vietnamese call the American War made sense to me. No military explanation explained our loss. It was as if something in the very nature of Vietnam had drawn us there, without us understanding it. It was as if the cascade of disastrous decisions led us to a brink, a doorway, a liminal space, a world between worlds, to an experience that confounded our expectations and turned our certainties about the world upside down.

The white man strategy of dominant force, dominant technology, dominant rhetoric and calculus—in short, of *hubris*—fell to something larger than ourselves and we did not even know how to see it. In this sense, Vietnam was our *nemesis*. It was not our arch-enemy—it was not our enemy at all—but it was, and still is, the thing that brings—or at least has the potential to bring—our *hubris* back into balance. And, I believe, it is not too late. The lessons have always been freely given and—perhaps this was what makes it difficult to see them—the lessons hide in plain sight.

In my first weeks in Hanoi, I took a class at the Cooking Centre led by the director of the school. We had been to the market, the one with the piles of plucked chickens, the mounds of fresh vegetables, and the frogs, and she was explaining the five tastes that make up the basis of Vietnamese cuisine: sweet, sour, spicy, salty, and bitter. The most difficult of these tastes for Westerners to accept, she said, is bitter. We take our bitter things—coffee or chocolate, for instance—and sweeten them until the bitterness is covered or gone. We reject even the idea of bitter, which we associate with something to be avoided or escaped.

Meanwhile, as she talked, one of the chefs was pounding the leaves of wild cosmos in a large mortar and pestle, adding more leaves and crushing them until he was satisfied. He poured off the thick, dark green liquid he had collected into sake cups and passed the cups around. As an encouragement, he taught us the Vietnamese toast, *"Mot, hai, bat, zho!"* and we downed it. It had a strong vegetal taste and was so bitter it made my spine shiver.

The chef, laughing at our reactions, was already chopping the leaves of the same bitter plant. He then made an omelet, Vietnamese style, beaten eggs with the chopped leaves mixed in and cooked flat in a skillet. When it was set, he cut the omelet into pieces with scissors and sprinkled them with lime juice. We each took a piece, dipped it in chili salt, and ate it. It was delicious, satisfying in a way my body craved, and each taste distinct and recognizable. Bitterness had not been treated as an enemy, something to be denied. Instead, the other tastes had been engaged to bring bitterness into balance.

I wondered if there might be more to avoiding or suppressing bitterness than simply missing an interesting taste. In an evolutionary way, bitter plays an important role in warning humans away from poisonous substances. Perversely, humans have difficulty generalizing these lessons: the bitterness of war has not stopped it. Wars are still started by those who will not fight in them and fought by young people who do not foresee the cost. But the lesson in bitter I learned that day in Hanoi provided a clue: it was not the war itself, not the memory of the nightly body counts, or the harrowing images, relentless casualties, the violence and destruction, that had caused the lasting damage. That lasting damage, what haunts us still, could not be dismissed by saying "it was war," or "it all happened long ago." Time does not heal all wounds. Time strips away superficial reminders, claims remaining witnesses, and provides the space for reconstructed history, but it does not take away the core memory. Time does not take away bitter.

I had hated the bitterness of that war, but I had clung to it, too, nursing it, denying it, letting it disturb my sleep. I had fought it and let it justify my actions, but I had never *owned* it. I had never recognized it as a part of myself, as playing a role in making up who I am.

So, as I had done when I was first invited to Hanoi and had felt the first panic attacks, I turned and faced it. For three days, I told myself, just three days, I would drop my pretenses, let down my guard, and surrender to everything bitter had to teach me. The three days turned into a week, and then two.

In an orgy of pain and tears, I tasted *bitter*, felt it, let it make my spine shiver. I let my anger at the lies run freely, my horror at chemical defoliants, and my loathing that their use was still being hidden behind self-delusion. I let go of decades of stiff upper lip, of stubborn optimism, of trying to find hope within despair.

Images swam before my eyes. Fragments haunted me.

A woman crouched in the water of a rice paddy, sheltering children as best she could, her face contorted in anguish, watching what was coming toward her from the sky. Another woman wearing a conical hat, allowed to live for no particular reason. Two desperate Vietnamese girls, maimed and scarred, waiting to be chosen by two American soldiers who had not learned that what they were doing was despicable.

An old man walking along a path toward his home from his field, the one his ancestors had worked and still guarded from their tombs. He held a lifetime's knowledge of rice-growing, weather, and seasons. His killers could not even agree if he should die, but he did, in the end, simply because he walked and was Vietnamese. His body would be counted at least once, recorded in the day's tally that appeared on television screens on the other side of the world, proof the war was going well.

Some of the men on the ground saw the beauty of the land they had come to destroy, the vibrant greens, the rocky cliffs that fell down to the sea, the conical hats and gentle water buffalo. The men who flew the machines that ripped into the villages, blew up the mountains, or poisoned the fields were perhaps too high up to notice.

I stopped believing that there could be a world without war. I surrendered to cynicism, tasted the gall, wallowed in failure and mortality. I let myself believe that that was all there was, that to be human was never to be able to stop Perpetual War, or to defeat the forces of greed and cowardice. I was Persephone, abducted into my own personal Underworld, by Hades, the god of death, leaving the earth in the darkness of winter.

Once having yielded to years of pent-up bitterness, I wondered if I would ever reemerge. Was this to be the fruit of my years of work? Would I end up more lost in anger than I had begun? It felt as if I would be a late casualty of the nihilism of a long-ago horror still haunting the present.

At last, exhausted, I had a vision:

I was on a path through dense jungle. I carried a torch and had brought with me some unlikely totemic animals. We had come to the village of my nightmare, the one from which I had awakened screaming in Hanoi. This time, instead of standing outside, lost in terror, I went through the gate. I found the water buffalo that had been tortured. I called to it, and it rose, and came with us. I found the children torn apart by the tank. I called to them and they came with us. I found the old woman with the hole in her shoulder. I called to her. She rose and took the torch from my hand. We walked the path, as we were meant to do, together.

I had searched for answers in errands in Hanoi, in deserted landing zones, in bustling markets, in the welcome of the people. I had beseeched Quan Am, asking for her favor, her protection, her wisdom. Now I learned to look the Underworld in the face, to see *bitter,* to know it, and to accept it. I was Persephone, not victim but Queen, walking toward her destiny with open eyes. The Underworld became for me not a place that was Other, to which we exile those who have journeyed there, but a part of the whole, a part of myself. In my anguish and in my searching, I allowed *bitter* to come into balance.

And so in the end, I was where I had started. I had asked to hear Mark's story. As a result, he gave it to me. We had learned to speak and to listen, learned to respect both the bridges we built and the gulf that lay between us. That is, really, all we can do for one another in this life. We can listen, hear one another deeply, rejoice together, grieve together, tell the stories, bear witness.

As a part of this project I had gotten to know many men whose names are on The Wall. I got to know them decades after their deaths and only through the stories told about them. I imagine them. I see in my mind's eye the mortal wounds. In a strange and mystical way, I am present at their deaths. I watch their bodies leave the field, feel the vacancy left by their sudden absence. I know something about their being in this life through the stories of their leaving it. Occasionally I speak to them. "If you want me to say something on your behalf, find a way to let me know," I say. "Gently, though," I add, knowing what might ensue if they were to unleash their pent-up opinions through me. They do not say much to me. Even after all this time, they keep their distance. I don't blame them. There is so much I will never understand.

Where I live there are deep gorges, carved by ancient glaciers, where people love to hike and swim. Sometimes, intentionally or not, someone will get in trouble in these gorges and then helicopters fly over my house. I hear them coming, hear the beat of the blades growing louder and I remember when chopper blades beat over rice paddies. Time disappears. I am attacker and attacked, technocrat and farmer. I am rage and love, hatred and forgiveness, despair and hope. They were all there, mixed up, in that war. So many years later they are there still. And though there is still no sense to be made, Quan Am still pours the waters of compassion over the world.

Acknowledgments

"War is too strange to be processed alone."
Phil Klay, Iraq veteran and author

This book could not have been attempted, let alone written, without a community of people engaging the content and upholding the authors.

During the course of the project, Susan's home in Ithaca became the studio, workshop, and social space in which during the day Susan and Mark called the war into life and at night dispelled the ghosts by making curries and watching classic movies. We thank Susan's husband Joe for guarding the space, her daughter Elizabeth for believing in us from the beginning, and her son Daniel, daughter-in-law Tali, and grandson Benji for reminding us that we do the work not only for ourselves but for the next generations.

By engaging issues of "war, peace, compassion, and forgiveness," the monthly dinner discussions of the New Moon Group provided critical support as the book evolved.

The Ithaca Warrior Writers inspired Susan to found a sister writing group for civilians, called Writing War, to confront war and its echos not as an act of generosity but as our shared duty as citizens.

In all three of these groups we are particularly grateful to Deborah Allen, Kevin Basl, Chuck Geisler, Mike and Linda Hoffman, Barbara Kane Lewis, Jim Murphy, John Suter, Mary Beth Tierney, Joe Shedd, Melissa and Hurf Sheldon, and Fred Wilcox.

The Tuesday Morning Writing Group, especially Adam Perl and Susan's longtime writing partner Stephen Clancy supported the work professionally and emotionally, often making just the right observation to move the writing through a challenge.

Among those whose contribution directed, redirected, or deepened the journey we thank John R. Peters-Campbell, whose invitation to visit Hanoi was Susan's 'call to adventure'; John W. Fisher, who readily and skillfully took up our request to navigate the mysteries of travel in Vietnam; and Joseph Wallace-Williams, then of Holy Cross Monastery, who, while keeping Susan company as various medical personnel addressed a broken wrist, led her toward a profound level of understanding of what, in the end, the book meant.

We deeply appreciate the support of veterans with whom Mark served and who, over the course of the project became friends. We especially thank Marvin Hasenak (as well as his wife Sharon), Robert Meager, and Robert Alekna. These men answered questions, provided professional and personal encouragement, and never questioned the presence of civilian woman in the story.

Special thanks to Robert Alekna, John Ulloa, and William Anderson for their work identifying the casualties of February 13, 1968.

A deep bow of gratitude goes to Dang Anh, Luu Trung Kien, and Tran Van Hai, our guides in Vietnam. We continue to benefit beyond measure from their knowledge, their energy, their wisdom, and their generosity of spirit.

For invaluable contributions to the beauty and professionalism of this book, we thank editor Elisabeth Chretien of Chretien Wordsmithery and Anna Gallow of Flourish Design Studio, Ithaca, New York. Both women understood the book from the beginning and supported its vision through their skills.

We owe a special debt of gratitude to Fred A. Wilcox, who patiently mentored the book through its many stages and championed the unusual synergy between the points of view of the authors.

About the Authors

SUSAN R. DIXON

As a writer and editor, museum curator and teacher, Susan R. Dixon has studied the effects of haunting memory, the consequences of suppressed secrets, and the healing power of storytelling. She received her B.A. from the University of North Carolina at Chapel Hill, her M.A. from George Washington University, and her Ph.D. from Cornell University. She leads a writing workshop for civilians reflecting on war and maintains a blog for *Seeking Quan Am* at www.seekingquanam.com and her own blog at www.susanrdixon.com. She lives in Ithaca, New York, the heart of the Finger Lakes Region.

Photo by Tom Hoebbel, Tom Hoebbel Photo and Video, Ithaca, New York.

MARK M. SMITH

During his three years in the Army, Mark Smith rose from Private to Staff Sergeant/Platoon Leader. He spent twelve months in A Company, 1/5 Cavalry, 1st Air Cavalry Division, eight months in West Berlin as part of Berlin Brigade, and eight more months in C Company, 2/7 Cavalry, 1st Air Cavalry Division. He won the Bronze Star, the Air Medal, the Combat Infantryman's Badge, six campaign stars for the Vietnam Service Medal and the Presidential Unit Citation. Despite much heavy action, he was never so much as scratched.

After serving two tours in Vietnam and working as North and South Carolina Coordinator for Vietnam Veterans Against the War, he pursued a career in newspaper journalism. He worked as a reporter and photographer and later an editor in Shallotte, North Carolina; Hamilton-Wenham, Massachusetts; Ossipee, Wolfeboro, Laconia and Lebanon, New Hampshire; White River Jct., Vermont.; and Las Vegas and Pahrump, Nevada. He lives in Sparta, North Carolina, just off the Blue Ridge Parkway.

www.ingramcontent.com/pod-product-compliance
Lightning Source LLC
Chambersburg PA
CBHW071148070526
44584CB00019B/2714